ECOLOGICAL-EVOLUTIONARY THEORY

ECOLOGICAL-EVOLUTIONARY THEORY: PRINCIPLES AND APPLICATIONS

Gerhard Lenski

Paradigm Publishers

Boulder • London

Copyright © 2005 by Paradigm Publishers

Published in the United States by Paradigm Publishers, 3360 Mitchell Lane, Suite E, Boulder, Colorado 80301 USA.

Paradigm Publishers is the trade name of Birkenkamp & Company, LLC, Dean Birkenkamp, President and Publisher.

Library of Congress Cataloging-in-Publication Data

Lenski, Gerhard Emmanuel, 1924–
Ecological-Evolutionary theory : principles and applications / Gerhard Lenski.
p. cm.
Includes bibliographical references and index.
ISBN 1-59451-100-4 (hc : alk. paper)
1. Human evolution—Philosophy.   2. Social evolution—Philosophy.   3. Human ecology.
4. Social ecology.   I. Title.
GN281.L45 2005
599.93'8'01—dc22

2005004261

Printed and bound in the United States of America on acid-free paper that meets the standards of the American National Standard for Permanence of Paper for Printed Library Materials.

Designed and Typeset by Straight Creek Bookmakers.

09 08 07 06 05
1 2 3 4 5

For Ann,
without whose encouragement and support this volume would
never have been completed

Upon this gifted age, in its dark hour
Rains from the sky, a meteoric shower
Of facts. . . .
They lie unquestioned, uncombined.
Wisdom enough to leech us of our ill
Is daily spun, but there exists no loom
To weave it into fabric.

—Edna St. Vincent Millay

CONTENTS

Part II: Applications

Religion and Technological Innovation, 227
War and Human Nature, 228
Population Growth and Quality of Life, 229
The Social Impact of Advances in the Technologies of Health
    and Sanitation, 230
Concluding Remarks, 231

FIGURES AND TABLES

xi

PREFACE

Many years ago, when I was a novice graduate student in sociology, one of the first lessons I learned was that evolutionism was *passé* and that functionalism was the coming thing. All of the evolutionists of the past had been mere armchair theorists whose speculations lacked the kind of solid empirical foundation science demands. As Crane Brinton contemptuously put it, "Who reads Spencer today?"

We students, I'm afraid, were a gullible lot. We saw what we were told we should see and, like the people in the old story, enthusiastically praised the emperor's new clothes.

It was only a decade later, after many semesters of teaching the introductory course and finding myself frustrated year after year by the task of making sense of the discipline of sociology to yet another group of students, that I began to see merit in the work of the older evolutionists whom I had earlier rejected. Several experiences along the way still stick in my memory.

For example, I remember one student in particular. In a very large class of 200 or more, he stood out because of the perceptive questions he would ask and the insightful comments he would make at the end of class sessions. At the end of the final lecture, I remember that he waited patiently at the edge of a group of students that had gathered to ask questions about the final exam. When the last of them left, he stepped forward to say how much he had enjoyed the course. But he said there was just one question he had not been able to answer. As I preened myself and looked forward to putting the capstone on his wonderful experience, his question totally deflated me, "What is sociology?"

This question was especially unsettling because I had already picked up signals in previous semesters that this was a problem that bothered a number of students. As a result, I had introduced a new lecture at the beginning of the course in which I carefully explained what sociology was all about. But clearly that had not done the trick. The diffuse and disjointed nature of the materials we discussed, and the absence of a meaningful theoretical framework to integrate them, left far too many students puzzled about the discipline itself and wondering whether there even was a discipline underlying all of the diverse materials.

About this same time, I remember another incident that occurred in a coffee shop where a young history instructor and I were commiserating with one another over the hard lives we led. Each of us was sure his own responsibilities were the more onerous. At one point, however, after I had made what I thought was a singularly telling point, my friend said, "But the trouble with teaching introductory history courses is that they are all simply the study of one damn thing after another."

Like St. Paul on the road to Damascus, I was struck by this statement; it hit me like a blinding light, a revelation. For the first time, I understood the problem that troubled my students. Sociology, taught from a functionalist perspective, was simply the study of one damn thing after another: some things about the family, some things about communities, some things about ethnicity, some things about conflict, some things about cooperation, some things about this, and some things about that. Truly a thing of shreds and patches. But in Yeats's immortal words, the center would not hold. In fact, there was no center except for the unhelpful assertion that every social process and every social arrangement serve some function for somebody.

About this time, I discovered Walter Goldschmidt's slender little classic *Man's Way: A Preface to the Understanding of Human Society.* It provided a fresh and exciting approach to the study of human societies—an openly evolutionary approach that integrated an amazing range of materials into a coherent and meaningful whole. In short, it had the center that functionalism lacked.

In those days, Goldschmidt was a voice crying in the wilderness. Most social scientists shared Brinton's contempt not only for Spencer but for evolutionists as a whole. But Goldschmidt's primer made sense in a way that the popular theories of the day did not.

Also about this time, I encountered V. Gordon Childe's volume *Man Makes Himself.* It provided an exciting historical dimension that was largely implicit in Goldschmidt's work. As I began incorporating these new materials into my thinking and teaching, I began finding all kinds of things falling into meaningful patterns and relationships.

During these same years, I was regularly leading a graduate seminar in social stratification, or social inequality. Here, too, I found the greatest problem was that of establishing some kind of theoretical integration of the wealth of diffuse materials.

In those days, the two alternatives appeared to be functionalism and Marxian theory. But both left much to be desired. In an effort to develop a more solid foundation for the study of inequality, I began reading historical and ethnographic monographs as widely as possible. In time, this led to the publication of *Power and Privilege* in 1966, a volume that was explicitly evolutionary in its approach.

From there, it was a short step to the publication of the first edition of *Human Societies* in 1970. This volume was an attempt to formulate a modern evolutionary theory and use it to provide what I hoped would be a more intellectually stimulating introduction to the discipline of sociology than the standard textbooks of the day, with their eclectic and largely descriptive surveys of contemporary American society. I also hoped that *Human Societies* would help students to see how materials from such seemingly disparate fields as sociology, anthropology, archaeology, history, political science, economics, and even biology could all be brought together into a single theory capable of explaining the incredible transformation of human life during the last 10,000 to 12,000 years and of providing new and useful insights into the process of change in our own day.

In the years that followed the publication of the first edition of *Human Societies,* I sought to test various aspects of my new version of evolutionary theory, which I came to call ecological-evolutionary theory. I also published several papers in which I argued for changes in sociological theorizing (e.g., Lenski, 1976, 1988), and *Human Societies* has appeared in a succession of new editions, most recently in 2004 (Nolan and Lenski, 2004).

For a number of years, however, various friends and colleagues have suggested that I should pull together into a single, definitive summary statement as many as possible of my thoughts on ecological-evolutionary theory that have, until now, been scattered in a variety of publications. This volume is a response to those suggestions. I hope that it will stimulate others to explore the more controversial elements, and also to expand the theory into areas that I have either neglected or barely touched upon. For I truly believe that ecological-evolutionary theory has a rich potential and will pay handsome dividends to those who invest time and effort in its development.

Gerhard Lenski

PART I

Principles

1

EVOLUTIONARY THEORY: AN INTRODUCTION

One of the more surprising developments in the social sciences in recent decades has been the revival of interest in evolutionary theory. After more than half a century of rejection—even ridicule—evolutionism has again become a viable option in both anthropology and sociology, while in archaeology it has become the dominant theoretical paradigm.

This is hardly what anyone anticipated in the half-century following World War I. Evolutionism had been tried and found wanting—and, indeed, in the harsh and unsentimental world of science, theories that have been discarded almost never get a second chance. Evolutionism was seen as a matter of interest only to students of the history of social thought and a few surviving proponents, such as V. Gordon Childe, William F. Ogburn, and Leslie White. But even Childe and Ogburn came to express reservations toward the end of their careers. Crane Brinton summed up the prevailing view of the period when he wrote, "Who now reads Spencer?"

Yet, somehow, despite the odds, evolutionary theory is flourishing again, and not only in the social sciences. In biology, its position is stronger now than it has ever been (Mayr, 1978, 1982), and evolutionary theories have even been adopted in the physical sciences (Calvin, 1969; Dickerson, 1978; Holland, 1984; Laszlo, 1987; Novikov, 1983; Strom and Strom, 1979).

Owing to the unusual history and scope of evolutionary theories, several questions need to be addressed before we can proceed to the first major task of this volume—namely, examination of the basic principles of the new evolutionary theory in the social sciences. Specifically, we need to consider the relation of this theory to other evolutionary theories, past and present.

3

First, we must ask how this theory is related to evolutionary theories in the biological and physical sciences. Are they linked merely by a dubious metaphor, as Nisbet and others have alleged, or are there more substantial ties? Then, how is this new social science version of evolutionary theory related to the older evolutionary theories of the nineteenth and early twentieth centuries? Is it merely a revival of these older theories, as Nisbet, Peel, Utz, Bock, and others have charged, or are there important differences? And, finally, what has been responsible for the surprising revival of interest in evolutionism in the social sciences? Why has evolutionary theory proved an exception to the general rule that scientific theories are rarely resurrected once they have been abandoned?

The Family of Evolutionary Theories

As the presence of evolutionary theories in all the major branches of science indicates, the new theory of societal evolution, which is the primary concern of this volume, is part of a larger family of related theories. The relationship of these theories is based on two things: (1) They share a common objective, and (2) they provide substantive grounding for one another.

The basic objective of all evolutionary theories is to explain processes of change, and more especially cumulative, macrochronic, and macrostructural change. *Cumulative* change is a distinctive kind of change associated with systems composed of multiple, interrelated parts. Within these systems, some parts change while others remain unchanged. Thus, cumulative change is a process that combines elements of continuity with elements of change; many parts of the system are preserved for extended periods while new parts are added and other parts are either replaced or transformed. Cumulative change is also a process in which the characteristics of a system at any single point in time have a significant impact on the system and its characteristics at successive times. The classic definition of biological evolution as "descent with modification" illustrates this type of change, but the distinctive nature of cumulative change is best understood when it is compared with noncumulative patterns of change, such as cyclical change (e.g., the annual cycle of seasons) or stochastic change (e.g., successive rolls of a pair of dice).

As noted, evolutionary theories are also concerned primarily with *macrochronic* and *macrostructural* change, which is to say that they are efforts to explain the more basic long-term transformations that have been observed within a particular field of study. Thus, evolutionary theories in astronomy, for example, seek to explain the major structural changes that stars and star systems have undergone since the beginning of the universe (Novikov, 1983). In chemistry, evolutionary theories are designed to explain the basic changes that have occurred in the chemical composition of the earth and its atmosphere since their formation, especially the emergence of organic molecules from inorganic materials and the emergence of simple one-celled organisms from organic molecules (Calvin, 1969).

In the biological sciences, evolutionary theories are concerned with the processes of reproduction, variation, and selection and their consequences for the changing patterns of plant and animal life from the time when life first appeared on our planet (Mayr, 1978). And in the social sciences, evolutionary theories seek to explain the various transformations that have occurred in our own species' way of life from earliest Paleolithic times to the present. Where other theories are content to deal with structural and functional relationships and with limited sequences of change, evolutionary theories insist on the necessity of explaining the most basic developments that have occurred over the total span of the history of various phenomena, be they star systems, chemical systems, life systems, or the social and cultural systems that humans have created.

This is not to say that evolutionary theories and theorists are uninterested in shorter and more limited sequences of change. On the contrary, these are often matters of great concern, as will become evident later in this volume, for they provide some of the best opportunities for testing evolutionary theories. However, when analyzing these more limited patterns of change, evolutionists seek to establish the larger evolutionary context within which such developments occur and to utilize this information as an important aspect of their analysis.

Two other concepts that are shared by all the members of the family of evolutionary theories are divergence and emergence. *Divergence* is the process by which phenomena become increasingly dissimilar over extended periods, as in the case of the Indo-European languages or of Darwin's finches. Biologists refer to this tendency as "adaptive radiation." The fantastic diversity of both the world of nature and the world that humans have created are ever-present reminders of the process of divergence, as well as a measure of its importance.

The concept of *emergence* is essentially a special case of the more general concept of divergence. Emergence is the process by which significantly new structures and new processes evolve out of older structures and older processes, as when the first amphibians evolved from marine animals. Although the boundary separating emergence from other forms of divergence is fuzzy and difficult to specify, it is clear that some forms of divergence have had vastly more important consequences than others. Thus, the evolution of the first amphibians was far more significant for the subsequent development of life on this planet than was the evolution of the umpteenth species of Darwin's finches.

Of all the instances of emergence, the most important are those that underlie the distinctions we make between physical, chemical, biological, and sociocultural evolution. In each instance, an important threshold was crossed and *an entirely new mode of evolution was set in motion*. Thus, stellar evolution laid the foundation for chemical evolution, which, in turn, laid the foundation for biological evolution, which, eventually, led to the evolution of human societies. In other words, one of the basic principles of modern evolutionary theory is that *the evolutionary process itself evolves* (Boulding, 1970; Lenski and Lenski, 1974).

It follows that the various evolutionary theories are not only linked by similar objectives, principles, and concepts, but more importantly they are linked substantively in a causal process in which each new mode of evolutionary change has laid a foundation for the next mode of such change. For students of human social and cultural evolution, this means that they cannot ignore the biological foundations on which societal evolution rests; in short, theories of societal evolution must be grounded in, and compatible with, theories of biological evolution. This does not mean, however, that a reductionist approach to this relationship is justified, as sociobiologists have sometimes assumed. The concept of emergence is an important reminder of the fundamental error involved in such an approach.

A final feature shared by all of the newer theories of evolution is a commitment to *probabilism* (Lenski, 1970; Mayr, 1978). In this connection, bear in mind that deterministic models of change and development are universally rejected. As a result, the study of evolution, whether in astronomy, chemistry, biology, or the social sciences, is destined to remain an inexact science, since exact sciences require that processes have deterministic outcomes (Boulding, 1970). Sometimes, of course, the probabilities associated with specific evolutionary processes are so high that the distinction between probabilism and determinism has little meaning, but these are exceptions to the more general pattern.

In addition to the elements that all evolutionary theories share, there are others that are shared by some of them. The best example of this is the concept of transmittable systems of coded information, which are records of prior experience (i.e., DNA and symbol-based cultural information). These systems are essential components of evolutionary theories in the biological and social sciences, but they are absent in the physical sciences. Because of this important distinction, and because societal evolution is a direct outgrowth of biological evolution but only an indirect outgrowth of chemical and physical evolution, theories of societal evolution resemble theories of biological evolution much more closely than they do theories of chemical or stellar evolution. Thus, while social scientists may safely ignore the latter, they cannot ignore many aspects of the theory of biological evolution.

Older and Newer Evolutionary Theories Compared

The newer evolutionism of recent decades owes an enormous debt to scholars of the eighteenth and nineteenth centuries who pioneered in the formulation of evolutionary theory—scholars such as Turgot, Ferguson, Millar, Robertson, Spencer, Tylor, Morgan, Lamarck, and Darwin. These, and others like them, laid a foundation on which modern theories of evolution build. Above all, they established the cumulative nature of change and identified the basic processes of divergence and emergence. They also discovered many of the more specific mechanisms governing evolutionary processes.

Yet, having acknowledged our debt to these scholars, we need to recognize that the newer evolutionism differs from the older in significant ways. In the biological sciences, for example, the rise of the new science of genetics has had profound consequences for evolutionary theory. One reason evolutionism went into eclipse in Darwin's later years and for many years thereafter was because he and other evolutionists of his day had no adequate explanation for the process of variation. Darwin's theory of natural selection could explain the elimination of various forms of life, but how and why did new forms arise? The new science of genetics, with its discovery of the processes of mutation, recombination, and genetic drift, provided answers to these questions.

While there has been no development in the social sciences with as profound an impact as this, more recent evolutionism in sociology, anthropology, and archaeology differ in several fundamental respects from their nineteenth- and early-twentieth-century predecessors. Above all, the older evolutionism generally lacked a satisfactory explanation of the *causes* of societal development and growth. As Marvin Harris (1968) has noted, early evolutionary theory in the social sciences tended to be either eclectic or racialist in its explanations. Modern evolutionary theory, in contrast, explains the most basic patterns and trends in human societies and their cultures in terms of some combination of the following: (1) humanity's common genetic heritage, (2) the various technologies our species has fashioned to enhance this heritage, (3) the resources and constraints of the biophysical environment, (4) the resources and constraints of the sociocultural environment, and (5) the impact of the process of intersocietal selection. This newer emphasis is the result of a number of significant developments in the social sciences, most notably the striking advances in archaeology, the growing appreciation of the explanatory power of ecological perspectives, and, not least of all, the experience of societies themselves in the last hundred years.

A second important difference between the older and newer evolutionary theories in the social sciences involves the concept of progress. In the older evolutionism there was a pervasive tendency to see progress in almost every sphere of life, from the technological to the moral. Contemporary evolutionists do not share this view. Over many extended periods, societal evolution seems to have resulted in a *deterioration* in the quality of life for the great majority of people, and *lowered* standards of morality as well. These trends are especially evident in the period from the end of the hunting and gathering era (ca. 7,000 B.C.) to the modern era (Lenski, 1970: 468–477). Furthermore, some contemporary evolutionists regard a catastrophic end to human history (e.g., via a nuclear holocaust) as a distinct possibility. Thus, when the term "progress" is used by evolutionists today, it refers to certain specific developments with a clear directional component (e.g., an increase in the division of labor) rather than to an improvement in the quality of life, as most nineteenth-century evolutionists would have meant the term. The closest today's evolutionists come to the older view is when some of us assert that the basic trend in sociocultural evolution has been a progressive expansion of the store of information available to the human societies viewed as a whole. This assertion, however, contains no assumptions about moral progress or any other form of human betterment.

Third, the newer evolutionary theory rejects the determinism that was often present in the older evolutionary theory. This change is largely a result of the tremendous impact that statistical theory has had on the social sciences since World War II. Even in situations where reliable quantitative data are lacking, contemporary evolutionists formulate their theoretical models in probabilistic terms.

Finally, compared with the work of Spencer, Tylor, Morgan, Sumner, and other nineteenth-century evolutionists, the newer evolutionism rests on a firmer and richer foundation of archaeological, ethnographic, and historical data. These data have greatly enhanced our understanding of the limits that various subsistence technologies set on development in other aspects of life, and of the varying probabilities that apply to the social and cultural options that fall within those limits.

In view of these changes, it is a serious mistake to suppose that contemporary evolutionary theory is simply a revival of earlier theory. While the new evolutionary theory incorporates many ideas developed in the past, the basic theoretical framework differs in fundamental ways from the theories of Spencer, Tylor, and others of the past.

Why the Revival of Evolutionary Theory?

This brings us to the last of our preliminary questions: Why the revival of evolutionary theory? What makes it more attractive today than in the recent past?

A number of factors, it seems, are responsible. To begin with, breakthroughs in various areas of science have removed serious impediments to the growth and development of evolutionary theory. Genetics is a good example of this, providing, as it has, an answer to a fundamental question that the older Darwinian theory could not address.

In the social sciences, the discovery, since World War II, of several techniques for accurately dating archaeological remains (e.g., the radiocarbon, potassium-argon, and fission-tracking techniques) has been especially important. Previously, it was impossible to establish a reliable chronology for the first 99.9 percent of our species' span of existence. This meant that reliable ordering of sequences of events in widely scattered excavation sites was usually impossible. Even when linkages between multiple sequences could be agreed upon, there was no way of determining with any accuracy the actual time spans involved. Thus, prior to the discovery of these new techniques, impasses were reached with respect to a number of critical questions relevant to evolutionary theory.

Our knowledge of human societies has also been enlarged enormously by other developments too numerous to review here in entirety or in detail. Several, however, merit mention. These include the important work of the Leakeys and other physical anthropologists who have contributed so much to the understanding of our more remote prehistoric ancestors; the work of Jane van Lawick-Goodall and other primatologists who have revolutionized thinking about our closest primate relatives; the work of George Peter Murdock and his associates and successors who have systematized and quantified much of the data concerning modern preliterate societies; the research of the new breed of social historians that has so greatly increased our understanding of the daily lives of ordinary people in agrarian societies of the past; the work of sociologists, anthropologists, and others since World War II who have added so much to our knowledge of less developed societies; the work of political scientists and historians who have brought to light the realities of life in Communist societies; and, finally, the work of UN bureaucrats and others who have supplied us with a vast body of comprehensive and systematic data on nearly all societies of the present era. Collectively, such work has made it possible to rebuild evolutionary theory in the social sciences on a far more solid empirical foundation than was possible fifty or a hundred years ago.

Important as these contributions have been, the revival of interest in evolutionary theory in the social sciences might not have occurred if we lived in a more tranquil or more stable era. The twentieth century, of course, was anything but tranquil or stable. On the contrary, the social and cultural change of that period was more rapid, more pervasive, and more critical than in any previous century. The struggles of the less developed nations, and the problems associated with these struggles, have been especially important in reviving interest in the classic issues of nineteenth- and early-twentieth-century social science. Modernization theory, world-system theory, and dependency theory have been other important responses to the issues raised by the divergent trajectories of human societies in recent centuries, and all of them can be considered *mesochronic* evolutionary theories (i.e., theories concerned with *intermediate-length* patterns of change). The revival of interest in the larger questions of classical theory was also stimulated by the emergence of Communist societies and the controversies they generated, and by the conflict between revolutionary socialist, democratic socialist, and liberal capitalist ideologies.

In view of the revolutionary nature of the modern era, it was unfortunate that, in the early decades of the last century, sociology and anthropology abandoned the diachronic perspective of evolutionary theory and adopted the synchronic perspective of structural-functionalism. Because of this, the important dimension of time either was eliminated from social theory and research and replaced by correlational analysis (as in survey research), or its use was restricted to the briefest of intervals—sequences measured in decades at most. Longer sequences, and the larger issues associated with them, were largely ignored or were dealt with in superficial terms (e.g., in simplistic comparisons of traditional and modern societies and of *Gemeinschaft* and *Gesellschaft*).

Structural-functional theory possessed another feature that helps to explain the revival of interest in evolutionary theory: It tended to focus on the internal dynamics of social systems to the neglect of relationships between systems and their environments. One consequence of this was a built-in bias toward reductionist strategies in both theory building and research. Classic issues concerning total societies and their development were subtly transmuted into questions about social institutions and other subsocietal systems, and these, in turn, into questions about social roles and individual attitudes and behavior.

Under the circumstances, it was hardly surprising that as scholars found themselves confronted from time to time with one or another of the larger questions in their disciplines, some turned to ecological and/or evolutionary theory. These included Otis Dudley Duncan, William Catton, Amos Hawley, Talcott Parsons, and Robert Winch in sociology; Julian Steward, Walter Goldschmidt, Elman Service, Marshall Sahlins, Robert Carneiro, and Marvin Harris in anthropology; Robert Adams, Robert Braidwood, and Kent Flannery in archaeology; and Kenneth Boulding, economist-turned-sociologist—to name but a few of the more prominent early contributors. Despite important differences among them, each contributed to the revival of interest in evolutionary theory in the last half-century.

When one studies the work of these scholars and others who share their concerns, it is not hard to discern the outlines of an emerging paradigm that combines elements of structural-functional theory, ecological theory, Marxian theory, and evolutionary theory. This new paradigm shares with traditional structural-functional theories a concern for the internal processes of social systems, for relations among the parts of these systems, and for relations between parts and the whole. But it adds to this a number of other important features: (1) a greater appreciation of the role of conflict within and between groups; (2) a greatly heightened concern with macrosystems, especially total societies and the global system of societies; (3) a heightened concern for the relation of these systems to their environments, both sociocultural and biophysical; (4) a concern for the longer-term processes of change in these systems; (5) a much greater appreciation of the importance of technological innovation in societal development; and (6) a more realistic view of the impact of genetics on human nature.

Thanks to these elements, the social sciences are now able to provide *a reasonably reliable and comprehensive map of the most important features of the social universe from prehistoric times to the present and, more important, a theory capable of explaining those features.* This is something they were unable to do in the recent past, and their inability to perform these elementary yet basic tasks contributed far more than most have recognized to public skepticism concerning these disciplines and their claims to scientific status. In many ways, the social sciences in most of the twentieth century were like biology before Linnaeus and others provided the first reasonably reliable and detailed map of the biological universe, and before Darwin provided the first theory capable of accounting for many of its basic features. Now, however, and at long last, social scientists have the tools that are needed not only to identify the major "social phyla" in their universe and map relations among them but also to explain many of their most important features. And, since evolutionary theory, more than any other, offers the kinds of conceptual tools and resources needed to map this universe, the revival of interest in this line of theory should come as no surprise.

Aim and Plan of This Volume

The primary aim of this volume is to provide a systematic and comprehensive statement of an ecologically oriented evolutionary theory that may prove useful in this new century. Because this is an effort to *build* theory, and not simply a survey or history of theory, I have drawn selectively from the work of others, incorporating those elements that seem most useful while omitting others that seem less promising or relevant. The scholars to whom I am most indebted (or, at least, most aware of indebtedness) are Adam Ferguson, John Millar, Thomas Malthus, Charles Darwin, Herbert Spencer, Karl Marx, Friedrich Engels, Gaetano Mosca, Robert Michels, Albert Keller, V. Gordon Childe, William Ogburn, George Peter Murdock, George Gaylord Simpson, Leslie White, Julian Steward, Amos Hawley, and Marvin Harris.[1]

I offer this list in the probably futile hope of discouraging those critics of evolutionary theory (e.g., Levine, 1982; Peel, 1971) who persist in tracing the lineage of the present theory exclusively back to Herbert Spencer, or alternatively to Spencer and Sumner. The heritage of this theory is far richer than their putative genealogies suggest, and far more of a synthesis of previous work than they have recognized or acknowledged.

This volume differs substantially from *Human Societies* (Lenski, 1970; Lenski and Lenski, 1974–1987; Lenski, Lenski, and Nolan, 1991–1995; Nolan and Lenski, 1999, 2004). Much of that volume in its various editions has been devoted to a survey of the enormous and varied body of evidence on which modern evolutionary theory rests. In the present volume, I assume that readers have access to that evidence and limit myself to a more detailed discussion of the theory itself than was appropriate in *Human Societies.*[2]

Part I of this volume lays out the basic principles and concepts of an ecologically oriented evolutionary theory of societal development. It specifies the nature of the relationship between biological evolution and sociocultural evolution and establishes the emergent properties of the latter. And, perhaps most important, this section establishes the distinction between specific and general evolution (Sahlins and Service, 1960), which is to say, between the processes of continuity and change in individual societies and those in the total global system of societies. Much of the criticism of the older evolutionary theory has been due to the failure of earlier theorists to clarify this distinction, and much of the criticism directed at contemporary evolutionary theory is based on the failure of critics to grasp the paradoxical nature of the relationship between these two levels of the evolutionary process.

Part II of this volume shifts the focus of attention from an exposition of general principles to an analysis of a series of specific problems and issues. One chapter involves the application of evolutionary theory to the analysis of a single society, ancient Israel, and its development. Two others focus on sets of societies, Communist societies, industrializing horticultural societies, and industrial agrarian societies. A fourth focuses on a major transformation in the evolution of the global system, the remarkable rise of the West in recent centuries.

---

1. This ordering is roughly chronological and not based on any judgment as to the relative importance of their contributions.

2. Those who are not familiar with the supporting evidence for the theory will find it helpful to examine *Human Societies* in conjunction with the reading of the present volume.

Part II is designed to show how the application of evolutionary theory can lead to insights that tend to be missed otherwise. Too often, I have found, the graduate training that most sociologists have received in recent decades makes it extraordinarily difficult to grasp the value of a macrochronic, macrostructural theory or to understand how such a theory can be tested. I hope that the examples I have chosen (which are intentionally as diverse as possible) will help some, at least, to discover the potential benefits of this kind of theory and arrive at a greater understanding of how such a theory can be applied and tested.

Part II also provides an opportunity to demonstrate how evolutionary theory permits one to juxtapose the most general analysis of trends in the global system of societies with analyses of various specific problems in individual societies, all the while working within the framework of a single integrated and coherent theoretical system. One of the greatest attractions of the present theory, I believe, is the opportunity it provides for moving from one level of analysis to another, without slipping into reductionism or mere *ad hoc* generalization. Related to this, I further believe, is the fact that the new evolutionary theory provides sociology with its best hope for overcoming its present fragmented and anarchic state. This theory has a remarkable capacity for absorbing and integrating diverse theories of more limited scope.

This is not to suggest that the new evolutionary theory can explain all of the infinite variety of problems that have been raised concerning human societies and their component elements. Such an ability is beyond the power of any theory. What we can hope for, and what I believe the present theory can provide, is a parsimonious and internally consistent explanation of most of the basic features of the global system of societies and of individual societies and sets of societies. Indeed, it can provide a meaningful map of the social universe throughout history and prehistory—something that has been lacking in sociology since the demise of the older evolutionism. I also believe that the present theory offers sufficient flexibility to allow modifications to be made in the light of new evidence and valid criticism without, at the same time, creating so much flexibility that it degenerates into mere eclecticism (Harris, 1979). In short, I believe this theory offers a unique opportunity to enhance our understanding of the crucial processes of continuity and change at work in the complex and fascinating world of human societies.

2

PROBLEM AND METHOD

The basic aim of the present theory can be stated quite simply: It is *to explain as many as possible of the more important characteristics of human societies, both individually and collectively, past as well as present, as parsimoniously and as falsifiably as possible.* Why, for example, have some societies been large and others small? Why have some had a complex division of labor and large urban populations while others have had neither? Why have some had substantial inequality among their members while others have had little? Why have some been warlike and expansionistic while others have been peaceable and content to live within their boundaries? In short, the new evolutionary theory seeks to provide a theoretical foundation for a comprehensive science of human societies.

Because the characteristics of human societies are so numerous and varied, it is imperative, at the outset, to establish priorities to guide theory construction and related research. Not all of the characteristics of human societies are equally important from an explanatory standpoint. Some are epiphenomenal in nature and can be safely ignored, especially in the earlier stages of theory building and research. Leisure activities, for example, while important to the individuals involved, are not as important to an understanding of societies and their development as the production of goods and services and governance.

It is also important to recognize at the outset that the new theory is concerned with the characteristics of societies at three levels: (1) individual societies, (2) sets of societies, and (3) the global system of societies. This approach draws attention to a paradox that has long been a stumbling block in efforts to construct a science of societies. Before we turn to these matters, however, it may be wise to spell out several assumptions that underlie the theory.

Epistemological Assumptions

Every theory rests on a foundation of epistemological assumptions, and the present theory is no exception. Many of its assumptions are so generally acknowledged and accepted that it would be tedious and counterproductive to discuss them here. Some are not, however, and need to be made explicit.

To begin with, it should be noted that ecological-evolutionary theory (as I have called the present theory) assumes that *valid theory construction in the social sciences requires frequent and continuous alternation between the processes of induction and deduction.* Neither process alone is sufficient, as is evident from the failure of countless efforts to build a viable theory of human societies "from the bottom up" by a process of induction or "from the top down" by the use of deductive logic. Because of the fantastic complexity of sociocultural systems, we are compelled to shuttle back and forth endlessly between tentative theoretical assertions and empirical tests of those assertions, with the latter often leading to modifications of the theory and those, in turn, leading to new empirical tests.

In short, theory must be *open-ended.* This is one of the important differences between science and religion and quasi-religions, such as the "scientific socialism" of Marxists of the recent past. The new evolutionary theory embraces the processes of self-correction and modification that are necessary consequences of a method involving the use of both induction and deduction.

Second, ecological-evolutionary theory assumes *the necessity of the comparative method.* To say that the method is comparative is merely another way of saying that the methodological basis of the theory is the same as that which underlies all of the sciences. From the perspective of science, nothing can be understood except when seen in relation to other things. No science can be based on the study of a single tree, a single star, or a single society, since all the characteristics that the sciences consider important—force, mass, speed, temperature, age—are abstractions derived from a process of systematic comparison. In fact, it seems safe to say that the degree of scientific understanding of any entity or phenomenon tends to be proportional to the range and diversity of entities or phenomena to which it has been compared.

Unfortunately, this principle has often been ignored by sociologists, especially in the United States since World War I. Ever since the rise of the Chicago school in the 1920s, the attention of most American sociologists has been focused on their own society, a tendency that Everett Hughes was once led to characterize as "ethnocentric sociology." This tendency was greatly strengthened by the rise of functionalist theory, which sought to replace the older and more focused concept of "human societies" with the extremely abstract concept of the "social system" as the basic unit of analysis in sociological theory. By shifting the focus of theoretical concern to this vastly more inclusive concept, it became tempting to believe that theory could be constructed satisfactorily merely by comparing various social systems within a single society. Thus, the comparisons of primary groups with bureaucracies, for example, could substitute for the comparison of one kind of society with another.

Had this logic been made more explicit, its inadequacy would have become obvious. Instead, it remained largely unstated with the result that a subtle, but profound, change occurred in the nature of the problems sociologists studied. Increasingly, American sociology became, as Hughes observed, the study of American institutions and American organizations. Worse yet, it became the study of *contemporary* American institutions and organizations, as functionalist theory legitimized static, structural analyses in which the time dimension was ignored or largely neglected. Thus, the study of change—especially macrochronic change—almost disappeared during the heyday of functionalism.

Ecological-evolutionary theory seeks to restore the comparative study of human societies to its former place at the core of sociology. The theory assumes that subsocietal systems, such as families, religious groups, and work groups, cannot be adequately explained without substantial understanding of the societal systems in which they are embedded, and this understanding can come only from the systematic, comparative study of *the universe of human societies, past as well as present.* One reason for the frequent allegation that American sociology is little more than common sense packaged in obfuscating jargon is the failure of American sociologists to employ the tools of the comparative method. For, while substantial knowledge of one's own society is acquired by most people simply as a part of the socialization process, systematic knowledge of human societies as a whole, and the relevance of this knowledge to one's own society, is not.

Third, the new evolutionary theory assumes *the necessity of incorporating the time dimension into both theory and research.* No amount of knowledge of the characteristics of a society, or set of societies, at any single point in their history can substitute for knowledge of these characteristics over the entire history of the society, or set of societies. Data pertaining to change are especially important in efforts to explain the characteristics of societies. In fact, the experimental method—the most powerful tool available to science—presupposes the possibility of observing and measuring phenomena at two or more points in time.

Unfortunately, data on extended sequences of change that measure up to the rigorous requirements of the experimental method are rarely available in the social sciences, and methodological compromises are unavoidable. Where better data are lacking, we are forced to rely on correlational data and on data for which many relevant controls are lacking. Such efforts, though subject to criticism by purists, can be justified on the grounds that some evidence is better than none at all, and that weak inferences based on such evidence are better than pure speculation or the refusal to deal with important questions merely because the evidence leaves much to be desired. Moreover, there is a measure of protection against possible abuse in such cases, since multiple imperfect tests of hypotheses are often possible. Furthermore, elements of a theory that are based on limited evidence and weak inferences must always be congruent with other elements of the theory that rest on firmer foundations.

Fourth, modern evolutionary theory assumes that *human societies are systems, but imperfect systems.* In other words, it assumes that human societies are entities made up of interrelated parts, and that this is critical to an understanding of their various characteristics. They are not simply aggregations of unrelated elements in chance conjunction with one another, as are the contents of a typical trash container. Thus, students of human societies cannot safely adopt the reductionist strategy of analyzing only the components of societies in the expectation that the sum of the explanations of the components will be the explanation of the society as a whole.

At the same time, however, it is important to keep in mind that human societies fall far short of what we expect of a true, or ideal, system. The actions of the parts are not nearly as well coordinated as we find them in mechanical or electronic systems, and the interests of the members of human societies, unlike those of the members of certain insect societies, often lead to intrasystem conflict. Failure to take these facts into account can lead to a very misleading view of human societies, especially the larger, more complex, and interdependent of them. Thus, while it is necessary to take account of the substantial interdependence of the parts of every human society, it is important not to exaggerate the degree of that interdependence (W. Moore, 1963).

Fifth, the new theory is committed to what Marvin Harris (1968, 1979) has called the *etic principle.* In other words, the scientific community—rather than the members of the societies whose organization and activities are being analyzed— is considered the ultimate judge of the adequacy of categories, concepts, and explanations relating to individual societies or sets of societies. Thus, evolutionary theory today differs from ethnomethodology, symbolic interactionism, deconstructionism, and other subjectivist theories. Members of societies may suggest categories, concepts, or explanations, but they are not considered the best judges of their adequacy.

Finally, the theory presented in this volume is *probabilistic and nondeterministic.* The theory does not claim that it will ever be possible to explain and predict with precision all of the characteristics of human societies. On the contrary, it assumes that many of them will remain unexplainable and unpredictable. In part, this is due to the phenomenon of emergence, which, as we have seen, is an essential element of the evolutionary process. Also, because of the complex nature of human societies, the relatively small number of cases available for study and analysis, the imperfections in the data sources, and the impossibility of controlled experimentation, formulations of relations can rarely be both precise and highly specified at the same time. Finally, there is an inevitable tradeoff between the goal of explanatory parsimony and the goal of explanatory adequacy: Striving for adequacy alone leads to a theory that explains everything in terms of everything. In effect, the development of a parsimonious theory of human societies requires that some information be deliberately ignored. For example, while there is reason to believe that every individual and every event in a society has some influence, however minuscule, on the subsequent development of that society, ecological-evolutionary theory makes no attempt to take all of these forces into account. However, by excluding them from its *explanans,* the theory necessarily introduces an element of unpredictability into its analysis.[1]

Basic Units of Analysis

As is evident by now, human societies are the entities whose characteristics the new evolutionary theory is designed to explain and predict. Although the theory deals with other elements of social organization ranging from the nuclear family to the global system of societies, these are always viewed from the standpoint of their relation to individual societies.

The concept of "societies," it should be noted, is not unique to the social sciences. Entomologists, primatologists, and others in the biological sciences (e.g., Emerson, 1959; Kummer, 1971; Wilson, 1971, 1975) view *human* societies as a species-specific instance of a more general phenomenon that includes such diverse entities as colonies of insects, schools of fish, flocks of birds, herds of elephants, packs of wolves, and colonial invertebrates of various kinds (e.g., corals, sponges, the Portuguese man-of-war). Edward O. Wilson (1975) has defined "society," in this generic sense, as "a group of individuals belonging to the same species and organized in a cooperative manner."

This definition, while appropriate and adequate for other species, is not sufficiently specific when applied to humans, since it fails to differentiate between the larger and more inclusive groups to which the term is customarily applied by social scientists (e.g., American society, Roman society, Incan society) and the many subgroups, such as families, communities, and specialized associations of various kinds, that these larger groups contain.

To avoid confusion, sociologists need to increase the specificity of the more general definition. Thus, *to the degree that an aggregation of people is politically autonomous and engaged in a broad range of cooperative activities, it can be considered a society*). Societies are, in effect, *the primary organizational subdivisions of the human population as a whole.* While a few other kinds of organizations (e.g., religious groups) sometimes have larger numbers of members, these are highly specialized entities that lack the broad and comprehensive range of cooperative activities that are an essential element of societies.

---

1. The exclusion of variables from the *explanans* is not done capriciously. Decisions to include or exclude variables are based primarily on judgments concerning their relative predictive power across the entire spectrum of human societies. While this approach may mean less predictive power in the case of certain societies, or certain developments within those societies, it ensures greater predictive power overall. A second consideration that influences decisions is the quality of available evidence relating to different variables, with preference given to those for which the evidence seems more reliable.

In practice, it is sometimes difficult to apply the present definition of societies, since self-governance exists in varying degrees. Some small and less-developed societies have gradually been absorbed over an extended period by larger and more powerful neighbors (e.g., native American groups). In such cases, it is all but impossible to specify the precise point at which the smaller entity ceased to be a society, but that level of precision is seldom necessary.

The present definition of human societies, it may be noted, differs significantly from the customary anthropological definition that equates societies with linguistic and/or cultural groupings. (Ember and Ember [1981], for example, define a society as "a territorial population speaking a language not generally understood by neighboring territorial populations.") Such a definition creates several problems. To begin with, it is incompatible with the definition that biologists have found to be most fruitful: The linguistic and cultural groupings that anthropologists call societies frequently lack the element of cooperation that is the foundation of the biological definition. Incompatibility with the biological definition is not a fatal flaw *per se;* but when the definition also shifts the focus of analysis from critically important entities to others whose impact is much more limited, its usefulness becomes doubtful.

It is no accident that nation-states rather than linguistic/cultural groupings are the primary units of most analyses of the modern world. Thus, although North and South Koreans share a common language and cultural heritage, there has been no cooperation between them for decades and they obviously function as separate and discrete social entities. To a slightly lesser degree, the same is true of the English-speaking peoples who are scattered in various nations around the world, the Spanish-speaking peoples of Europe and the New World, and the Arab-speaking peoples of North Africa and the Middle East. Cooperation among the members of these more inclusive populations has been far more limited than that among members of nation-states, and consequently their impact on the world scene has also been more limited overall. In fact, as recent events in the former Soviet Union and Yugoslavia remind us, the chief importance sociologically of linguistic and cultural groups has been that they sometimes give rise to the formation of new nation-states.

What is true today has also been true in the past: Political boundaries have tended to define the limits for most kinds of cooperative activities, and the social entities defined by these boundaries have generally been more effective bases for organizing such activities than have the entities defined by linguistic and other cultural criteria. Thus, the failure of the Crusades, for example, seems to have been due as much to the political divisions within the Christian camp and their resulting inability to cooperate with one another as to the military might of the enemy. A common faith was not enough to prevent Christians from the West from plundering and destroying the Christian Byzantine Empire, despite the threat from nearby Muslim forces. Even among peoples who have been technologically and organizationally much less advanced, political boundaries have usually defined the outer limits of the more extensive kinds of cooperative activities.

Definitions based on political boundaries provide two other important advantages from the standpoint of theory and its development. First, it is generally much easier for researchers to agree on the boundaries of politically defined populations than on the boundaries of linguistically and culturally defined populations, thus enabling them to apply the definitions in a consistent manner. And, second, vastly more data are available concerning politically defined populations than are available for linguistically and culturally defined populations. These are vitally important considerations, since without consensus concerning the basic units of analysis in a field of study, and without an adequate body of relevant data, theories cannot be tested and knowledge in the area cannot be advanced.

Thus, without minimizing or denying the importance of linguistic or other cultural criteria, or their usefulness for certain purposes, the present theory employs a political criterion in its definition of societies.

Before concluding this discussion of the units of analysis, it may be noted that ecological-evolutionary theory is concerned with *sets of societies* as well as individual societies. Most of these sets are analytical constructs, such as modern industrial societies, agrarian societies, and hunting and gathering societies. One set, however, is an entity in its own right, a system of interactive parts: This is the global system of societies, which consists of the totality of human societies. In this connection, it should be noted that one of the greatest challenges confronting the new evolutionary theory—and every other sociological theory, for that matter—is to explain the characteristics of the different levels of social organization without slipping either into a reductionist mode of analysis that ignores the systemic properties of the higher level or into an overly reified mode that exaggerates the impact of the system on its constituent elements.

Dependent Variables: Characteristics of Individual Societies

The most striking characteristic of human societies has almost certainly been their enormous variability. This is especially evident when they are compared with societies established by members of other species. While it would be a mistake to imagine that one society of a given species of termites is a carbon copy of other societies of that same species, or that one society of elephants is exactly like other societies of elephants, these would be far less serious errors than to assume the same concerning human societies.

There is no better indication of the tremendous variability of human societies than their size. Chinese society and Indian society today each have more than a billion members and a number of other societies have populations of 100 million or more. In contrast, ethnographers and others have reported the existence of societies with populations of twenty or less, and between these extremes, every possible level has been found at one time or another.

What is true of population size is true of scores of other characteristics: (a) Levels of production and consumption of goods, (b) levels of wealth and income,

(c) extent of occupational, organizational, and regional specialization, (d) levels of intrasocietal inequality in power, privilege, and prestige, (e) size of territories, and (f) magnitude of resources controlled are but a few of the many important variables with ranges rivaling or surpassing those of population size.

One of the most important of the variable characteristics of societies is the amount of energy its members consume. No human activity—not even thought— is possible without energy, and the quantity and nature of the energy available to the members of a society profoundly influence their patterns of life. In the smallest and technologically least advanced societies, energy has been derived almost totally from food and has equaled as little as 40,000 calories per day, or perhaps even less. In contrast, members of American society derive most of the energy they consume from inanimate sources, especially natural gas, petroleum, and coal. American society currently consumes on a daily basis more than 60 quadrillion calories of energy from the inanimate sources alone, or roughly 1.6^{12} times more energy than the smallest and least advanced societies.

As humanists remind us, the variability of human societies is not limited to characteristics to which we can apply numbers and measure quantitatively. It also manifests itself in religious beliefs and practices, patterns of political organization, art forms, and more. With respect to religion, there have been societies that practiced animism, ancestor worship, polytheism, henotheism, monotheism, and atheism, both exclusively and in various combinations. Moreover, when these categories are examined more closely, further variations appear: Monotheism, for example, includes Zoroastrianism, Judaism, Christianity, Islam, and the many sects to which each of these has given rise. Political systems have been almost as varied, ranging from the participatory democracies of some societies of hunters and gatherers to the extraordinarily powerful and centralized autocracies found during certain periods in the Ottoman Empire or in Mughal India, for example, or more recently in Germany under Hitler, the Soviet Union under Stalin, or China under Mao. In politics, as in religion, general labels often suggest greater uniformity than actually exists. Thus, although Britain and the United States are both commonly labeled "western democracies," the specifics of their political systems vary substantially.

Because the variability of human societies is so great, some deny the possibility of a science of human societies. This is the view not only of most humanists but of a number of social scientists as well, and it is especially evident among area specialists, historians, and ethnographers who have devoted their careers to the study of some single society and who, therefore, are extremely sensitive to the unique features of that society. Such specialists often react vigorously—even contemptuously—to efforts to establish generalizations that include "their" society, and many challenge the validity of any generalization pertaining to human life and human societies.

Given the enormous variability of human societies and the limited number of well-documented cases available, it is clear that a science of human societies cannot be constructed in the same manner as certain of the physical sciences, such as chemistry, which are concerned with problems involving units of analysis available in virtually unlimited quantities and possessing only a small number of characteristics requiring explanation. In the study of human societies, unfortunately, there are far too many variables and far too few degrees of freedom for the experimental method to be applied even in *post hoc* statistical analyses.

Yet, that said, it is equally true that there are striking patterns present in the data pertaining to human societies that cannot and should not be ignored. There are significant correlations of many kinds that cry out for interpretation and explanation—even when interpretation and explanation require the exercise of inference.

Since at least the middle of the eighteenth century, Western scholars have recognized an interesting set of correlations involving *the basic mode of subsistence in societies and a broad set of other important characteristics.* Thus, as early as 1748, Montesquieu was able to write:

> There is this difference between savage and barbarous nations: the former are dispersed clans, which . . . cannot be joined in a body; and the latter are commonly small nations, capable of being united. The savages are generally hunters; the barbarians are herdsmen and shepherds. (p. 176)

Two years later, in 1750, A.-R.-J. Turgot noted the relation between a society's mode of subsistence and its population density and patterns of social organization. For example, in comparing pastoral and agricultural societies, he wrote that the practice of agriculture permitted the earth

> to sustain many more than were required to till it. Hence, to a greater extent than among pastoral peoples, men were free for other work: hence, towns, commerce . . . a greater ability in war, the division of labor, the inequality of men, domestic slavery, and precise ideas of government. (Harris, 1968: 28)

The recognition of correlations such as these between a society's basic mode of subsistence and its other characteristics gave rise to a taxonomy of human societies that persisted well into the twentieth century. In its simplest form, it differentiated among savage, barbarian, and civilized societies, with the former being identified with hunting bands and the latter with nations of plow agriculturalists containing small urban and literate minorities. Some writers even took note of finer distinctions, differentiating, for example, between pastoralists and preplow horticulturalists, whom others lumped together in the category of barbarians.

Critics of the comparative method, as this mode of analysis has come to be known, have been quick to point out various exceptions to generalizations, such as those of Montesquieu, Turgot, and their successors, and also to point out that some characteristics of societies bear little or no relationship to a society's mode of subsistence. Nevertheless, despite this, the existence of numerous strong and intriguing correlations cannot be denied and remain a challenge to the social sciences.

Important linkages have also been observed between the geographical location and biophysical environments of societies and various features of the societies themselves. Thus, the societies of Africa and the New World never achieved the same levels of size and organizational complexity as some of the societies of Asia and Europe prior to the modern era. Societies in arctic regions and in tropical rain forests have been especially small and organizationally underdeveloped. In contrast, societies that have developed in broad river basins or in proximity to navigable bodies of water have generally enjoyed greater levels of wealth and cultural development than have societies that lacked these attributes. These correlations, too, are a challenge to the social sciences that should not be ignored.

Lastly, there are correlations between the religions of societies and their level of social and economic development. In the nineteenth and early twentieth centuries, various scholars observed that Christian societies, and more especially Protestant societies, were economically and otherwise more advanced than non-Christian and non-Protestant societies (e.g., Weber, 1958). The least advanced societies were those that practiced animism. Between these extremes there have been societies with other universal faiths, such as Islam and Buddhism. Once again, although there was great disagreement concerning the cause of these correlations, there was little disagreement regarding the correlations themselves.

Second, in addition to the search for explanations of the features of societies shared by sets of societies, the present theory seeks to explain unique, but important, characteristics of individual societies. The Indian belief in the sacredness of the cow, for example, is peculiar to that society and has played, and still plays, an important role in the life of that society. What was the origin of this belief? Why did it spread, and how has it managed to persist even in times of famine when thousands of people starved rather than kill and eat a cow? Similarly, how does one explain American society's adoption of a republican form of government in the eighteenth century, a time when monarchy was the prevailing form of government throughout the civilized world? And what factors were responsible for the early adoption and spread of the democratic form of government in American society? These and countless other important features of individual societies are among the facts that every theory of human societies must address. We cannot expect, of course, that any single reasonably parsimonious theory will explain all such facts, but the aim of every theory is to explain *as much as possible, as parsimoniously as possible,* and the present theory is no exception.

Third, ecological-evolutionary theory is challenged to explain *societal universals*—those characteristics that vary little, if at all, from one society to the next. Thus, in every society of which we have knowledge, there has been a division of labor along the lines of age and sex. Certain activities have been defined as the responsibility of men, others as the responsibility of women, and some as the responsibility of both, or either. Similarly, some activities are defined as the responsibility or prerogative of one age group or another. In addition, language, kinship ties, ritual, traditions, and customs are present in every society even though the specifics vary. These, too, require explanation.

Finally, because the present theory is an evolutionary theory, it directs attention to patterns of continuity and change in the characteristics of individual societies. In some societies, especially contemporary societies, change is a pervasive feature of life. In most societies of the past, however, change was far less frequent.

Most of the changes that have occurred in human societies have been of little or no importance from the standpoint of the survival and well-being of the society as a whole. This is true, for example, of such things as changes in the pronunciation of words, most changes in the content of myths and legends, minor changes in customs and moral codes, and changes in social practices that reflect merely the growth or decline in the influence of specific individuals and their varying traits of personality. Such changes have little or no impact on a society's size, productivity, mode of organization, or other sociologically important characteristics.

In contrast are changes that give rise to permanent alterations in the basic structure and functioning of the society. Sometimes these are the result of prior changes in either the biophysical or sociocultural environment of a society (e.g., a change in climate that affects food supplies or alters relations with neighboring societies). Such changes may also occur in response to some significant invention or discovery. Depending upon the nature of the change involved, the position of the society may be either enhanced or weakened. This more consequential kind of change, while relatively infrequent until the modern era, has been far more important for the populations involved and also for social theory.

Changes of the first kind (i.e., minimally important changes) are of little concern to evolutionary theorists: They are like the physicist's noise that has to be screened out in the search for signal. This is not always easy, however, especially when one is examining ongoing processes of change. What seems initially to be signal (i.e., a significant change with lasting consequences) often proves later to have been mere noise. There have been countless instances of this in the last century, as evidenced by many seemingly significant elections in industrial societies and political coups in Third World societies.

Dependent Variables: Characteristics of Sets of Societies

Since the days of the Greeks, scholars have recognized that individual societies share many of their characteristics with other societies and that these shared sets of characteristics can serve as a useful basis for defining sets of societies for purposes of analysis. Thus, Hippocrates, writing several centuries before the Christian era, argued that societies could be usefully differentiated on the basis of climatic conditions. The members of societies in warm climates, he argued, tended to be clever, but they were also weak and wicked, while the members of societies in cold climates tended to be strong and stupid. Somewhat immodestly he argued that the members of societies in temperate climates—such as his fellow Greeks—

combined the good qualities of both the others, but not their weaknesses. In later centuries, others from ibn-Khaldun to Ellsworth Huntington carried on and extended this tradition of analyzing sets of societies classified on the basis of geographic characteristics.

Not long after Hippocrates, Plato and Aristotle thought it important to differentiate between sets of societies defined on the basis of political or constitutional characteristics. Thus, Aristotle, in *Politics,* distinguished among monarchical, aristocratic, and democratic societies, and subdivided each of these on the basis of whether the polity served the common good or merely the special interests of the dominant faction or individual. This mode of classification, too, with various modifications and refinements continued to be popular until recent times, especially in political science.

Religion is another criterion that has often been used to define sets of societies for scholarly analysis. For centuries, western scholars have speculated about the differences between Christian and non-Christian societies, and this line of thought has often been extended to discussions of differences between more specific religious traditions. Thus, Protestant societies have been compared with Catholic, and Confucian with Puritan, as in the Weberian tradition.

Another widely used taxonomy of societies since the eighteenth century has been the one developed initially by Montesquieu, Turgot, and others, a system of classification that, as noted earlier, is based on societal modes of subsistence. While this method of classifying societies has undergone considerable modification and refinement since Montesquieu and Turgot, the basic underlying concept remains the same and the taxonomy continues to have great utility.

Working with different kinds of data, archaeologists of the nineteenth century developed a classification of societies based on the kinds of materials used in the manufacture of tools and weapons. The pioneer in this tradition, Christian Jurgenson Thomsen, a Danish museum curator, differentiated among Stone Age, Bronze Age, and Iron Age societies. Later, each of these categories was further subdivided, and this mode of classification remains in use today. Following the lead of V. Gordon Childe, however, a growing number of archaeologists have sought to link their discipline's traditional taxonomy with that derived from the work of Montesquieu and Turgot, with the result that now one often encounters taxonomies that are based on a combination of criteria involving both subsistence technology and materials technology.

Linked to these last two types of taxonomies, but distinct from both, is that developed in the nineteenth century by Marx. Marx classified societies on the basis of technology (the "forces of production") and social organization (the "relations of production"). Thus, the Marxian taxonomy divided societies into ones practicing primitive communism, the domestic mode of production, the Asiatic mode, the Germanic mode, the Slavonic mode, feudalism, capitalism, socialism, and advanced or modern communism (Marx, 1964, 1970). In recent years, neo-Marxists have proposed a number of additional categories to remedy deficiencies in the classical scheme. Accordingly, efforts to explain the failures of Soviet and other socialist societies led to discussions of developed socialist societies, bureau-cratic state socialist societies, deformed workers' societies, and others (cf., e.g., Evans, 1977). In addition, Immanuel Wallerstein (1974) has introduced the concepts of core societies, semiperipheral societies, and peripheral societies.

During the nineteenth century, many social scientists sought to establish a taxonomy based on the dominant mode of social organization in societies. Thus, Sir Henry Maine contrasted societies organized on the basis of status with those organized on the basis of contract; Ferdinand Toennies contrasted *Gemeinschaft* with *Gesellschaft;* and Emile Durkheim (1893) contrasted societies based on mechanical solidarity with those based on organic solidarity. In recent decades, Morton Fried and Elman Service refined and extended these earlier, simplistic formulations. Specifi-cally, Service (1962) proposed the following taxa: egalitarian clan societies (i.e., all clans equal), hierarchical clan or gens societies (i.e., one clan or gens superior to the others), chiefdoms, paramount chiefdoms, minimal states, and states.

One of the more obvious tasks for theorists is to explain and predict how these different systems of classification, and the various sets of societies they have generated, are related to one another. How strongly are they correlated? Can the sets generated by one system of classification be regarded as by-products of the sets generated by another? If we are ever to have a science of human societies, it is essential that we come to understand the relationships among the various taxono-mies and, more especially, the variables on which they are based.

One possibility that needs to be considered is that some of the sets em-ployed today are actually *subsets* of another more inclusive set. Thus, it is possible, for example, to consider socialist and capitalist societies as subsets of industrial societies. Similarly, Christian, Muslim, Hindu, and Confucian societies may be regarded as having been subsets of agrarian societies.

There is, unfortunately, a powerful temptation in modern sociology to ig-nore such questions, or to resolve them by recourse to statistical analysis. Neither of these "solutions" is satisfactory, however, because the problem is too important to be ignored and the quantitative data we possess are not adequate to the task of resolving the issue statistically (i.e., the relationships are only correlational). The solution lies instead, I believe, with the careful development of a general theory of societal adaptation and evolution and with an equally careful examination of *all of the relevant data*—nonquantitative as well as quantitative.

Dependent Variables: Characteristics of the Global System of Societies

Last, but by no means least, ecological-evolutionary theory must explain and pre-dict the important features of the global system of societies. As indicated above, this is not simply another set of societies. Unlike the sets we have just considered, the world system is more than an analytical construct: As its name indicates, it is a functioning system composed of interactive parts—namely, individual societies.

Two striking characteristics of the global system are (a) the extent to which it has been transformed and (b) the temporal pattern of this process. Prior to the modern era, most societies had *direct and sustained* contact with only a small number of neighboring societies; relations with more distant societies were indirect and mediated by intervening societies. Now, however, thanks to revolutionary advances in the technologies of transportation and communication made in the last century, most societies interact directly and in a sustained way with most other societies.

Much of the change in the global system is impossible to quantify, but there are important exceptions. For example, we now have reasonably accurate estimates of world population at several scattered points in history. One of these is the end of the hunting and gathering era, roughly 10,000 years ago. Estimates for this period are based on information about the extent of the territories inhabited at the time and their carrying capacity, with the latter based on numerous observations of modern hunting and gathering peoples living under similar conditions. The best estimates today range from 3 to 9 million. By the beginning of the Christian era, 8,000 years later, world population had grown to approximately 300 million, and during the next 1,700 years, by the eve of the Industrial Revolution, it grew to 750 million. Now, hardly more than 300 years later, it is over 6 billion and growing at a rate of approximately 75 million per year! Indeed, as these figures indicate, for most of the last 10,000 years (see Table 2.1) human population has been increasing at an exponential rate.

Energy consumption is another fundamental feature of the world system for which there are reasonably good estimates. Prior to the discovery of the uses of fire around 500,000 B.P. (Before the Present), food was the only source of energy in human societies. Assuming an average individual consumption of 2,000 calories per day by a population numbering half a million (a generous estimate for the time; see Hassan, 1981: ch. 12), we arrive at an estimate of energy consumption for the entire human population of 10^9 calories per day. Harrison Brown (1954) calculated that the use of fire and the domestication of animals (beginning about 10,000 B.P.) raised the daily consumption of energy for a part of the world's population to about 10,000 calories per day. Thus, by the start of the Christian era,

Table 2.1. The Growth of Human Population, 8000 B.C. to 2000 A.D.

Date	Population
8000 B.C.	3–9,000,000
1 A.D.	300,000,000
1650 A.D.	545,000,000
1750 A.D.	750,000,000
1850 A.D.	1,170,000,000
1950 A.D.	2,500,000,000
2000 A.D.	6,075,000,000

Sources: Dumond (1975); Hassan (1981); Grauman (1968); *Statistical Abstract of the United States, 2002.*

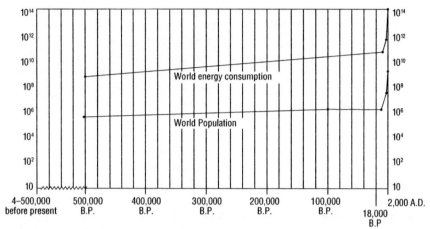

Figure 2.1 Log of world population and log of world energy consumption from 500,000 B.P. to the present

when the use of fire in human societies was virtually universal and animal domestication was practiced by a substantial percentage of societies, world energy consumption must have totaled approximately 2.5×10^{12} calories per day, or roughly 2,500 times the amount consumed 500 millennia earlier. Finally, individual consumption currently averages 50,000 calories per day worldwide, or 2.3×10^{14} calories per day—nearly a hundred-fold increase in just the last 2,000 years and more than a two hundred thousand-fold increase in the last 10,000 years.

Plotting these values graphically (see Figure 2.1), we see how the explosive acceleration in the rate of world energy consumption and population growth in the last 10,000 years, and especially in the last 200 years, brought to an end the pattern of gradual change that had prevailed for hundreds of millennia. The rapid nature of this acceleration, it should be noted, is understated visually in the diagram because of the logarithmic transformations of the measures of world population and world energy consumption. Without these transformations, it would be all but impossible to graph the trends on a normal-sized page. In interpreting Figure 2.1, the reader should also keep in mind that the trend lines cover only the most recent 10 to 12 percent of hominid history. If the trend lines were carried back to the point where our ancestral line had its beginnings 4–5 million years ago (i.e., if the figure were eight to ten times wider than it is), these lines would come close to the bottom of the chart. This is a further reminder of the unique character of the recent past.

The pattern of slow and gradual change over millions of years, followed by an explosive rate of change in recent millennia, is evident also in a number of other areas where quantification is much more difficult or impossible. The trend in the production of goods and services, for example, closely parallels that of energy consumption, since levels of production are highly correlated with the amounts of energy consumed. Not surprisingly, these trends are paralleled by trends in the accumulation of wealth in general and of capital goods in particular. Their rate of increase has been especially explosive in recent millennia, since accumulation was all but impossible until the beginnings of plant cultivation allowed for a more settled way of life. And, finally, the volume of illth, or waste and injurious products (e.g., harmful drugs), has also grown exponentially in recent times.

Many important trends did not even commence until the last few thousand years. For example, the first urban settlements (i.e., communities in which the majority of residents are free of the necessity of producing their own food and fibers) do not appear in the archaeological record until the last 8,000 to 9,000 years, and until recently their growth was slow. The best available evidence suggests that as recently as 200 years ago, no more than 5 percent of the human population lived in such communities, with the largest having a population of only about a million. Today, in contrast, nearly half of the world's population lives in urban communities, the largest of which, Tokyo, now has more than 34 million inhabitants.

The rise and spread of urban communities is closely linked to other important trends. Writing and monetary systems, for example, are both products of urban life, though neither appeared until thousands of years after the first urban settlements. The increase in the division of labor is another trend that has been largely dependent on the expansion of urban settlements. Judging from archaeological evidence, and from studies of nonurban societies that have survived into the modern era, it appears that, prior to the emergence of the first towns and cities, occupational specialization was based mainly on age and sex distinctions. Occasionally, preurban societies have had headmen and shamans who performed specialized tasks on a part-time basis, but specialization rarely went beyond this. In contrast, urban communities, from the outset, utilized full-time specialists of various kinds, ranging from religious and political functionaries to artisans, merchants, soldiers, and household servants. Since the beginning of the Industrial Revolution, occupational specialization has increased enormously. Although there is no measure of the extent of occupational specialization in the global system as a whole, the U.S. Department of Labor has identified more than 20,000 full-time occupational specialties in this one society alone.

The expansion of the division of labor is not merely a matter of increased occupational specialization, however. It also takes the form of increased organizational, regional, and even *societal* specialization. Over time, an extraordinarily complex division of labor has developed among both specialized associations (e.g., labor unions, universities, churches) and communities (e.g., political centers, resort communities, fishing villages, university towns). Regional and societal specialization is largely economic in nature, with different regions within societies, and different societies within the global system, specializing in the production of various types of goods and services. Communal and societal specialization have roots that go back to the hunting and gathering era, as indicated by archaeological evidence of early intersocietal trade. Associational specialization is more recent, and has been dependent on the rise of towns and cities. In all cases, however, the degree of specialization has risen exponentially, with the most dramatic increases occurring in the recent past.

The enormous increase in the division of labor within societies has been possible only because of the increased size of societies themselves. Prior to the beginnings of horticulture, the largest human settlement of which we have knowledge had an apparent population of 400 to 600 (Pfeiffer, 1978). Because of its location, however, it appears that this was merely a temporary convergence of several different societies that were attracted to the site by a rich seasonal salmon run. Studies of hunting and gathering societies of the modern era indicate that their populations have averaged no more than 25 to 50 (Hassan, 1981: ch. 6; Lenski et al., 1995: table 5.3), and rarely numbered as many as 100. Based on all we know about these groups, it seems unlikely that the limits on growth were very different in the past (Hassan, 1981: ch. 6).

Since the beginnings of horticulture, however, the average size of societies has steadily increased, with the increase having been especially pronounced since the rise and spread of industrialization. Today, the populations of societies average 20 to 30 million. This growth in numbers has been paralleled by growth in territorial size and in organizational complexity.

Not every sociologically important variable, however, is characterized by a pattern of continuing and exponential growth. One extremely important exception is the number of societies themselves. Prior to the beginnings of plant cultivation 9,000 years ago, the trend was upward, so far as one can judge today. This was due to the more or less continuous spread of human population into new territories and a process of frequent societal fission. This upward trend was almost certainly an irregular one in which periods of relative stability were punctuated periodically by surges following the initial entry of human groups into vast new territories, such as the Americas and Australia.

This upward trend was finally reversed sometime in the last 10,000 years as the process of forming *multicommunity* societies began and an ever-increasing number of smaller societies were conquered by, or otherwise absorbed into, more expansive neighbors. This trend has continued to the present day, with the result that the 100,000 or more societies into which the world system was divided just 9,000 years ago has been reduced to fewer than 300 today.[2] As we shall see in

---

2. No one knows exactly how many societies were in existence at the end of the Paleolithic, but modern estimates of the human population at that time, based on knowledge of the areas occupied and the levels of population density possible in hunting and gathering societies, indicate numbers in the range of 3 to 9 million, as noted earlier. In addition, modern studies of societies dependent wholly or largely on hunting and gathering indicate an average size of 25 to 30. Putting these figures together, we arrive at an estimate of 100,000 to 300,000 societies around 8,000 B.C. Since then, the number of societies has shrunk dramatically. There are today less than 200 independent nation-states and perhaps another 50 to 100 small, preliterate groups that still enjoy sufficient political autonomy to justify classifying them as societies.

Chapter 6, this development has been of critical importance to the overall transformation of the global system.

Another reversal of note is the declining level of *intra*societal inequality that has been associated with the rise and spread of industrialism in the last 100 years. Since early in the horticultural era, societal growth and development was always linked with increases in inequality within societies. Horticultural societies, for instance, were less egalitarian than hunting and gathering societies, and inequalities in agrarian societies were even more pronounced.

Had this trend continued, the level of inequality in modern industrial societies would have become substantially greater than in agrarian societies. This has not happened, however. Inequalities in the distribution of income and wealth (as measured by the Gini Index and similar measures of overall distribution) in advanced industrial societies, though enormous, are less than they were in agrarian societies of the past and still are in industrializing agrarian societies today. Political inequality, too, though still substantial, has been significantly reduced in all industrial societies.

Within the last quarter-century there has been an important reversal in another historic trend: A decline in the rate of population growth, begun in the late 1960s, promises to be the beginning of a new long-term trend. During the period from roughly 2,000,000 B.P. to about 10,000 B.P., the rate of population growth appears to have increased gradually from 0.00007 to 0.00150 percent per year (Dumond, 1975: 717). From 10,000 B.P. to 1960 A.D., the rate of growth increased much more rapidly, and by the early 1960s world population was increasing annually at a rate of 2.0 percent. Since then it has dropped back to a level of 1.2 percent. Given the many problems that population growth creates and the technological resources now available for controlling it, it seems unlikely that the long-term trend will again be reversed. In fact, one can now even begin to contemplate the possibility of a reversal in the growth of world population itself, and not simply in its rate of increase.

Another recent reversal involves the extent of societal diversity. For most of the last 10,000 years, human societies have grown increasingly varied, especially in terms of size and complexity (see Figure 2.2). Now, however, the point has been reached where all of the smallest and least complex societies seem destined for extinction. In fact, it seems unlikely that any reasonably pure hunting and gathering society (i.e., one that is substantially unmodified by contact with more advanced societies) still survives intact, and the future for other preliterate societies is not much brighter.

Having emphasized the change that has occurred in the global system, it is necessary to emphasize once again the importance of continuity in the human record. During the vast span of the Lower Paleolithic that encompassed all but the last 2.5 percent of hominid history, there was what one writer (Hawkes, 1963) has called an "almost unimaginable slowness of change." Patterns of life in the global system, insofar as they can be inferred from the archaeological record, persisted not merely for centuries and millennia, but for tens and hundreds of millennia.

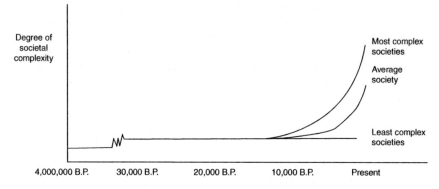

Figure 2.2 Changing patterns of societal complexity 4,000,000 B.P. to the present

In the last 10,000 years, the dramatic increase in the rate of change has tended to obscure the still-widespread evidence of continuity, yet tangible proof of it is all around us. Social institutions such as marriage, the nuclear family, government, and religion can all be traced back to the earliest of written records, and many have persisted far longer. Social roles such as husband, mother, priest, king, artisan, and servant have endured for millennia, and we still use many of the same kinds of tools—hammers, axes, knives, and saws—as did our distant ancestors. These serve as a powerful reminder of the essentially *cumulative* nature of the evolutionary process itself, a process by which older, simpler elements of social and cultural systems are absorbed and incorporated into newer, more complex systems. Thus, even supersonic jet airplanes, a classic symbol of innovation and modernity, incorporate many ancient elements, including the basic principles of metallurgy, the wheel, the chair, the window, the handle, numbers, letters, and more. Similar examples abound. For this reason, *it is a great mistake to think of the rate of continuity as the inverse of the rate of change where evolutionary processes are involved.*

The Great Paradox

One of the more important challenges confronting the new evolutionary theory and other macrosociological theories is that of explaining a curious paradox— namely, that in the vast majority of individual societies of which we have knowledge, the forces of continuity have prevailed over the forces of change, whereas in the global system of societies, the forces of change have prevailed for at least the last 10,000 to 20,000 years. This raises an interesting and important, but generally neglected, question: *How has it been possible for the system as a whole to change so dramatically when the vast majority of its constituent parts were successfully resisting change?*

Answering this question is crucial to the defense of evolutionary theory, since one of the most frequent criticisms directed against it is that it exaggerates the importance and power of the forces promoting change in societies. Critics of evolutionism argue that the forces of tradition have been far more powerful within the vast majority of individual societies and that evolutionists have overgeneralized on the basis of the experience of a small number of modern industrial societies—two observations, the critics argue, that invalidate one of the basic assumptions of evolutionary theories. This criticism has been extremely effective, since evolutionists have been slow to recognize the existence of the multiple levels of organizational reality they have been trying to explain and, more importantly, the possibility of divergent patterns on different levels.

Recognizing clearly the nature of the problem involved (i.e., the fact that two different levels of social reality are involved) is an essential first step in building a satisfactory theory of human societies and their development. Resolving the paradox is the critical second step, and one that the new theory must take if it is to win general acceptance.

3

THE BIOLOGICAL FOUNDATIONS OF HUMAN SOCIETIES

The first substantive premise of ecological-evolutionary theory is that *human societies are a part of the larger world of nature and cannot be understood adequately unless this fact and its many implications are taken fully and explicitly into account.* Thus, ecological-evolutionary theory strives at the outset to specify the relationship of humans to the rest of the natural order, especially the biotic world.

This task of specification is best accomplished by starting with the taxonomic "map" that biologists have developed for the biotic realm as a whole. Viewed from this perspective, human societies are seen to be a part of the animal kingdom and, within that kingdom, they are part of the chordate phylum, the vertebrate subphylum, the tetrapod (or quadruped) superclass, the mammalian class, the primate order, and the anthropoid suborder. What all this means is that humans have much more in common genetically with other anthropoids than with the rest of the primate order, more in common with other primates than with the rest of the mammalian class, more in common with other mammals than with the rest of the tetrapod superclass, more in common with other tetrapods than with the rest of the vertebrate subphylum, more in common with other vertebrates than with the rest of the chordate phylum, more in common with other chordates than with the rest of the animal kingdom, and more in common with other animals than with plants, bacteria, and nonliving things.

For sociologists and for sociological theory, matters can be greatly simplified if we think of the characteristics of humans and human societies in terms of three basic groupings: (1) those that are shared with all other forms of life, (2) those that are shared only with our closer kin in the animal kingdom, and (3) those that are unique to our species. This approach enables us to identify and specify the important biological foundations on which human societies rest. Later, we will consider some of the ways in which societies are influenced by the bio-physical environment.

Characteristics Humans Share with All Other Species

Viewing the biotic world in all its diversity, we may find it hard to believe that there is anything that is common to all forms of life. Yet, beneath their obvious and enormous differences, the human, the housefly, the rose, and the amoeba are alike in a number of important ways.

To begin with, all living things share the same underlying structure. Every organism is composed of one or more cells, and all cells are composed of the same basic materials: water, minerals, and organic compounds, such as carbohydrates, fats, proteins, nucleotides, and their derivatives. In addition, the same basic activities go on within every organism. First, there is metabolism, which includes nutrition, respiration, and synthesis, on which the survival and well-being of the organism depend. Because of metabolism, all organisms depend on their environment for food that can be converted to energy and for other vital resources. Second, most organisms are genetically programmed to respond to most external and internal stimuli in a self-preserving and self-serving manner.[1] Third, every organism has a capacity for reproducing itself in substantially greater numbers than are needed for simple replacement if all offspring were to survive.

The explanation of these and other common characteristics among otherwise vastly dissimilar forms of life is that all life on our planet is descended from a common source and subject to the same common evolutionary forces. As George Gaylord Simpson (1951: 281) once wrote, "all living things are brothers in the very real, material sense that all have arisen from one source and been developed within the divergent intricacies of one process."

The key to understanding biological evolution lies in the basic units of heredity known as genes. Genes, as we have discovered in recent decades, are complex chemicals that are present in every cell of every organism, and they contain, in coded form, information that profoundly influences both morphology and behavior. Sometimes the influence of the genes is deterministic; other times it merely predisposes the organism to act or develop in certain ways, while providing latitude for alternative courses of action or development.

From a functional standpoint, the gene pool of a population of organisms is *a vast storehouse of information* that has been acquired over countless generations through the trial-and-error process of mutation and natural selection, and the

---

1. Altruistic behavior also seems to be genetically programmed into some species, but even in these species it is often less frequently activated than self-preserving behavior and tends to be restricted to closely related individuals, as in maternal defense of immature offspring.

population's survival depends on it. Much of the information contained in the gene pool appears redundant, some of it irrelevant, and some even harmful, but this in no way diminishes the critical importance of the information system as a whole.[2]

As the process of natural selection implies, the genetic heritage of every species is influenced by its ancestors' interaction with the various environments they encountered. The biophysical environment is the testing ground for every population and its genetic heritage. Reproductive success is generally considered the best measure of the fitness, or overall adaptation, of an organism.

Adaptation is an important concept in the biological sciences, but it is sometimes used in ways that confuse more than clarify. Writers often fail to distinguish between long- and short-term adaptation. What is adaptive for a population or species in the long term is not always adaptive in the short term, and *vice versa*. For example, many species have adapted to their environments by becoming increasingly specialized, using an ever-more limited set of resources more and more effectively (Cooper and Lenski, 2000). In the short run, this can be highly adaptive. In the long run, however, it can prove disastrous if environmental changes reduce or destroy the limited set of resources on which the population has become dependent. Should that happen, the entire population may be wiped out.

As this reminds us, adaptive change is always governed by immediate circumstances and forces operative in the short run. If such change also proves beneficial in the long run, that is in some sense accidental and, in fact, the outcome of a succession of short-run processes. This is the essential insight that underlies Darwin's important concept of natural selection. It is only the human observer with his or her concepts of time, change, and history who is tempted to think of genetic change in populations as though it were influenced by long-term considerations or teleological processes.

From studies of the interaction of populations and their environments, biologists have constructed their most basic paradigm. As Figure 3.1 indicates, the phenotypic properties of biological populations—that is, their morphology and behavior—are viewed as products of the interaction of their genetic heritage, or genotype, with their environment. These phenotypic properties of the population

---

2. In recent years, geneticists have increasingly distanced themselves from the view that all genetic material is useful or adaptive. Various explanations have been advanced to account for the existence of apparently maladaptive and nonadaptive genes, including "hitchhiking" and "selfish" genes. In the case of "hitchhiking," natural selection affects clusters of linked genes, such as adjacent genes on the same chromosome. When selection favors a beneficial mutation in one gene, nonadaptive mutations in nearby genes can be "dragged along" if there is a net benefit (Charlesworth and Charlesworth, 2002). "Selfish" genes are, in effect, parasites that persist when there is an opportunity to produce extra copies of themselves relative to the rest of the genome. For example, some genes that reduce the fitness of individual organisms spread by a process called "meiotic distortion," in which these genes manage to hijack the genetic process so that they are included in more than half the gametes (sperm or egg cells) produced by a parent that has only one copy of the "selfish" gene (Lyttle, 2002). In the case of redundant genes, current theory suggests that they may sometimes have utility in much the same way as back-up electrical systems in a hospital (Krakauer, 2002).

Time 1   Time 2

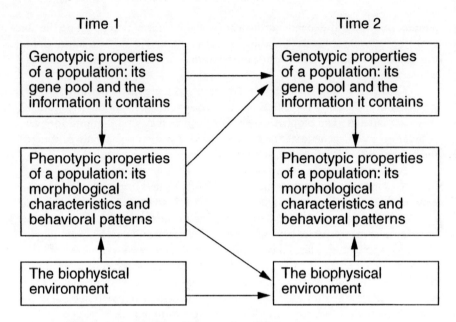

Figure 3.1 The basic biological paradigm and model

have no *direct* effect on the phenotypic properties of subsequent generations in this most general model. They have only an indirect effect that is mediated either through the gene pool or through the environment. Thus, by the process of natural selection, organisms that bear certain genes develop morphological characteristics and behavioral patterns that enable them to be either more or less successful reproductively than others of their species. This causes their genes to become either more or less common in the population, and this, in turn, influences the phenotypic properties of the population in subsequent generations. Alternatively, the behavior of populations may alter the biophysical environment to greater or lesser degree (e.g., beavers dam streams, predators check the growth of prey populations), and these changes may later have an impact on the morphology and behavior of the population itself.

This paradigm is of far greater importance to the study of human societies and their development than is generally acknowledged. For if the first premise of ecological-evolutionary theory is sound,[3] human populations are subject to the influences of genetics and environment just as all other populations are. Acknowledging this in no way commits ecological-evolutionary theory to reductionism, however, because the ways in which the paradigmatic model operates for different species varies greatly (see below). But these differences must be recognized for

---

3. See the first paragraph in the chapter.

what they are—namely, variations on a common theme, not totally different and unrelated processes.

Characteristics Humans Share with Certain Other Species

As we have noted, humans are most closely related to other members of the primate order and, more generally, to other members of the mammalian class. This is important, because it directs attention to some of the more distinctive features of our species' genetic heritage and to certain evolutionary processes of special relevance to the understanding of human societies and their evolution.[4]

First, we are reminded that our species is located in a part of the animal kingdom in which the *societal mode of life* is prevalent. As E. O. Wilson (1975: 456) has observed, "Even the so-called solitary species [of mammals], which display no social behavior beyond courtship and maternal care, are characterized by relatively prolonged interactions between the mother and offspring." Moreover, in many mammalian species, this relationship has become the basis of more complex and elaborate social systems.

The mammalian and primate heritage of our species also points to another important component of human life, our dependence on *learning* as a source of information. Viewed from a broadly comparative evolutionary perspective, learning appears to have been an emergent mechanism that supplemented the older mechanisms by which species acquired information. Reliance on learning as an adaptive mechanism has proven an extraordinarily important trait and its genetic basis can be seen in the evolution of mammalian and primate nervous systems and brains.

Closely linked to learning and the societal mode of life are the complex and efficient systems of *communication* that distinguish mammals in general, and primates in particular, from most other species. Mechanisms of communication among them take many forms, including sounds, smells, grimaces, gestures, and larger bodily movements (i.e., body language), used both individually and in various combinations (J. Turner, 2000). These mechanisms are all genetically fixed in the sense that the mechanism and the information it conveys cannot be altered voluntarily by individuals. Although limited in this way, these systems of communication still allow members of many mammalian species to transmit substantial amounts of information, especially the expression of psychological states, such as fear, anger, submissiveness, sexual arousal, and affection. The importance of this for the coordination of the actions of the members of social species is obvious.

Finally, our species' genetic heritage and our location within the animal kingdom appear to underlie our *strong feelings of individual identity and self-interest,*

---

4. In recent years, a number of sociologists have used this comparative approach to gain an understanding of the biological foundation of human life. Sometimes, however, this work has been flawed by the adoption of the overly deterministic approach of sociobiology. For a more balanced approach, as well as a detailed critique of sociobiology, see Maryanski and Turner (1992).

as well as the antisocial individualism that is a recurrent feature of human life (Maryanski and Turner, 1992). Biologists report that most social invertebrates, as well as fish and amphibians, apparently lack the ability to recognize and distinguish between individuals. In contrast, the power of "personal recognition is widespread and possibly a universal phenomenon among birds and mammals, the two vertebrate groups containing the most advanced forms of social organization" (Wilson, 1975: 382). This power of personal recognition and the strong feelings of individual identity and self-interest associated with it are both in no small measure *by-products of learning*. Where members of a species are dependent to any great degree on information gleaned through individual experience—experience that cannot possibly be shared in its entirety—differences among members of the group are bound to be enlarged and recognition of these differences is inevitable.

As the foregoing suggests, the *combination* of these four important mammalian traits—social organization, dependence on learning, powers of communication, and individuation—is not simply coincidence. Rather, these traits seem to have evolved more or less in concert, mutually reinforcing one another, to produce the distinctive kind of social systems found among mammals in general and primates in particular. These systems differ profoundly from those that have evolved in most other parts of the animal kingdom, especially among the colonial microorganisms and the invertebrates, where individuality is almost totally suppressed and learning and intelligence play little or no role.[5]

All this has had profound implications for human societies. Human societies depend far more on learning and communication than do other mammalian and primate societies, and they enjoy the benefits and pay the price of a vastly heightened and intensified process of individuation. Because differences among the members of human societies are so much more pronounced, and so much more important to the individuals involved, human social systems are *much less well-coordinated systems* than the Portuguese man-of-war and corals, or even termite colonies and wasp societies. Within human systems, individuals enjoy a degree of autonomy and freedom of action that is lacking in most nonmammalian societies (bird societies are a notable exception) and is far less pronounced even in most mammalian societies.

These aspects of our species' genetic heritage are crucial to an understanding of human societies, because they are responsible for the intragroup tension and conflict that are so characteristic of them. *Homo sapiens* is, by nature (i.e., by genetic endowment), simultaneously a cooperative social animal and an individualistic, self-seeking animal. This, more than anything else, creates the drama in human life and its uncertainties. And it is this, above all, that justifies William

5. The presence of the societal mode of organization in such diverse parts of the animal kingdom as fish, insects, mammals, birds, and colonial invertebrates is an example of convergent evolution and is indicative of the great adaptive value of intraspecies cooperation. This repeated *independent* evolution of societies in the animal kingdom also explains why mammalian societies are different in critically important ways from most nonmammalian societies. (See Maryanski and Turner [1992] for a critique of the tendency among sociologists to assume that humans are genetically programmed to be highly social animals.)

Graham Sumner's apt characterization of human societies as systems of "antagonistic cooperation" (Sumner, 1906: 32).

Earlier, I said that the basic paradigmatic model of the biological sciences can and must be modified to take account of differences that exist within the biotic realm. Building on the present brief survey of the more important consequences of our species' primate and mammalian heritage, we can now consider the first of these modifications.

One of the most important features of Figure 3.1 is the absence of any *direct* causal link between the phenotypic properties of a population at Time 1 and the same properties at Time 2. With the emergence of learning and, later, with the emergence of systems of communication in the animal kingdom, this relationship changed, necessitating modification of the basic model in order to take this into account. With the development of learning, it became possible for populations to acquire information by methods other than mutation and natural selection. For the first time, a kind of Lamarckian evolution became possible, with changes in certain limited aspects of the behavior of a population occurring without prior changes in its members' genes. Still later, with the development of systems of communication, it became possible for some of the information acquired by learning to be transmitted from one generation to the next without resort to genetic mechanisms or processes.

Figure 3.2 summarizes graphically the situation in most mammalian and primate populations. Comparing Figures 3.1 and 3.2, we find that the latter is

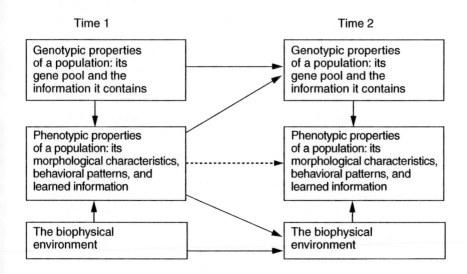

------------▶ = Learned information transmitted via signal systems

Figure 3.2 Modified paradigm and model appropriate to societies capable of learning and communication

merely a modification of the more basic model, not a totally new model. All of the essential elements in Figure 3.1 are incorporated in Figure 3.2. This, of course, is what we should expect when studying evolutionary processes in which the cumulative nature of change is its distinctive feature.

Characteristics Unique to Humans

Finally, the genetic heritage of every species contains certain elements that are unique to it alone. As we have seen, many of the most important attributes of our species represent an intensification of attributes that are important to mammals in general and primates in particular. Thus, while nearly all mammals, especially primates, rely heavily on social organization, learning, and communication as mechanisms of adaptation, and these give rise to powers of personal recognition and a sense of self-identity, these traits are far more pronounced in human populations. But why, we may ask, should this be true, and how did humans come to occupy the unique niche they do in the global ecosystem?

The answers will probably never be fully known, but recent research on the origins of the hominids provides a number of clues. For example, it now appears that one of the first major biological innovations in the hominid line was the shift to bipedal locomotion. This occurred long before the growth in cranial capacity or any other identifiable morphological change (e.g., Maryanski and Turner, 1992: 69).

Bipedal locomotion is thought by many to have been associated with a shift in habitat from arboreal conditions to more open grasslands where upright posture provided a selective advantage both in the search for food and in defense (i.e., by providing a larger visual field). More significant, however, an upright stance freed the already dexterous primate hands for new kinds of activities, and these provided a selective advantage to individuals with good hand-eye coordination and greater intelligence, thus setting in motion evolutionary trends with far-reaching behavioral consequences.

The most important trend may well have been the enhanced potential for toolmaking and tool-use. Modern research has shown that humans are not unique in their ability to make and use tools. But this research also makes it clear that humans are indeed unique both in the subtlety, complexity, and effectiveness of the tools they make and in the degree of their dependence on them. Whereas tool-use is an occasional and infrequent activity among chimpanzees, and of minor importance as an adaptive mechanism, it is a constant and ubiquitous activity among humans and a vital adaptive mechanism. Thus, the shift to bipedal locomotion seems to have stimulated early hominids to cross a critical evolutionary threshold that drastically altered the subsequent course of hominid history.

Another consequence of bipedal locomotion may well have been a strengthening of the social ties between adult males and females, a relatively weak link in most other primate social systems (Maryanski and Turner, 1992: table 2). Archaeological evidence indicates that from an early date hominids used their hands and arms to transport meat from the places where it was obtained to residential campsites elsewhere. As this is not the typical primate pattern (since primates usually eat food wherever they find it), the practice of these early hominids suggests that the meat was shared. If this inference is correct, it indicates that bipedal locomotion reinforced the basic thrust of mammalian and primate evolution in an important way, and contributed significantly to a key element in the development of the social foundation on which the subsequent growth and elaboration of human societies depended.

While much of the foregoing remains speculative, the record shows clearly that over the course of the last 4 million years, the hominids grew physically larger overall, with the growth in cranial capacity being especially pronounced. This trend seems not to have run its course until the emergence of *Homo sapiens* in the last several hundred thousand years.

The most important consequence of these developments was a major breakthrough in hominid powers of communication. In the earliest days of their history, there is no reason to believe that the hominids differed appreciably in this respect from modern chimpanzees and gorillas, their closest kin in the animal kingdom today. In other words, the earliest hominids probably possessed a complex repertoire of signals (i.e., mechanisms of communication whose meaning is genetically fixed) but lacked the power to create or use symbols (i.e., mechanisms whose meaning is established by their users). Somewhere in the evolution of the hominids, however, symbol-creation and symbol-use got their start. Where and when this happened is still anybody's guess (Washburn, 1978), but it was almost certainly a gradual process requiring substantial development of the cerebral cortex.

Eventually, however, symbol systems became far more complex and as this happened the foundation was laid for a radically new mode of evolution. *For the first time in evolutionary history, a species had the capacity to acquire vast stores of information that were separate and distinct from the information contained in its genes.* Learning and communication could now become tools to be used in a limitless process of information acquisition and cumulation, something never before possible.

With this new power at their command, the stage was set for the cultural explosion that has carried humans to the position of dominance they now enjoy in the world of larger vertebrates. Symbol systems made it possible to translate individual learning of every kind into forms that could readily be shared with others and, ultimately, with the entire human population. With this new "tool," human societies were able to expand into habitats previously closed to them, exploit new resources, and grow in numbers as no large-bodied animal had ever done before. Furthermore, they could now develop patterns of life as diverse as those of different species, while still preserving their genetic unity, something else never before possible in evolutionary history.

Figure 3.3 describes graphically the basic determinants of the phenotypic properties or attributes of human populations. The model is the same as Figure

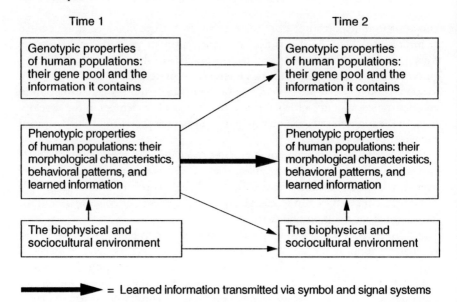

Time 1   Time 2

| Genotypic properties of human populations: their gene pool and the information it contains |
| Phenotypic properties of human populations: their morphological characteristics, behavioral patterns, and learned information |
| The biophysical and sociocultural environment |

= Learned information transmitted via symbol and signal systems

Figure 3.3 Modified paradigm and model appropriate to human populations

3.2 with two important exceptions. First, the relatively weak and limited direct link between the phenotypic properties at Time 1 and Time 2 has been enormously strengthened. And, second, the sociocultural environment has been added as one of the basic determinants of the phenotypic properties of human populations. In other words, the model has also been modified to take account of the enormous influence that human societies exert on one another.

Evolution as the Cumulation of Information

Before we continue examining the biological foundations of sociocultural evolution, it may be well to digress for a moment to consider the meaning of the concept "evolution" and the relationship between biological evolution and sociocultural evolution. Is it true, for example, as some (e.g., Nisbet, 1969) have claimed, that the concept of sociocultural evolution rests on nothing more than a dubious analogy, or is there a more substantial basis for invoking this concept?

Viewed from the perspective of the new science of genetics, it is clear that far more than analogy is involved. *Both sociocultural and organic evolution are processes by which populations have been formed and transformed in response to changes in the stores of heritable or transferable information they possess.* In organic evolution, it is the entire population of living things, human and nonhuman alike, that has been formed and transformed; in sociocultural evolution, it is the human population alone. Thus, both organic and sociocultural evolution may be defined as *the cumulation of heritable or transferable information within populations and its attendant consequences.* The term "information," as used today by evolutionists in both the biological and social sciences, refers to a record of experience that is stored in memory systems and subsequently influences the actions of individuals and populations. Information systems are important because *they are the ultimate mechanisms of adaptation.* All of the more obvious and familiar adaptive mechanisms, such as the turtle's shell, the skunk's scent, and the oyster's fecundity, are simply manifestations of these underlying and more basic mechanisms and are expressions of them. None of them would exist had not some ancestral population acquired, stored, and transmitted the requisite information.

As the science of genetics has taught us, the most basic information on which plant and animal populations depend is preserved in coded form in the chemical molecule DNA. Thanks to the processes of genetic mutation and natural selection, the gene pool of every plant and animal population is a record of solutions to challenges of the past that channel actions of the population in certain directions rather than others.[6] Without this information, no population could survive.

Somewhere in the distant past, the emergence of larger-bodied animals seems to have been associated with the emergence of an important new system of information gathering, the neurological. Key elements in the evolution of this new system were advances in sensory organs and the beginnings of the central nervous system and brain. Growth in the size of organisms obviously facilitated these developments, but it may also have necessitated it. Many smaller species of the kinds that had inhabited the planet up to that time were able to adapt satisfactorily to new challenges and new conditions relying solely on genetically encoded information. This was possible in many cases because of very high reproductive rates (e.g., a single housefly is theoretically capable of producing 6 trillion descendants in a year, were all its offspring to survive and themselves reproduce), which meant sufficient mutant genes to ensure fairly rapid genetic change, should environmental conditions change.

With the emergence of larger animals, it became possible, and ultimately necessary, to develop some added source of information to supplement the older genetic system. Larger animals could not produce vast numbers of offspring simply because the enormous physical resources that would be required were not available.[7] In this situation, the evolution of the central nervous system and brain

---

6. The term "actions," as used here, includes such things as ontogeny and metabolism as well as feeding, sleeping, breeding, and such.

7. Imagine, for example, the amount of food that would be required if every female in the various species of cats produced a million offspring every year, as oysters do. Even if the vast majority died within hours of their birth, the nutritional requirements would far exceed what is available. Multiply this by the nutritional requirements of all large-bodied species, and the impossibility of levels of fertility like those of oysters and houseflies becomes obvious.

and the pattern of behavior we call learning seems to have served the purpose and provided mammals and many other larger animals with a new, alternative mechanism for the acquisition of information and for adaptive change.

Now, for the first time, members of certain animal species could acquire information of adaptive value directly from their own encounters with the environment. Utilizing their neurological systems, individuals were able, through a process of trial-and-error learning, to discriminate between situations and experiences that were rewarding, or linked to rewarding outcomes, and others that were painful, or linked to painful outcomes. Moreover, they had an electrochemical record of these experiences and the related associations (i.e., memory) and it could serve as a guide to subsequent actions. In short, members of these species now had a far more flexible and adaptable source of information than that stored in genes.

The emergence of the neurological system of information was especially important from an organizational standpoint because it enabled members of numerous species to transmit certain limited types of information directly to others of their kind. Through the use of genetically fixed *signals,* individuals were able to exchange various kinds of information, even information about their inner psychological states (J. Turner, 2000). As noted previously, such information is especially valuable in social species, since it facilitates the coordination of the actions of the members and thus greatly enhances the value of group organization.

Finally, long after these other developments, hominid evolution added a third information system to those already in existence (see Table 3.1). The critical element in this new system was the capacity of humans to create and manipulate systems of *symbols.* This newest system of information is rooted in the older genetic and neurological systems, and would not be possible without them. But symbols, unlike signals, are not genetically fixed or determined. Thus, symbols are vastly more flexible than signals, and cultural systems are correspondingly more flexible than neurological systems. This has been especially important for the evolution of human systems of social organization, since the kinds of infor-

Table 3.1. Three Information Systems Compared

Type of Information System	Scope	Storage Mechanisms	Mode of Acquisition	Mode of Transmission
Genetic	All species	DNA	Genetic variation and natural selection	Reproduction
Neurological	Many animals	Brains and nervous systems	Trial and error, imitation, observation, reasoning	Signals
Cultural	Only humans	Brains, books, data banks, and other cultural mechanisms	Instruction, reasoning, research	Symbols

mation that can be transmitted by symbols is infinitely more varied and complex than those transmitted by signals.

With the emergence of cultural systems, a radically new mode of adaptation was established and the stage was set for hominid populations to move with amazing speed from their long-time position of relative obscurity to their present position of dominance in the vertebrate world. The emergence of cultural systems did not, however, free human societies from their dependence on genetic and neurological systems of information. On the contrary, these continued to be powerful forces in human life, but now they were supplemented and enhanced by a unique and powerful new informational resource.

The Nature of Human Nature

During the last half-century or more, the vast majority of social scientists have either ignored or minimized the relevance of biological factors for the understanding of human behavior. This has been motivated partly by abhorrence of racialist theories, partly by fear of intellectual imperialism by the biological sciences. But it has also been due in no small measure to the failure of social scientists to keep up with developments in the relatively new science of genetics.

While there may once have been some justification for the struggle to deny the importance of biological factors in human life, that time is now long past. *Biological factors do greatly influence human behavior, and continued efforts to ignore or minimize this fact only jeopardize the credibility of the social sciences.* Acknowledging the influence and importance of biological factors does not mean, however, that one must also accept racialist theories. Although the precise nature, extent, and social impact of racial differences remain unclear, it is impossible to deny the enormous importance and impact of our species' *common* genetic heritage, a heritage that is shared by all races.

Because of this heritage, human societies are part of the great web of life and subject to all of its more basic laws. Thus, *any satisfactory theory of human societies must be both ecological and evolutionary in nature.* Human societies do not stand outside the evolving global ecosystem; on the contrary, they are an integral part of it. To ignore this fact and its many implications is to build sociological theory on a foundation of sand.

Acknowledging our species' involvement in, and dependence on, the evolving global ecosystem does not, however, commit us to biological reductionism. For it was the same distinguished evolutionist who wrote that "all living things are brothers in the very real, material sense that all have risen from one source and been developed within the divergent intricacies of one process" who also wrote that

> [t]o say that man is nothing but an animal is to deny, by implication, that he has *essential* attributes other than those of all animals. This would be false as applied

to any kind of animal. . . . As applied to man the "nothing but" fallacy is more serious than in application to any other sort of animal, because man is an entirely new kind of animal in ways altogether fundamental for understanding of his nature. (Simpson, 1951: 281 and 283–284)

In summary, then, human nature is an extraordinarily complex combination of elements, some that are shared with all other species, some that are shared with some others but not all, and still others that are unique and peculiar to *Homo sapiens*. To deny or ignore any part of this rich heritage in constructing social science theories is to deny or ignore elements of the real world that are altogether fundamental to the understanding of human life.

Having argued for the necessity of acknowledging the biological foundation of human societies, one must be careful not to exaggerate its influence. For example, while it is obvious that genetic differences between men and women underlie some of their behavioral differences, we know that this is not the whole story. Societal norms have often magnified the underlying differences by rewarding individuals for conforming to their group's gender-specific norms, and by punishing them for deviations. We also know that technological innovations can modify previously determinant relations between gender and behavior, as when the adoption of machine technology enables women, with the aid of forklifts, cranes, and other machines, to lift weights that even the strongest man cannot move unaided.

Despite the uncertainties and ambiguities that confront us, many of the more basic features of our species' genetic heritage and their implications are readily apparent and should take their place as integral parts of the explanatory structure of macrosociological theory.

First, *all humans have the same fundamental needs.* These include the basic physical requirements for food, water, sleep, oxygen, elimination, and so on that must be satisfied if we are merely to survive. We also have a variety of other needs whose satisfaction is not essential for individual survival or whose intensity varies greatly from one stage of life to another. These include sexual needs, the need for play, the need for new and varied experience, and the need for social experience (Dobzhansky et al., 1977: 224–225). That these needs have as much of a genetic basis as our more obvious "survival" needs is well documented. The need for new and varied experience, for example, has been tested in newborn infants, who, when offered a choice, are found to have a decided preference for visual variety and contrast and who also have a "bias to explore" that they seek to satisfy almost from the moment of birth (Pfeiffer, 1972–1978: 354ff.). Human infants also have such a compelling need for social contact and stimulation that, if it is not satisfied, they may not survive (Spitz, 1945).

Second, *for the most part, all humans have the same basic resources for satisfying their needs and desires.* These include such physiological endowments as legs, fingers, teeth, ears, bowels, heart, brain, and so on. The brain is a particularly impressive resource: It provides the means of recording "memory traces" equivalent to the content of 1,000 twenty-four-volume sets of the *Encyclopaedia Britannica* and is far more densely packed with information than a computer (Pfeiffer, 1972–1978: 429–430; Sagan, 1977: 47–48). In addition, everyone is genetically programmed for the automatic performance of a variety of essential activities, such as digestion, growth, and circulation, and has numerous invaluable reflexive actions and response sets.

The most distinctive of the resources humans possess and the most unique element in human nature is *the capacity to create and use symbol systems to process, store, and communicate information.* This is based on a variety of genetic attributes, including the organs of speech, such as lips, tongue, palate, sinuses, and vocal cords. Even more important are peculiarities of the human brain, especially the unique areas of the cerebral cortex that control speech and abstract thought (Curtis: 1975; 717–720; Weisz, 1967: 819). Linguists now believe that despite the great variability in the thousands of spoken languages humans have created, there is a single "deep structure" that is shared by all (Chomsky, 1957). In other words, our species' common genetic heritage does not merely bestow on us a generalized capacity for speech; it appears to determine even the basic structure of our languages.

Third, because of their genetic heritage, *humans everywhere are motivated to maximize pleasurable experiences and minimize painful and unpleasant ones.* This is a trait that we share with every other form of animal life. Although an individual's definition of pleasure and pain may be altered to some degree by experience (see below), the extent of such change is quite limited in most cases.

Fourth, *most humans have an enormous capacity for learning from experience and for modifying their behavior in response to such learning.* Learning is not merely a process of remembering what happened and when; it is also a process of evaluation based on the association of things and events with experiences of pleasure and pain. Because of these associations, patterns of action that are painful tend to be extinguished, and those that are pleasurable tend to be reinforced. And while an individual's definition of pleasure and pain may, itself, be modified to some extent with experience, the essential underlying process appears never to change.[8]

Fifth, *humans everywhere develop a variety of derivative needs and desires.* Because of the importance of learning, individuals develop new needs and desires as by-products of their social and cultural experiences. Because these experiences vary from individual to individual, and also because genetic variation plays some role in the process, the nature and intensity of these derivative needs and desires

---

8. As Maslow (1954: ch. 5) has suggested, individuals whose basic physiological and safety needs have always been easily satisfied are likely to become more concerned with the so-called higher needs, such as the need for esteem and respect or the need for "self-actualization," and, therefore, their concept of what constitutes pleasure and pain is likely to differ to some extent from that of others who have not had their basic needs satisfied so easily or so fully. But if Maslow is correct, all individuals have the same genetically based hierarchy of needs and thus are subject to the same essential process of redefinition.

are highly variable. Notable among them, however, is the need or desire to control other people and circumstances, to possess things, to obtain emotional gratification, and to discern order and meaning in life.

Sixth, *individuals are differentiated from one another both biologically and culturally in ways that societies cannot ignore.* Differences in age and sex are two of the most obvious. In addition, some individuals are severely handicapped, either physically or mentally, while others enjoy exceptional physical or mental endowments and the majority of us fall somewhere in between. These genetically based differences and the ones that result from differences in prenatal environment are subsequently compounded and modified in countless ways by differences in the postnatal environments to which individuals are exposed. The variability of human populations that results from all this is simultaneously an invaluable asset of human societies and the source of many of their most intractable problems.

Seventh, *humans economize most of the time, seeking the greatest return for the least possible expenditure of resources.* This is because their needs and desires almost always exceed their resources for satisfying them. Thus, to maximize the satisfaction of needs and desires, economizing is essential except when costs are trivial. Failure to observe this principle leads to frustration, disappointment, and unfulfilled needs and desires.

Eighth, *human action is governed by emotions as well as by reason* (J. Turner, 2000: 59–60). In other words, there is a nonrational component in human action. Emotions are activated by elements in what has come to be known as the "old brain," that part of the brain that we have inherited from prehuman ancestors and which has much in common with the brains of other species. Reason, in contrast, is centered in the "new brain," or cerebral cortex, which is proportionally far larger and vastly more complex in humans than in other species. Although we flatter ourselves by emphasizing the role of reason in our actions and proudly designate our species *Homo sapiens,* this is hardly a fully accurate characterization because, when our emotions are aroused, reason is often reduced to the role of providing comforting rationalizations for courses of action determined by emotions.[9]

Ninth, *early in life most humans acquire a highly developed sense of self and self-interest.* In part, this is instinctive and genetic, but it is also a product of learning. In fact, the development of a sense of self and self-interest is virtually a corollary of the remarkable human capacity for learning. *Learning, by its very nature, is a differentiating experience:* No two individuals ever share precisely the same set of experiences and, thus, no two individuals ever learn precisely the same things or interpret experience in exactly the same way. As awareness of this gradually penetrates our consciousness, the distinction between self and others grows increasingly salient. Moreover, early in life we discover that actions that are pleasurable to others are not always pleasurable to ourselves, and *vice versa.* Thus, the develop-

---

9. In this connection, it is interesting to note the old Wall Street adage that financial markets are driven by just two things: fear and greed.

ment of the distinction between self and others is soon followed by the development of the distinction between self-interest and the interests of others. These are among the earliest lessons that every human learns. Because of them, competition and conflict have been endemic in every human society, though their form and nature vary depending on circumstances.

The importance of these elements of human life is difficult to exaggerate; St. Paul and Marx to the contrary notwithstanding, new beliefs and new ideologies seldom succeed in creating the promised "new man."[10] Far too many social scientists, however, still cling to the comforting belief that the self-aggrandizing aspects of human nature can be eliminated by appropriate social engineering. One would suppose that the repeated failures, and sometimes tragic consequences, of modern efforts to overcome the self-serving tendencies in human nature would have disabused them of this belief, but unfortunately that has not been the case.

Tenth, and finally, *the concept of self and self-interest commonly expand and is modified as individuals mature.* This is an aspect of human nature that has often confused scholars and laypeople alike as they have tried to understand the nature of human nature. All of us are aware that people often sacrifice their own well-being for the sake of others: Parents do this for their children, children for their parents, friends for one another, soldiers for their buddies, and so forth. This seems to suggest that altruism is as widespread and important in the life of societies as self-serving action.

Appearances are deceptive, however. Closer examination of seemingly altruistic actions, such as those just mentioned, indicates that their frequency and importance are highly correlated with the closeness of the relationship between the parties involved. In other words, these are seldom *purely* disinterested actions; most are expressions of what is best described as *enlightened self-interest.* While it would be a mistake to deny the existence of some truly disinterested and altruistic actions, we need to beware of exaggerating either their frequency or their importance in the daily life of human societies.

One could easily extend this list of the characteristics of human nature by adding other, more specific elements, but that is unnecessary at this point. What is required is simply a specification of the more basic elements of the human condition to which every human society has had to adapt. They should, in fact, be *explicit* in every theory of human society, open to scrutiny and critical examination. Thus, if there are faulty assumptions, they can be challenged; if there are flaws, they can be corrected.

What social theory should not and cannot tolerate is the current widespread practice of leaving assumptions about human nature largely unstated and unexamined.

---

10. Although St. Paul and Marx differed profoundly in the beliefs to which they committed their lives, they did share one important conviction: Both believed that human nature could be radically transformed. St. Paul believed that faith in Christ could lead to the emergence of what he called "the new man in Christ," while Marx believed that establishment of socialism would lead to the emergence of "the new socialist man." Both would become exemplars of all the moral virtues.

Faulty assumptions lead to flawed analyses and inaccurate predictions, and these in turn lead to loss of credibility and public confidence. This is a matter of no small importance to the social sciences because it is still much too easy in these disciplines to build otherwise sophisticated theories and analyses on a foundation of covert assumptions about human nature that are much too sanguine and ignore masses of contrary evidence. Unfortunately, overly sanguine and romanticized views of human nature are so much a taken-for-granted part of the heritage of the social sciences that the problem passes largely unnoticed. Yet if the social sciences are ever to gain the kind of acceptance and recognition to which they aspire, this cannot continue.

Constants and Variables: A Brief Excursus

One of the more popular clichés in the social sciences asserts that constants cannot explain variables, that only variables can do this. This seductive half-truth is often invoked to justify neglect of human nature in social theory.[11] Before concluding the present discussion of the biological foundations of human societies, we would do well to confront this widespread misconception directly.

The importance of constants for the understanding of human societies should be evident whenever we consider empirical reality and attempt to explain the patterns we perceive. Rarely do we observe sociocultural systems and not find striking indications of the influence of biological constants ranging from the universal concern for food, water, and other material necessities to the equally universal presence of intrasocietal conflict and the division of labor along age and sex lines. In each instance, we find the same essential elements in every society. Were it not for the influence of largely unrecognized and unexamined biases, social theorists would long ago have formulated their explanations of social and cultural phenomena as responses to the interaction of both types of forces, constants as well as variables.

The continuing resistance to the incorporation of constants into sociological theory is especially surprising in view of the tremendous emphasis on statistical analysis that has become a part of sociological training in recent decades. One would suppose that individuals trained in regression analysis would be quick to recognize that constants are part of the essential logic of regression analysis and present in every regression equation. In the basic regression equation,

$$y = a + b_1 x_1 + b_2 x_2 \ldots + b_n x_n.$$

the intercept a and the coefficients b_1, b_2, and b_n are all constants. Regression analysis, therefore, should serve as a reminder that *the prediction and explanation of any variable compels us to take account of both variables and constants.*

---

11. The chief result of the acceptance of this half-truth has been to drive assumptions about human nature underground, where they remain unexamined.

This is not to say that human nature and our common genetic heritage as humans can be treated as a constant for all purposes. We know, for example, that there have been important morphological and behavioral changes linked to the evolution of the hominids from *Australopithecus* to *Homo sapiens sapiens.* Thus, depending on the time frame of the particular problem one is dealing with, certain aspects of our species' genetic heritage may become variables. Thus, too, anthropologists who seek to understand changes in hominid life over the last million years or more are obliged to treat certain aspects of our genetic heritage as variables.[12] But this is not a problem for sociologists and other social scientists who deal with events over a much more limited time span.

---

12. Similar adjustments must also be made in treating environmental characteristics and phenotypic characteristics of societies themselves. Depending on the time frame involved, a given characteristic may be either a constant or a variable.

4

DETERMINANTS OF THE CHARACTERISTICS OF INDIVIDUAL SOCIETIES: THE INDEPENDENT VARIABLES

No two human societies have ever been exactly the same; each is unique. Because of this, some scholars have concluded that a science of human societies is impossible. This view is certainly correct if one expects from science deterministic explanations of invariant causal relationships (*vide,* e.g., Baldus, 1990), but much of modern science does not conform to this model. Most of astronomy, geology, meteorology, and the biological sciences would not be considered sciences were this the standard that applied.

These sciences have all been forced to construct probabilistic theories to account for the characteristics of the things they study. Sometimes it is possible to assign fairly precise and stable values to the relevant probabilities, but often they can be expressed only in relative terms, as in the statement that under conditions A, B, and C, outcome X is more likely than Y or Z.

Not surprisingly, given the nature of the materials with which it deals, sociology falls in this category.[1] Moreover, because of the complexity of human societies and the multiplicity of forces that influence them, it is seldom possible to specify all of the relevant conditions. This means that conclusions about relative probabilities are subject to revision as new conditions are identified and taken

---

1. It should be noted, however, that there are at least a number of invariant relationships that exist within the framework of ecological-evolutionary theory. To cite a single obvious example: Urban communities cannot develop in a hunting and gathering society.

into account. On more than one occasion, social scientists have been obliged to make major revisions, sometimes to their great embarrassment. At the same time, however, there are other propositions that have required little or no modification despite prolonged and repeated testing.

Despite such difficulties, if our analysis has been correct up to this point, all of the characteristics of human societies can be accounted for as products of the interaction of information-bearing populations with their environments. To be even more specific, they are determined by the interaction of *three* kinds of information and *two* kinds of environment. In addition to the genetic and neurological systems of information (see the related sections below), human societies are influenced by cultural systems; and, in addition to the biophysical environment, they are influenced by a sociocultural environment.

One of the first concerns of macrosociologists, therefore, is to understand the nature of the influence exerted by each of these five sets of forces. In the discussion that follows, each is considered separately, but it is important to bear in mind that in the real world the several sets act in concert and rarely, if ever, is it possible to fully explain societal characteristics on the basis of any one of them alone.

The Genetic System of Information

As the analysis of the last chapter made clear, we can no longer think of human nature in John Locke's terms as a *tabula rasa* passively waiting for environmental forces to act on it and give it its character. There is far too much evidence now that humans enter this world equipped in countless ways with genetically based biases and tendencies, and, while many of these are modified during the socialization process, the biological materials are far more recalcitrant and far more resistant than optimistic social theorists and utopian political theorists of the recent past have imagined.

Although it is still not possible to specify precisely many of the ways in which the genetic system of information influences human societies, the broad outline of the relationship has become increasingly clear. For example, it is obvious that humans, like other organisms, have material needs that must be satisfied if they, and the societies of which they are a part, are to survive. When access to any essential resource becomes problematic, efforts to obtain it become a high priority on the societal agenda.

Abraham Maslow, the psychologist, speculated that humans share not just these basic material needs but a variety of psychic needs as well. According to Maslow, these are arranged in an inborn hierarchy, with the physiological needs for food, water, sleep, protein, and so forth being the most basic, followed in turn by safety needs, "belongingness" needs, esteem needs, and the need for self-actualization. So long as the basic needs are unsatisfied, they are dominant, but the more fully they are met, the more salient the higher needs become.

Although Maslow's theory as a whole can hardly be considered definitive, its basic concept is supported by research on the behavioral correlates of affluence and security. When the basic material needs of individuals and populations are ensured, they show increased concern for psychic needs of various kinds (de Graaf, 1988; Inglehart, 1971). From the standpoint of our present concern, however, Maslow's theory is important because it illustrates how highly divergent patterns of action and motivation can arise from a single, common genetic heritage.

Unlike the members of most other species, humans are poorly endowed with specialized biological tools to satisfy their needs and desires. Instead, they depend primarily on their ability to create cultural tools that can be used, in combination with their modest biological equipment, to achieve these ends.

Because the biological needs and resources of human societies are substantially the same everywhere, the cultures of all societies contain the same basic components. Thus, the culture of every society includes language, technology, morality, and ideology, together with such institutional systems as kinship, economy, polity, and religion. The presence of these elements in every society is no coincidence; each is a response to genetically based needs and desires and the inability of the human genotype to provide otherwise for their satisfaction.

Sometimes it is easy to see the dependence of cultural phenomena on the genetic system of information. The diurnal cycle of activity that is found, with minor variations, in every society is a good example of this. Essential economic activities in every society occur largely in the period between dawn and dusk, while the period from dusk to dawn is used primarily for rest and relaxation. The dependence of this cycle on the genetics of human vision and human metabolism is fairly obvious.

Similarly, it is not hard to see the dependence of the division of labor based on age and sex—a characteristic of all human societies—on the genetic system of information. For obvious reasons, adults assume responsibility for the more important and more difficult tasks, while children are assigned less important and less difficult ones, with the nature of the tasks linked to the level of their maturity. For equally obvious reasons, women have assumed primary responsibility for the care and nurture of the very young and for other tasks that are compatible with that responsibility. Men, in contrast, have assumed responsibility for those tasks that were least compatible (e.g., tasks requiring swift and unimpeded movement). They have also assumed responsibility for tasks requiring substantial upper-body strength for which they are, on average, better endowed genetically. And, while it is true that recent technological advances have substantially reduced the need for the sexual division of labor, the need has not been totally eliminated in even the most advanced industrial societies. It is also important to recognize that even if that point should eventually be reached, genetically based differences between the sexes would still be present and societies would still be obliged to maintain various technologies to offset and overcome the effects of those differences.

The relation of social and cultural universals to genetic constants is not always as obvious or direct as in the examples just cited. With respect to language, for example, it was long supposed that while the power of speech was genetically determined, the structure and content of languages were not. In recent decades, however, linguists, following the lead of Chomsky, have concluded that the "deep structure" of all languages is the same and, apparently, genetically determined. Basic syntax seems not something that children learn in the same way as they learn nursery rhymes. Rather, it is something they express spontaneously at the appropriate stage in the developmental process, just as they also begin to crawl and walk in response to inner forces and an inner clock. Dell Hymes (1968: 357) summed up this view of language and its relation to the genetic system of information when he wrote:

> To achieve the normal yet nearly miraculous result of an infinite capacity [for combining words] from a finite experience [of hearing them] . . . a child must be presumed to apply a native endowment, formulating theories to account for and go beyond the speech he hears. The rapidity and accuracy of a child's success, no matter what the language, indicate that all languages are of only one or a few fundamental types *and that the contribution of native endowment must be great.* (emphasis added)

Values are another aspect of culture for which the links to genetics have been far from obvious. In fact, many influential social scientists (e.g., Margaret Mead, Ruth Benedict) have made the concept of cultural relativism central in their work and have denied that there are any values shared by all societies.

This view, however, is no more than a half-truth. As Kenneth Boulding (1970: 31) observed some years ago, "Straight from the womb we like milk, dislike loud noises, and we dislike falling." No environmental conditioning is necessary to establish these preferences. More important still, many moral principles are shared by all societies. As Ralph Linton once noted, killing or maiming fellow members of one's own society without justification is universally condemned, even though the concept of what constitutes adequate justification varies. Similarly, every society has taboos against incest, even though the definition of forbidden consanguinity varies (though no society approves of sexual intercourse between mothers and sons). These are but two of a much larger list of universal moral precepts identified by Linton.

Cultural relativists, in their eagerness to challenge the traditional concept of moral absolutes, have ignored evidence of important similarities and uniformities. And, while it is most unlikely that there are specific genes, or sets of genes, responsible for specific moral principles, it does appear that the universality of moral codes as well as certain striking similarities among them are due to peculiarities of our species' common genetic heritage. Above all, these characteristics appear to be responses to our genetically based dependence on social organization and our lack of genetic programming of the kind required to hold intragroup conflict sufficiently in check to ensure the effective functioning of societal systems.

Regrettably, sociologists and other social scientists still cannot agree entirely on a list of the characteristics that all human societies share. The details of such a list, however, are less important than the underlying principle that human societies, despite their great variability and flexibility, are not infinitely variable or infinitely flexible. At numerous points, and in numerous ways, their development is constrained by their members' genetic heritage.[2]

While most social scientists would probably not challenge this assertion, many would respond by asking, "So what? What difference does it make?"

For much of the research in which sociologists and other social scientists are currently engaged, and for much of the theory they have constructed, it may be true that little would be gained by pursuing the biological bases of sociocultural patterns. There are, however, exceptions and some of them are extraordinarily important to the social sciences and their credibility. An instance of this is the claim of many modern utopians, echoed by many social scientists, that with a little social engineering (i.e., with modification of key social institutions) a radically new kind of society is possible—one in which liberty, equality, justice, and brotherhood are all combined with material abundance, and in which the ancient evils of poverty, oppression, exploitation, and injustice are abolished forever.

For obvious reasons, this idea is enormously appealing. But social scientists have an obligation to ask hard questions concerning all ideas about human societies, not simply those they find personally distasteful. Questions need to be asked not only about the costs, psychic as well as economic, of the revolutionary struggles required but, more important still, about the feasibility of the kind of society envisioned.

To answer the latter question, we are compelled to draw on all that is known today concerning the determinants of human nature, and it is no longer defensible merely to restate the views of optimistic philosophers of the eighteenth century and utopian theorists of the nineteenth, who knew nothing of the science of genetics or of the experience of societies created in the twentieth century by revolutionaries who acted on their vision. Social scientists today have a responsibility to rethink, in the light of this new evidence, all of the assumptions concerning human nature handed down from the past.

Although it is not possible to prove conclusively the impossibility of creating a complex, harmonious, and productive society of the kind that modern utopians seek to create, the record now provides abundant evidence that the obstacles to its creation, and the costs its creation would entail, are vastly greater than its proponents ever acknowledged, and also that the results of repeated attempts to create the ideal society have been quite different from what proponents have

---

2. When I was first writing this sentence, I started to say that human societies are constrained "by forces beyond their control." Recent advances in genetic engineering suggest, however, that we are approaching the threshold of an era in which it will be possible, through feedback from the cultural system, for humans to manipulate their own genotype.

promised.[3] This does not mean that social conditions cannot be substantially improved or that the *status quo* is inevitable, but it does mean that many constraints exist that utopian ideologies have never taken sufficiently into account.

Before concluding this discussion of the influence of genetics on the life of human societies, I need to be explicit about one aspect of the analysis that has been largely implicit up to this point. In emphasizing the *constraining* role of genetics, I may seem to have denied or minimized its contribution to the diversity and creativity of human societies and to the process of societal change. This was not my intent, nor would it be justified. I have merely sought to redress the balance by focusing attention on a badly neglected, but highly important, set of consequences of the genetic system of information. It should go without saying that all the richness and variety of human societies and their cultures are dependent on our species' unique genetic heritage: Cultural systems are possible only because of peculiarities in the evolution of human anatomy and physiology, especially in the brain and vocal apparatus. To acknowledge the diversifying influence of cultural systems of information (see below, under "The Cultural System of Information") is to acknowledge also the contribution of genetics to societal diversity, creativity, and change. Thus, in a curious way, this constant element in the human equation is key to the explanation of the most variable features of human life.

Finally, the genetic system of information contributes to societal creativity in yet another way that should not be underestimated. Humans, like other living things, have a capacity for reproduction that, unless checked in some way, leads to population growth, and sooner or later population growth upsets the critical balance between numbers and resources on which key elements of every social system are based. Although recent research indicates that there are spontaneous biological processes triggered by insufficient female body fat and by lactation that reduce fertility rates in human populations, other research (Divale, 1972; Whiting, 1964) indicates that most societies have had to develop cultural mechanisms, such as abortion, infanticide, and coitus interruptus, to constrain population growth. And, since none of these practices is valued for its own sake, there is good reason to believe that the genetically based threat of increased numbers has caused the members of many societies to be alert to more attractive alternatives (e.g., methods of increasing the food supply) that might preserve or restore the balance between numbers and resources. In short, *genetically based population pressures have probably been one of the most powerful spurs to human creativity and societal change.*

---

3. With respect to the last point, one need only recall the disillusionment of western Marxists, first with the Soviet Union, then with China, and later with Cuba, North Korea, and other revolutionary socialist societies (e.g., Hollander, 1981; Huberman and Sweezy, 1967). It is no accident that revolutionary socialists have always judged capitalist societies on the basis of the *abstract ideals* of revolutionary socialism rather than on the basis of the *realities* of actually existing revolutionary socialist societies. Nor is it surprising that an endless succession of justifications have had to be found to explain the disappointing record of these societies.

The Biophysical Environment

No population of organisms is self-sufficient. Each depends on its biophysical environment for the vital necessities of life and for all the other resources on which health and happiness depend. Because of this, human societies have always differed from one another to greater or lesser degree.

These differences have been especially pronounced in technologically limited societies. More advanced societies have generally found ways to compensate technologically for deficiencies in local environments, but this has not been possible in simpler societies. The latter have been much more dependent on resources within their immediate area, and on resources that were readily accessible and did not require much processing or modification. As a result, patterns of life in hunting and gathering societies (technologically the least developed) have varied considerably in response to differences in the biophysical environments to which they have had to adapt. Thus, housing, clothing, diet, and numerous other aspects of life among the Eskimo have differed greatly from their counterparts among hunting and gathering peoples living in tropical rain forests and in temperate regions, and these differences obviously reflect the influence of the biophysical environment.

Biophysical environments not only differ in the kinds of challenges they pose and in the resources they afford to technologically primitive societies, they differ also in *their potentials for indigenous societal development.* This is especially evident in desert, arctic, and mountainous regions, where obstacles to social and cultural expansion and development are obvious. But, as Betty Meggers (1954) pointed out long ago, other areas, chiefly in the tropics, are incapable of supporting sustained and intensive cultivation of the kinds of plants that are necessary for human subsistence. Thus, indigenous development in these areas has been limited to the horticultural level with its system of slash-and-burn or swidden cultivation based on gardens that must be relocated every several years.[4] A third type of environment identified by Meggers is capable of sustained and intensive cultivation of subsistence crops (e.g., wheat, rice, and other grains), but only when subjected to advanced techniques, such as crop rotation, fertilization, irrigation, and fallowing, that maintain the fertility of the soil and control the spread of weeds. In this kind of environment, advanced societies can develop by means of cultural diffusion, though not by indigenous growth. Finally, there are a few areas in the world in which sustained and intensive plant cultivation has been possible with relatively primitive techniques, as in the Nile valley where the annual flood ensured continuous soil fertility and the control of weeds. The "cradles of civilization," Meggers argued, were all in such areas.

---

4. As Meggers noted, these areas are often capable of supporting the sustained cultivation of certain tree crops, such as cacao, coffee, citrus fruits, and bananas, as well as jute, "but with the possible exception of the banana, none of these could provide an adequate subsistence base."

Later, William McNeill (1976), the historian, called attention to another important environmental constraint on societal growth and development: viruses, bacteria, and other microparasites that prey on human populations and their domesticated animals. In some regions, these invisible predators have taken an extremely heavy toll, not just in human lives but in human vitality as well. Survivors have often been left in a weakened condition and unable to work effectively.

Until the invention of the microscope and the beginnings of modern medical science, the problem of micropredators was completely beyond conscious human control.[5] Thus, the effect of this constraint on growth and development in tropical societies has been much greater than on societies located in temperate regions, where, as McNeill stated, "intelligence could play freely on the parameters of human life that mattered most. As long as men and women could see food and foe, they could invent new ways to cope with both" (p. 28). The importance of this principle is hard to exaggerate.

Because of these differences in the developmental potential of various territories, change has been greater, and development more rapid, in some societies than in others. Societies confined to harsh environments where there was no possibility of plant cultivation (e.g., Siberia and the Canadian north) have generally experienced a high degree of continuity in their basic social and cultural arrangements, regardless of almost everything else except, in recent decades, contact with advanced industrial societies. To a lesser extent, the same has been true of tropical regions infested with micropredators and handicapped by poor soils. In contrast, societies in temperate regions, where the effects of micropredators were much less serious and topography, soils, rainfall, and climate conducive to plant cultivation, have long enjoyed the possibility of substantial and sustained social and cultural development.

Because societies are adaptive mechanisms that mediate relations between a population and its environment, patterns of continuity and change in the environment necessarily affect patterns of continuity and change within societies. On first consideration, the biophysical environment gives the impression of granitic, rock-like stability. Many geological features persist over expanses of time that dwarf the life span of even the most durable of human societies. Yet, if we look more closely, we see that initial impressions can be deceptive, diverting attention from various changes that are highly relevant to the life of societies. Temperature and rainfall, for instance, can vary greatly from month to month and year to year, as farmers know from bitter experience. Variations in the timing of the first and last frosts of the year create other problems. Even when these aspects of the environment are manageable, variations in viral, bacterial, and insect populations often prove disastrous.

Since many of these kinds of variations are recurrent, societies have learned to compensate for them (e.g., by preserving an extra season's supply of seed in

---

5. The only defense was genetic adaptation, as in the spread of the sickle-cell gene in malarial regions.

farming communities). More serious, and less easily compensated for, are longer-term trends in temperature and rainfall. Sometimes, as in Greenland in the fourteenth century, entire territories have had to be abandoned because of changes that tipped the scale beyond the point where survival was possible. In less extreme cases, as in Iceland, changes in climate have led to substantial fluctuations in population size, as well as in other aspects of life (Tomasson, 1980).

Not all of the changes in the biophysical environment to which societies have had to adapt have been due to spontaneous natural forces. Many have been due to human activity. One of the more serious instances of this was the drastic reduction in the supply of big-game animals approximately 10,000 years ago, which some (e.g., Harris, 1977) believe was responsible for the beginnings of farming in many areas—a development that was the basis of a profound social and cultural revolution. Other instances of major environmental change brought about by human activity include the loss of fertile farmlands in the Middle East through the adoption and misuse of irrigation systems, and the destruction of forests throughout much of China and the Mediterranean world during the agrarian era. In each instance, these societally induced changes in the biophysical environment had serious repercussions on the societies and peoples involved.

Human societies have often been slow to recognize the limitations inherent in the biophysical environment. Many species of plants and animals have only a modest capacity for reproduction and, when exploited beyond that limit, are doomed to extinction. Minerals and various other physical resources are nonrenewable, and once they are exhausted societies are forced to find more costly substitutes or to do without. These limitations, which are an inherent feature of the biophysical environment, have been important constraints on the growth and development of societies, both individually and collectively.

The Sociocultural Environment

Every human society is also confronted with a sociocultural environment. The importance of this is difficult to exaggerate, for, as McNeill (1976) has observed, the only serious threat from large-bodied predators that most human societies have faced for thousands of years has been the threat posed by other human societies.

Other human societies are not simply a threat, however; they are also a resource. Cultural information obtained by members of one society is often transmitted—intentionally or unintentionally—to neighboring societies. In many societies (perhaps most), cultural diffusion has been a far more important source of useful information than independent discovery and invention (Linton, 1936).

As Amos Hawley once pointed out, not all environments are equally conducive to the acquisition of information from other societies. The most favorable locations have been at the intersection of major trade routes, where exposure to people and goods from other societies is maximized. It was no accident, therefore, that the Middle East, where trade routes from Asia, Africa, and Europe intersected, was at the forefront of societal growth and development for thousands of years. It was also no accident that societies in places like Australia and Siberia were among the least developed.

As these examples remind us, the influence of location is modified by, or interacts with, the influence of technology—a topic that will be examined more closely later in this chapter. For now, however, suffice it to note that changes in the technologies of transportation and communication can alter drastically the relative advantage or disadvantage of specific locations. North America is a classic instance of this: Prior to the modern era its very existence was unknown in the rest of the world. Today, thanks to advances in transportation and communication, it is an integral part of the global system. In contrast, these same advances have greatly eroded the locational advantages so long enjoyed by the Middle East.

During the last 5,000 to 7,000 years, the sociocultural environment has changed dramatically for societies all around the world. Advances in the technologies of transportation and communication have greatly increased the volume of societal interaction as well as opportunities for cultural borrowing. Thus, while the Middle East has suffered recently in *relative* terms, it has gained enormously in *absolute* terms. Its access to the store of cultural information of other societies is far greater today than it ever was in the past, even in the days when it was at the hub of international trade and commerce.

The advances in transportation and communication responsible for these developments have been a mixed blessing. Societal leaders have found it all but impossible to control the flow of information entering their societies from abroad. Many times, this new information subtly subverts established institutions and leads to more far-reaching changes than anyone anticipated. Developments in eastern Europe and China during the 1980s are illustrative of this. Even today, scholars and social planners find it impossible to anticipate all of the second-, third-, and higher-order consequences of major innovations.

Early advances in transportation and communication that paved the way for increased cultural borrowing also facilitated the emergence of wars of conquest. Because of this, thousands of tiny societies of hunters and gatherers and of simple horticulturalists have either been destroyed or been absorbed by their technologically more advanced and more powerful neighbors. Many of the latter, in turn, have fallen victim to other, still more powerful, expansionist neighbors. As noted in Chapter 2, the number of societies in the world system has been reduced by more than 99 percent in the last 10,000 years. This development has had far-reaching consequences for the world system, and some of these will be examined in a later chapter.

The Neurological System of Information

Human societies are unique because of the enormous store of learned information their members possess. Some animal societies possess modest amounts of learned information, but even the smallest and most limited of human societies possess vastly more. The explanation for this lies in the ability of members of human societies to create symbol systems and cultures. Because of symbol systems, it has been possible to convert the information acquired by individuals through personal experience into forms that can be shared with others. In fact, this is precisely what happens to most of the useful information that is acquired by individuals within human societies. Thus, in the analysis of human societies, as contrasted with the analysis of individual members of these societies, it is not necessary to differentiate between the neurological and cultural systems of information. The socially useful and important elements of the former are almost always converted into elements of the latter with the result that an analysis of cultural systems subsumes neurological systems.

The Cultural System of Information

The cultural system of information occupies a unique place in ecological-evolutionary theory: It is part of both the *explanans* and the *explanandum.* This is because the cultural characteristics of a society at any one point in time exercise a powerful influence on its cultural characteristics at later times (see Figure 3.3 in the previous chapter), and also because cultural systems are made up of interacting elements whose relations with one another are matters of considerable theoretical interest and importance.

The kinds of information that cultural systems contain are extraordinarily varied, including everything from technology to morality and from kinship systems to art. Not all elements of cultural systems, however, are of equal importance when judged from the standpoint of their impact on one another and, more important, their impact on societal development. Some have many other elements dependent on them, while others have relatively few. Changes in the former tend to have many and far-reaching consequences, while changes in the latter have fewer and less important ones.

Although social scientists have generally been reluctant to acknowledge the degree of its influence (Merrill, 1968), *technology* appears to have been the most important component of cultural systems if importance is judged by the magnitude of the impact of components on the life of human societies as a whole, past as well as present (*vide* Heise, Lenski, and Wardwell, 1976). This should not be surprising, however, since technology is *information about the ways in which the resources of the environment may be used to satisfy human needs and desires.* In other words, it is *the critical interface between the biophysical environment and all the other components of sociocultural systems, and therefore influences virtually every aspect of human life.*

The technologies of *energy* and of *materials* have been especially important. All human activity depends on the availability of energy—even thought requires energy!—and the nature and quality of the materials available to the members of a society greatly influence the kinds of tools and machines they can construct to harness energy for human purposes.

Technology is, in effect, *a cultural extension and functional equivalent of that part of our genetic heritage on which human survival and physical well-being depend.* Together, genetics and technology channel the activities of the members of a society as they seek to manipulate the biophysical environment to obtain and transform the material resources required to satisfy their needs and desires. Since the Upper Paleolithic began nearly 40,000 years ago, technological advance has all but eliminated the need for genetic change as an adaptive mechanism and *technological advance has come to play essentially the same role in the adaptive process of human societies that genetic change has always played for the populations of other species.* This does not mean, however, that genetics no longer influence the life of societies and their development. On the contrary, our species' genetic heritage continues to have a profound influence on every aspect of life, as the earlier discussion of the nature of human nature hopefully made clear. What has changed in the last 40,000 years is that technology has replaced genetics as the primary force responsible for the major transformations and changes in the life of human societies. Without the fantastic growth in the store of technological information that has occurred since the Upper Paleolithic, societies today would differ hardly at all from their prehistoric Stone Age counterparts.

Two basic principles define the role that technology, in concert with genetics and the environment, plays in human life. First, *technology, interacting with genetics and the biophysical environment, determines the outer limits of what is possible for the members of any society at any given time.* Second, *technology, again interacting with genetics and the biophysical environment, profoundly influences the choices that individuals and societies make among the options available to them.* This second principle is operative because these three factors determine the basic costs of every form of human activity. And, while individuals and societies are not obliged to choose the least expensive option every time, they cannot afford to ignore considerations of cost, since they are always faced with competing needs and desires and the resources for satisfying them are never abundant enough to cover the costs of optimal solutions in every case—or even in a substantial minority of cases. Thus, *the necessity of economizing greatly enhances the importance of technology and generates pressures leading to technological innovation.*[6]

Because there is no aspect of human life that is not profoundly influenced by technology,[7] major technological innovations send shock waves throughout the entire sociocultural system, creating the need for, and possibility of, thou-

---

6. This is not to say that technology alone determines the outcome. Ecological-evolutionary theory is not a theory of technological determinism, as some have claimed. For an early statement of my position on this issue, see Lenski (1970: 103–104, 116–117, and 139–142). This argument has been repeated in slightly varying form in subsequent editions. See also Lenski (1966: 438–441).

7. Even artists depend on the paints and other materials, and composers on the musical instruments, available in their day. See Chapter 12 for a more detailed discussion of this and related points.

sands of adaptive changes. This is especially true of major innovations in the technologies of energy and materials. One does not need to minimize or deny the impact of innovations in religion, politics, economics, and other aspects of sociocultural systems to recognize the unique impact of technological innovations.

In an effort to explain why technological innovations are so important, Walter Goldschmidt (1959: 115–116) called attention to the "snowballing tendency" that seems to be inherent in technological advance. Goldschmidt argued that some of the more immediate effects of technological advance include growth in the size of societies and other social aggregates, more permanent settlements, increased production and consumption of goods, increased division of labor, and increased time for activities other than those that satisfy the essential physical needs of the population. These effects, in turn, Goldschmidt stated, increase the probability of further technological advance and further social and cultural consequences.

The *cumulative character* of technological innovation that Goldschmidt and others have noted is one of the things that most distinguishes it from most other kinds of innovation. Many of the most important changes in other aspects of culture are either cyclical or nondirectional in nature. Thus, for example, students of the family have long drawn attention to the cyclical tendencies in standards of sexual conduct. Puritanical eras have often been followed by eras of laxer standards, and these, in turn, by a return to stricter standards. Similarly in politics, observers have noted endless shifts between more tyrannical systems of government and more democratic ones (Michels, 1915; Plato, n.d.). By itself, this kind of change is not likely to provide a foundation for the more fundamental social and cultural revolutions produced by technological innovations—revolutions that radically alter the place of human societies in the global ecosystem.[8]

Where cumulative change *is* observed in other areas of human life, it is usually the result of some underlying process of cumulative technological change. Thus, the enormous growth of human population during the last 10,000 years has obviously been dependent on an extended series of advances in subsistence technology. Similarly, the striking changes in western societies in the last 150 years—the enormous expansion of educational systems, the rise of the welfare state, changes in the role of women, and much, much more—would not have occurred were it not for the tremendous growth in productivity fueled by a succession of major advances in industrial technology.

Our current understanding of the cumulative character of technological change owes much to the work of William F. Ogburn. In his classic study of social change, Ogburn demonstrated that inventions are essentially new arrangements of already existing elements of technology. The automobile, for example, was a

---

8. They can, of course, produce revolutions that are awesome and overwhelming for those caught up in them, as in the French and Russian Revolutions. Such revolutions can even have important consequences for the course of world history, but it is difficult to argue that their impact can compare with the impact of major technological revolutions, such as the shift from hunting and gathering to plant cultivation and animal domestication (the so-called Neolithic Revolution) or the more recent Industrial Revolution.

Table 4.1. Number of Combinations Possible for Various Number of Units

No. of Units	Number of Combinations Possible									
	Two	Three	Four	Five	Six	Seven	Eight	Nine	Ten	Total
Two	1	0	0	0	0	0	0	0	0	1
Three	3	1	0	0	0	0	0	0	0	4
Four	6	4	1	0	0	0	0	0	0	11
Five	10	10	5	1	0	0	0	0	0	26
Six	15	20	15	6	1	0	0	0	0	57
Seven	21	35	35	21	7	1	0	0	0	120
Eight	28	56	70	56	28	8	1	0	0	247
Nine	36	84	126	126	84	36	9	1	0	502
Ten	45	120	210	252	210	120	45	10	1	1,013

novel combination of the gasoline engine, the carriage body, running gears, and the drive shaft, all of which were already in existence when Gottlieb Daimler constructed the first auto. The "only" thing that was new was the combination of elements, the automobile itself.

Because inventions are such an important part of the innovative process, and because they are novel combinations of already existing elements, the potential for technological innovation is an exponential function of the size of the store of information in existence in a society at any given time. Each new bit of information more than doubles the possibility of further inventions (see Table 4.1).[9] This means that there is *an inherent tendency for the rate of innovation in a society to accelerate as its store of technological information increases.* This, in turn, means that the potential for technological innovation and change in societies with advanced technologies is vastly greater than in societies in which the store of technological information is limited.

As Ogburn observed, the difference between these two types of societies does not end there. Technological advance has other consequences as well that stimulate further advance (see Figure 4.1). For example, advances in subsistence technology usually lead to population growth, which means an increase in the number of information-gatherers within a society and, therefore, a greater probability of further innovations. Advances in the technologies of transportation and communication are likely to lead to increased contact with other societies and, thus, to increased opportunities for the acquisition of useful new technological information by means of cultural diffusion, or borrowing from other societies. And, finally, advances in any kind of technology that satisfies human needs and desires is likely to generate a more positive attitude toward technological innovation in particular and social and cultural change in general, thereby weakening the forces of resistance to change. In short, *the more advanced the technology of a*

---

9. To be exact, the addition of the nth bit of information increases the number of possible combinations two-fold plus n-1.

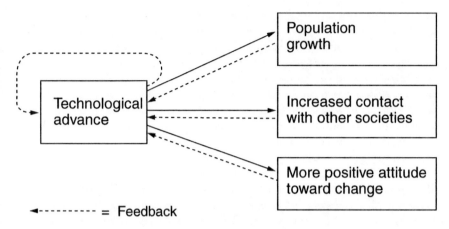

Figure 4.1 Some consequences of technological advance

society, the greater is the probability that values and attitudes supportive of change will gain ascendancy over those supportive of continuity.

Throughout most of history, however, the forces of continuity were dominant in the vast majority of societies. Homeostatic mechanisms are normally quite powerful within all of the information systems on which human societies depend. Within the neurological and cultural systems, one of the most powerful of these mechanisms is the *socialization process,* a process whereby individuals internalize much of their society's store of cultural information. Information, or cultural capital, has long been one of the bases of power, and power, in turn, tends to breed conservatism and a desire to preserve a rewarding *status quo* (Michels, 1915).

Ideologies have been another important homeostatic force, especially those supported by political elites or by large groups within societies. Most major religions, for example, have viewed the existing social order as the product of divine or supernatural forces and, therefore, something not to be tampered with (Lenski, 1966). Even revolutionary ideologies usually become conservative forces once their adherents gain control of a society. Marxism-Leninism is a classic example of this, having become a highly conservative force whenever its adherents came to power.[10]

Ideologies and the belief systems they embody are also important because they influence the judgments of individuals concerning the *psychic* costs and benefits

---

10. There have been a few instances, however, in which dominant ideologies have functioned as a force for change. Modern western market capitalism is probably the best example of this, supportive as it is of continuous economic growth. It should be noted, however, that market capitalism is, itself, the product of a prolonged period of technological advance and of the rewarding experiences (especially for elites, though not only for them) that accompanied it. In other words, it is yet another indication of the unique importance of technological advance in the overall process of societal change and development.

of various forms of activity. For this reason, we need to revise somewhat the statement earlier concerning costs and benefits and their influence on action. A more precise statement of the principle would be that *the interaction of genetics, technology, environment, and ideology determines the relative costs and benefits (psychic as well as economic) of alternative courses of action and, therefore, also, the choices that individuals and societies make among the options available to them.* The inclusion of ideology explains why individuals and societies do not always adopt the economically least costly solution to problems, and also why societies with similar technologies do not always have identical institutional systems.

Although it is important not to exclude ideology from analyses of the selective, or decisionmaking, process within societies, it is equally important not to exaggerate its influence as sociologists and others often do. If the present analysis is correct, *the exercise of ideological preferences for economically more costly solutions to problems is always limited by the availability of resources, and these limits are set by genetics, technology, and environment.* By itself, ideology cannot expand the limits of the possible; at best, it sometimes stimulates technological advance, and *this* may then extend the limits.

Ironically, one reason that the importance of ideology is so often exaggerated in the social sciences today is because technological advances of the last 200 years have enormously increased the size of the economic surplus in the societies in which most social scientists work.[11] Those societies now have an unprecedented supply of resources available after meeting all of the essential needs of their productive members and dependents, and much of this surplus can be allocated on the basis of ideologically based preferences—thus creating the illusion for those who focus on the handful of advanced industrial societies of the modern world that ideology is, and presumably always has been, the basic engine of social change and the basic determinant of the characteristics of societies.

Continuity and Change in Individual Societies: The Basic Dynamics of Societal Systems

One of the more challenging problems confronting macrosociological theory is that of providing an analysis of continuity and change that does not exaggerate the importance of the latter at the expense of the former. All of us today are products of an era of extraordinarily rapid and pervasive change, which makes it tempting to exaggerate the power of the forces promoting change and to underestimate the power of those promoting continuity.

---

11. C. P. Snow called attention to another major cause of the exaggeration of the role of ideology in his famous lecture on "The Two Cultures"—namely, the bifurcation and separation in the educational process in Britain and elsewhere between training in science and technology and training in the humanities.

Fortunately, an evolutionary perspective provides one of the more effective defenses against this, drawing attention, as it does, to the experience of *the totality of human experience from the Stone Age to the present.* As a result, one is quickly reminded that continuity, not change, has been the more salient feature of life in most societies throughout most of history, and helps us keep more clearly in mind the exceptional nature of the modern era. It also sensitizes us to an aspect of the problem that we might otherwise neglect—namely, the shifting balance in the relative importance of the two processes. This, too, is something that requires explanation.

If our analysis is correct up to this point, the ultimate sources of both continuity and change, and also of the shifting balance between them, are to be found in the interaction of the five sets of factors we have just considered: *the genetic, neurological, and cultural systems of information, and the biophysical and sociocultural environments.* This brings us back once more to human nature and the dependence of human populations on the environment.

Several aspects of human nature are especially relevant in any explanation of the sources of continuity and change. First, as we have seen, the common genetic heritage of our species motivates humans everywhere to strive to maximize pleasurable experiences and minimize painful and unpleasant ones. Second, it enables them to learn from experience and to modify their behavior in response to such learning. And, third, it leads them to economize most of the time.

But this is only half of the story. Life is not lived in a vacuum; pleasure, pain, and learning are all products of encounters with the environment, and economizing decisions always reflects its influence. Thus, the environment must also be taken into account in explanations of continuity and change, with several of its characteristics being especially important. First, and most important of all, the material resources available to human populations are finite, never infinite. Second, the environments themselves, both biophysical and sociocultural, exhibit elements of both continuity and change. And, finally, environmental change is partly endogenous, but partly a response to prior changes in human societies (e.g., population growth and technological innovation).

When one reflects on the nature of human nature and the environment, it is obvious that the potential for *both* continuity and change is always present in every society. Which occurs, or which is dominant in a given situation, depends on the specifics of the situation. For example, the economizing tendency that is so important a part of our nature causes us to develop many habitual patterns of action, but these persist only as long as environmental conditions make them rewarding. If conditions change, or we discover a more rewarding pattern of action, we are likely to modify our actions. Thus, human nature and the environment are like two-edged swords, sometimes promoting continuity, sometimes change.

From its inception, evolutionary theory has been associated with the concepts of change and progress, and not without reason. This is not to say, however, that evolutionists believe that change and progress are always dominant in individual societies, or even in the global system of societies. As noted earlier, continuity was the dominant feature of life in the vast majority of societies of the prehistoric past, and change in these societies was neither frequent nor important in most cases. Even in more recent times, continuity has been a striking feature of the life of most societies.

Few societies in history have experienced rates of change as great as those in western societies in the last 100 years, yet even among these societies social and cultural continuity plays an important role and some elements of social organization and culture have survived for centuries, even millennia. The calendar, the alphabet, the numeral system, many tools, many techniques of production, the institution of marriage, the family system, concepts of justice and morality, the concept of God and of life after death are all thousands of years old.

The causes of this continuity are not hard to find. They include the essential stability of the human genotype and the slowness of change in the biophysical environment. They also include the relative uniformity and stability[12] of the sociocultural environment of most societies prior to the last 9,000 years (i.e., before the emergence of the first farming societies) as well as certain characteristics of societies themselves, especially the socialization process, the development of social institutions, and the systemic nature of societies and their cultures.

As sociologists have long recognized, the socialization process is especially important in this regard. During the early years of life, individuals acquire much of the cultural information on which they depend throughout their lives, but during these early years, they have little or no control over the content of the information they receive and absorb. As they grow older, their ability to control the flow of information increases, but their rate of learning appears to decline, partly by choice, and partly because of physiological changes that reduce their ability to absorb new information. In addition, the most powerful members of societies are usually older persons who tend to have a lower capacity for absorbing new information (though often a greater store of information overall). Through their control of families, schools, religious groups, governments, and other organizations, these individuals greatly influence the learning process in the younger generation. Thus, the inverse relation between ability to absorb new information and ability to control the flow of such information promotes social and cultural continuity.

The systemic nature of societies and their institutions also ensures a substantial degree of societal continuity. Most of the parts of sociocultural systems are linked to other parts so that a change in one part necessitates or stimulates changes in others, thereby increasing the costs of change and the likelihood that older patterns will persist. The extent of such linkages and the magnitude of the obstacle they pose are illustrated by the difficulties that have been encountered in the effort to introduce the metric system in the United States. All kinds of equipment that has been engineered to specifications employing the traditional system of measurement would have to be replaced and an entire generation of people compelled to unlearn one system and learn another. During the transition period,

---

12. Stability in this context refers to the fact that all societies maintained the same technological infrastructure for millennia (i.e., the technologies of hunting and gathering), unlike the modern world where neighboring societies often change drastically, transforming the sociocultural environment.

maintenance workers would have to be equipped with two set of tools. Countless laws would have to be rewritten and endless records revised. In short, despite many obvious advantages, it is far from clear that the benefits of a shift to the metric system would outweigh the costs. The Chinese encountered a similar problem some years ago when proposals were made to replace their ideographic system of writing with a simpler alphabetic system. In the end, they found it more rewarding and less costly merely to simplify the older ideographic system.

Nevertheless, despite obstacles, change does occur, even in the most stable societies. Of course, much of the change is relatively inconsequential: Just as mutations occur randomly in a population of organisms because of imperfections in the processes of genetic reproduction, so nonadaptive innovations occur more or less randomly in human societies in the process of sociocultural reproduction. Changes that occur in languages over time are a classic instance of this. Contemporary Australian, Canadian, American, and British English all differ from one another despite the fact that they derive from a common source in the recent past. The same is true on a grander scale of the family of Indo-European languages. Comparable instances of nonadaptive change can be observed in myths and legends. So far as we know, most of these changes were not intentional (though some probably were, as in the biblical version of the story of the great flood), but resulted from defects in the process of transmission and reproduction.

Even when unintended and unimportant initially, cultural changes like these can assume importance later. If nothing else, they reinforce the boundaries between societies by differentiating members from nonmembers. Linguistic alterations are especially important in this respect, since nothing helps to identify "foreigners" more readily than their speech.

While nonadaptive innovations can sometimes have important consequences, they are much more likely in the wake of adaptive innovations. By definition, adaptive innovations increase the capacity of a society to satisfy its members' needs, at least in the short run, and adaptive innovations in the technologies of subsistence, transportation, and communication have often had far-reaching consequences for the entire life of a society. Discoveries, inventions, and other adaptive innovations obviously occur in response to unfulfilled needs and desires. But this raises further questions: Why does the rate of adaptive innovation vary as much as it does among societies? And, why does it vary from one period to the next within a given society? Part of the answer to these questions is that differences in the rate of adaptive innovation in societies are a function of differences in the rate of change in the environments to which they must adapt. Differences in the rate of change of the *sociocultural* environment are especially important, because cultural borrowing seems to be a more important source of adaptive innovation in most societies than independent inventions and discoveries and because changes in the sociocultural environment have been much more frequent and much more important than changes in the biophysical environment during most of the last 10,000 years.

Differences in the rate of adaptive innovation in societies are also greatly influenced by characteristics of the societies themselves. For example, because of the systemic nature of societies, there tends to be a "multiplier effect" in the process of innovation: Each change tends to increase the need for, and the possibility of, further changes. It is almost as difficult for a society to make a single adaptive innovation as it is for an individual to eat a single salted peanut. In addition, most discoveries have multiple applications: The discovery of the basic principles of metallurgy, for example, led to varied applications in fields ranging from art and religion to economics and warfare.

The best predictor of the rate of adaptive innovation in societies is *the size of the store of adaptive information already available to their members.* The size of this store of cultural capital available to the members of a society is important not only because of the potential such capital provides for inventions (which are, by definition, new combinations of existing information) but also because it tends to stimulate population growth, increase contact with other societies, and stimulate more positive attitudes toward innovation and change, and each of these developments increases the probability of higher rates of adaptive innovation.

There is no guarantee, of course, that the rate of innovation and the level of societal development will *always* correspond to the magnitude of the cultural capital a society possesses. There are too many instances in history in which less advanced societies have overtaken more advanced ones (Nolan, n.d.; Nolan and Lenski, 1985) to justify such an assumption. In the modern era, the societies of northwestern Europe have overtaken those of the Middle East, and more recently Germany, Japan, and the United States have overtaken Britain, which pioneered in the Industrial Revolution.

The reasons for developments such as these are still not fully understood, but technological innovations appear to have played an important role in many instances. Sometimes, they reduced the locational advantage of one set of societies while increasing it for another: Thus, the advances in maritime technology that enabled Europeans to bypass Middle Eastern merchants and trade routes all but destroyed the historic locational advantage of Middle Eastern societies and substantially reduced the historic disadvantage of western European societies. Other times, societies have invested so heavily in a current state-of-the-art technology that when a newer technology appeared, they were reluctant, or unable, to make the necessary capital investments and thereby lost the advantage they previously enjoyed relative to other societies that had not invested as heavily in the earlier technology. The experience of Britain and the United States in the steel industry in the recent past provides a good example of this: Newer technologies, such as continuous casting, rendered older plants economically noncompetitive, but the companies owning those plants were slow to abandon them because of the tremendous capital investment involved. By delaying the changeover, they gave Japanese and German competitors an opportunity to gain an advantage. Finally, the cost of wars and military preparedness has often taken a toll, draining resources from the productive sector. When this has happened, resources that might have been used to support research and development in the productive sector were often sacrificed, since they seemed less essential in the short run.

Intrasocietal Selection

Because of the process of innovation, the members of human societies are often confronted with alternative ways of satisfying their needs and desires, and the choices they make can result in the elimination of one or more of the alternatives. Many factors influence their decisions, especially the information available to them at the time as well as their judgments concerning probable benefits and costs of the various alternatives. In keeping with the economizing principle, individuals usually follow the course of action that promises the greatest rewards (psychic as well as material) for the least expenditure of resources.

This is not to claim, however, that intrasocietal selection is entirely a rational process. Far from it! Decisions are often made on the basis of incomplete or inaccurate information. In addition, unexamined assumptions and emotional factors influence judgments, and calculations of probable costs and benefits tend to be based on shorter-run and first-order effects, while longer-term consequences and unintended side-effects tend to be ignored, overlooked, or minimized.

Complicating matters further, it is extremely difficult in many areas of human activity to predict which of several possible alternatives is likely to prove most rewarding. When the choices involve competing ideologies (e.g., capitalism vs. socialism) and systems of social organization (e.g., parliamentary vs. other forms of governance), it can be all but impossible to tell in advance which will be more rewarding. By comparison, it is usually much easier to anticipate the relative costs and benefits of alternative technologies, *at least in the short run.* This is also true of systems of organization that have a single dominant purpose, such as profit-making. Here, too, alternatives can be subjected to repeated tests and their efficacy judged by a single, unambiguous standard. But where multiple and more or less equally important standards are involved, as with governments and ideologies, consensus is much more difficult to achieve. This is why groups and societies that have disagreed violently on matters of ideology and basic social organization (e.g., Soviet-bloc and the western democracies in the recent past, or Muslim fundamentalists and members of secular western societies today) have so often agreed on matters of technology and limited-purpose forms of social organization (e.g., the factory system or the command structure of armies).

One of the great ironies of societal evolution is that the process of intra-group selection among social and cultural alternatives does not always increase a society's chances of survival (Goldschmidt, 1959: 128), and may even reduce them. This is because the principles governing the selective process on the *intra*societal level are different from those that operate on the *inter*societal level (see Chapter 6). Within societies, decisions are usually based on individual or group (especially elite group) self-interest, and this often conflicts with the interests of society as a whole. One need only recall the eagerness with which western businesspeople have sold high-technology items with deadly military applications to hostile governments, or the preference of most members of industrial societies for things that contribute to self-gratification rather than for things that strengthen their nations economically, militarily, or morally (see Galbraith, 1958: ch. 18).

Human Societies as Imperfect Systems

Usually, when we think about systems, we think in categoric terms: Either something is a system, or it is not. As with many concepts, however, it is better to think in variable terms. In other words, a system exists *to the degree that* the actions of the parts are coordinated with one another. Defined in this way, it is clear that human societies are *very imperfect systems*—far less perfect than most of the things to which this concept is usually applied (e.g., mechanical and electronic systems, or even insect societies).

This suggests the need for caution in applying the concept "system" to human societies if we are not to distort our image of social reality at the outset. For example, to say that a society adapts to its environment in a certain way does not mean that the process is beneficial for all members. In class-structured societies, wars of conquest have often been rewarding for the dominant classes but costly for others, just as actions that benefit the dominant religious or ethnic group in a pluralistic society may be hurtful to minorities.

Whenever inequalities in power exist in a society, the life of the society and its development invariably reflect these inequalities. Thus, in the process of intrasocietal selection, for example, the probability that any specific alternative will be adopted is a function not only of the number of people who expect to benefit from its adoption but of their relative power as well. This principle also governs the formulation of societal policies, even in such vital matters as war and peace. As functionalist theories have demonstrated repeatedly, failure to keep this principle clearly in mind can give rise to very misleading conclusions.

Societal Progress, Stasis, and Regression

By now it should be clear that there is nothing inevitable about societal growth, development, or progress—even when the idea of progress is narrowly defined so as to mean simply an increase in the store of useful information. If growth, development, or progress have seemed normal or natural to some, it is only because of the peculiar vantage point from which they have viewed human history.

Earlier, I noted that there were between 100,000 and 300,000 societies in existence at the end of the hunting and gathering era. While this was the largest number in existence *at any single time,* because the life span of societies is limited to centuries or millennia, over the total span of human existence there have almost certainly been well over 1 million societies. Compared to this, the number of societies in existence today (perhaps 200) is minuscule. Moreover, the current universe of societies is highly unrepresentative of the total universe. Societies today are, on average, far larger, far more complex, far more productive, far more powerful, and *far more subject to change* than societies of the past.

Change has always been present to some extent, but the *rate* of change has usually been incredibly slow by modern standards, and much—perhaps most—of the change that occurred was nonadaptive and organizationally inconsequential. In other words, much of the change had little or no effect on the basic nature of societies or their relation to their environments, except, perhaps, to increase the social distance between them and their neighbors. Thus, *stasis,* not change, has been the usual state of affairs among human societies throughout most of history. Only in the last 10,000 to 20,000 years, at most, have growth, development, and progress (in the limited sense of an increase in the store of useful information) become dominant in even a minority of societies, and only in the last 100 years or so have growth, development, and progress (in the limited sense) become dominant in the majority of societies.

But having recognized this, we must also recognize that the progressive minority of societies has had a disproportionate impact on history and especially on the modern world. It is this once tiny minority of societies that has shaped, and is shaping, the world we live in today. Thus, the importance of these societies for theory and for life is out of all proportion to their numbers.

Finally, we must note that just as there is nothing inevitable about societal progress, so, too, there is nothing inevitable about societal continuity. Regression is also a possibility. The Roman Empire in its later years provides one of the more familiar instances of this, but there are many others. Students of Chinese history and the ancient Middle East have long recognized cyclical alternations between periods of advance and prosperity and periods of decline and hardship. Even in the last 100 years, there is clear evidence of societal regression, as in the case of Germany and Japan in the 1940s, Cambodia or Kampuchea in the 1970s, and a number of African societies in more recent years.

The more carefully one examines the historical record, the clearer it becomes that the range of possibilities open to human societies is extraordinarily varied and that any appearance of inevitability in societal progress, advance, and development is just that—an appearance and an illusion. Regression and stasis are just as normal and just as natural as societal progress, even when that term is narrowly defined, and over the total span of human history, they have been far more frequent. These are facts that macrosociologists should not ignore.

An Initial Model of the Determinants of the Characteristics of Individual Societies

The ultimate aim of theory in any field of study is to provide a framework within which otherwise scattered bits and pieces of information can be interpreted and understood. Without such a framework, information tends to multiply rather than cumulate, and it becomes extraordinarily difficult to advance much beyond common sense in efforts to interpret materials.[13]

---

13. Unfortunately, most sociologists have been slow to recognize this. For many years now, efforts to construct comprehensive theories of human societies have been treated dismissively as efforts to build "grand" theory, when the real problem was the assumptions on which these theories were based and their inability to provide a foundation for the kind of multilayered theory that protects against crude overgeneralization.

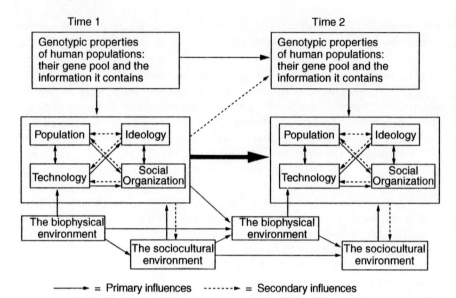

Figure 4.2 First-stage ecological-evolutionary model of the determinants of the characteristics of individual societies

The study of human societies is no exception. Here, as elsewhere, a theoretical framework is essential, both as a guide to research and as an aid in the interpretation of our otherwise fragmented store of information.

Ideally, theory should take the form of a set of highly specified equations that fit all of the relevant data. This is not possible, however, partly because of the extraordinary complexity of the relationships involved, partly because of the small number of well-documented cases, and partly because of the impossibility of manipulating the relevant variables experimentally. Nevertheless, it is possible to discern the basic outlines of a theoretical model that can account for many of the most important features of individual societies and thus provide the kind of comprehensive framework for the discipline that macrosociology requires.

Figure 4.2 is such a model, specifying as it does the four major components of societal systems and their relations to one another and to three crucial extrasocietal determinants. As is evident, this is a more highly specified version of the general model shown in Figure 3.3. Phenotype has been divided into population, ideology, technology, and social organization, and environment has been broken down into biophysical and sociocultural components. In addition, technology is identified as the critical interface between the biophysical environment and the other parts of the phenotype, and is shown as having a greater influence on social organization and ideology than either of them has on it. The thick, solid arrow linking the sociocultural system at Time 1 to the sociocultural system at Time 2 calls attention to the important phenomenon of *autocorrelation* that has been observed repeatedly in time-series studies of human societies. Correlations between measures of the same variable at successive points in time are usually so high that it is often difficult to assess the relative strength of other influences. This is especially true when the time intervals employed are relatively brief.

Autocorrelation needs to be recognized as something more than a method-ological inconvenience, as it is usually regarded; it is also a substantive finding with important theoretical implications. Above all, it is a reminder that there is a powerful social and cultural counterpart to the physical phenomenon of inertia and the biological phenomenon of homeostasis. Sociocultural systems tend to persist over time and resist change. Thus, the social and cultural characteristics of a society at any given time are never merely responses to current environmental and genetic circumstances and influences; they also include responses to circum-stances and influences operative in the past.

René Dubos (1968: 270), the noted biologist, captured this aspect of hu-man life in a remarkable way when he wrote, "The past is not dead history; it is the living material out of which man makes the present and builds the future." This is why synchronic and ahistorical analyses of the kind that have been so popular in American sociology are so disappointing. No matter how skillfully they capture the interplay of current forces, they fail to do justice to the heritage of the past and its continuing influence on societies. (See Chapter 10 for an im-portant instance of this in the world today.)

Before we leave Figure 4.2, there are two other points to be noted. First, the model shown in the figure is not meant to be exhaustive; it is simply a first-stage model that can be expanded to handle greater detail as the need arises. In other words, it is a foundation on which to build, not a finished structure. For example, although the initial model lumps all elements of technology into a single compo-nent, it is helpful or even necessary for certain purposes to differentiate between the technologies of production and the technologies of transportation and com-munication. From a developmental standpoint, the former appear to be the more basic, but it is clear that significant feedback effects have also been at work. In a similar manner, more detailed specifications can be added to each of the other components of the model.

While it is important to recognize the necessity of adding greater specificity to the model when dealing with specific problems, it is even more important not to lose sight of the basic model and the map it provides of relationships among the major components of societal systems and the primary forces acting on them. Failure to develop this kind of map may well have done more to impede the advance of sociology than all of the discipline's other failings and shortcomings combined.

Second, as the figure indicates, the influence of technology on other ele-ments of sociocultural systems is not always direct. Its impact on various aspects of social organization and ideology is often mediated by other elements of these same variables. By overlooking or ignoring these *indirect* effects of technology, many have been misled into believing that social organization and ideology are the principal sources of change in societies.[14]

For those who find ecological-evolutionary theory attractive, the model shown in Figure 4.2 can provide an aid to research and to the analysis of individual societies. Above all, it identifies the most important elements that must go into such an analysis and the nature of relationships among them. While not all of the elements of the model have to be dealt with explicitly in every analysis of every society, all should be kept clearly in mind. In short, those who seek to explain the characteristics of individual societies should bring to the task:

1. a conception of *human nature* that is informed by the new sciences of genetics and primatology as well as by the unhappy results of utopian social experiments in the twentieth century that assumed human nature was highly malleable;
2. a sensitivity to the influence of the *biophysical environment,* both as a resource for and a constraining influence on societal development;
3. a sensitivity to the influence of the *sociocultural environment,* again both as a resource for and a constraining influence on societal development;
4. an appreciation of the special role of *technology* as the interface between the biophysical environment and other aspects of sociocultural systems, as a factor limiting the developmental possibilities of a society, and as a force influencing a society's choices within the limits of the possible;
5. an appreciation of the importance of *population size* and its influence on all of the other components of societal systems;
6. a concern for the *interaction of societal systems of social organization and ideology* and for the possibilities of *feedback* between them and between both of them and technology and population; and, finally,
7. an appreciation of the impact of *a society's cultural heritage* and a recognition of the importance of taking the longer historical view even when attempting "merely" to explain the contemporary scene.

This approach to macrosociology may itself sound utopian, but if the analysis thus far has been correct, neglect of any of these elements of the model is likely to lead

---

14. For example, if one hopes to explain the striking changes in the role of women in industrial societies in recent years it is not enough merely to invoke the new feminist ideology or the success of recent feminist organizations. The question remains, Why did the new ideology and new organizations arise when they did and why have they been so successful at this time? Was it simply a matter of more skillful leadership or better organization? Or was it the new technologies that have liberated women from bondage to the extended cycle of child-bearing and child-rearing and have allowed them to become competitive in the new workplace where brains are usually more valuable than brawn? This is not to suggest that technological innovation and change have been *sufficient* causes. Clearly, they have not. But they have been *necessary* causes, and very important ones at that. Ecological-evolutionary theory does not deny or minimize the contribution of social organizational and ideological variables in processes of social change; but it does encourage much greater attention to the facilitating role of technological innovation, which extends the limits of the possible in human societies and thus plays a critical role in most of the more radical transformations in human societies.

to misinterpretations and faulty conclusions. As theologians have long recognized, sins of omission are no less serious than sins of commission; neglect of relevant variables, or constants, can bias conclusions no less than faulty analysis or errors in logic. In fact, there is good reason to believe that the limitations and shortcomings of contemporary sociology are due much more to the former than to the latter.

Excursus: Toward Greater Specification of Fundamental Relationships—Four Equations

Shortly before the end of the eighteenth century, Thomas Malthus published the first edition of his controversial *Essay on the Principle of Population as It Affects the Future Improvement of Society.* In it, he argued that the growth of population, unless checked by disasters, such as war, famine, and pestilence, will always exceed the growth in food supply, and thus prevent any permanent improvement in standards of living. Algebraically, Malthus's thesis can be rendered:

$$\text{Standard of living} = \frac{\text{Resources}}{\text{Population}}. \quad (1)$$

Despite its now obvious flaws, Malthus's essay made a lasting contribution to our understanding of an important aspect of societal dynamics. More than any other work, it drew attention to the consequences of population growth and to one of the causes of differences in living standards. Later scholars, writing with the advantage of greater hindsight (i.e., with greater awareness of the substantial improvements in living standards in western societies that were occurring), came to see the necessity of adding technology to the picture. Thus, when William Graham Sumner formulated his law of population a century later, he argued that "[p]opulation tends to increase up to the limit of the supporting power of the environment *on a given stage of the arts* [i.e., the practical arts, or what we now refer to as technology], and for a given standard of living" (Sumner and Keller, 1927: 46; emphasis added). In other words,

$$\text{Population} = \frac{(\text{Resources})(\text{Technology})}{\text{Standard of living}}. \quad (2)$$

Transposed, this equation can be restated for present purposes:

$$\text{Standard of living} = \frac{(\text{Resources})(\text{Technology})}{\text{Population}}. \quad (3)$$

Sumner's formulation was a major advance over Malthus's, since it provided an explanation for the extended and substantial improvements in living standards enjoyed by western societies in the time since Malthus first formulated his theorem. Nonetheless, Sumner's formulation is not the final word on the subject. It, too, can be improved in several ways.

First, the concept "standard of living" creates a problem. As economists have noted, it implies a unitary phenomenon, when, in fact, the living standards of different segments of a population can vary enormously, with most people living in abject poverty while a few enjoy enormous riches. This problem can be avoided if we replace "standard of living" with "economic surplus," a measure of the capacity of the economy to produce goods and services in excess of what is required to keep the producers of essential goods and services productive.

This points the way to a second important change—namely, the inclusion of capital as a major variable on the right side of the equation. Productivity is obviously a function of capital; societies short of capital are obviously handicapped in their ability to produce goods and services. Moreover, in recent decades we have come to recognize that the capital on which a society's level of productivity depends is not simply economic ($Capital_a$ in Equation 4 below); productivity also depends on *human* capital ($Capital_b$ below), the skills and knowledge that members of a society possess. In the modern world, measures of literacy and of formal education are useful approximations of human capital, though both leave something to be desired since definitions of literacy and the quality and content of educational systems vary considerably from society to society.

Third, we need to add an error term to cover the effect of all the other variables that influence the size of the economic surplus in societies. Individually, none of these appears to be as important as the variables already specified. Collectively, however, they are too important to be ignored. This brings us to a fourth, and final, equation, which, as we shall see in Chapter 10, has great relevance for macrosociological theory:

$$\text{Economic surplus} = \frac{(\text{Resources})(\text{Technology})(\text{Capital}_{a+b})}{\text{Population Size}} + e. \ (4)$$

Equation 4 is extremely important for both theory and research. Other variables may have a greater influence on one or another of the attributes of societies, but differences in the size of the economic surpluses of societies appear to be the most powerful influences shaping *the totality* of their attributes. In other words, this equation specifies a set of variables that has to be taken into account in any effort to explain or understand the more basic attributes of any society (or any set of societies). To neglect any of these variables in theory construction, or in research, is equivalent to attempting to construct a multistory building without first laying a proper foundation. The importance of this equation will become evident in the chapters that follow.

5

CHARACTERISTICS OF SETS
OF SOCIETIES

Since the demise of the older evolutionism, most sociologists have shown little interest in mapping the universe of human societies and in developing a comprehensive taxonomy of human societies.[1] Most have been content to define sets of societies and create categories and distinctions on an *ad hoc,* case-by-case basis. As a result, categories have multiplied to the point that the field is now inundated with countless overlapping and often incompatible sets of societies: industrial societies, urban societies, urban-industrial societies, postindustrial societies, modern societies, postmodern societies, postmaterialist societies, capitalist societies, monopoly capitalist societies, socialist societies, developed socialist societies, traditional societies, core societies, semiperipheral societies, peripheral societies, feudal societies, preindustrial societies, First-, Second-, Third-, and Fourth-World societies, dependent societies, developing societies, less developed societies, liberal democratic societies, welfare state societies, Marxist societies, totalitarian societies, authoritarian societies, western societies, Pacific-rim societies, Arab societies, Middle Eastern societies, Islamic societies, Latin American societies, and more.

Without denying the utility of many of these *ad hoc* categories for middle-level theory and research, *ecological-evolutionary theory postulates the need for a systematic and comprehensive classification of the total universe of societies, with the system of classification grounded in a general theory of human societies and based on clearly specified covering principles.* Sociology today desperately needs a "map" of the total universe of human societies, not unlike the taxonomic "map" of the

---

1. Despite the length of this chapter, much of the material is highly condensed and abbreviated, especially the discussions of each of the sets of societies. For more detailed analyses of the sets, see Nolan and Lenski (2004: chs. 4–14) or Lenski (1966: chs. 5–12).

universe of species that biologists have developed since the days of Linnaeus. Without such a map and the fundamental questions it poses about relations among species, it is hard to imagine that evolutionary theory could have developed as it has in modern biology.

Mapping the universe of relevant phenomena has been critical in the advance of knowledge and the development of theory not only in biology but in all of the sciences whose explanatory and predictive powers have proven greatest. Thus, it is hard to imagine the successes of modern chemistry without the periodic table. Similarly, much of the most important research in physics in recent years has been directed toward the goal of completing the theoretical map of subatomic particles; and in biology and psychology in recent years, major efforts have been under way to map the human genome and the brain.

Not infrequently, the mapping process in science leads to startling conclusions—conclusions that are not only counterintuitive but that radically transform our understanding of some important aspect of the world of nature. In geology, for example, the spatial and temporal mapping of rock formations around the globe eventually led to the discovery of tectonic plates and the realization that the positions of the continents have not been fixed immutably but have changed enormously over time. The evolution of species is another striking example of a counterintuitive insight that resulted from the mapping process. But even when the results of mapping are less dramatic, they can contribute to important advances in our understanding of the causal processes that have shaped the world around us.

Unfortunately, few sociologists in the last seventy-five years have had much appreciation of the importance of developing a *truly comprehensive* map of the social universe. Interest in the comparative study of human societies all but disappeared in the years following World War I with the rise of the Chicago school and its program of research focused on small-scale social systems (i.e., communities, neighborhoods, and interpersonal relations) in one's own society.[2] Following World War II, Robert Merton's (1949) advocacy of middle-range theory and research seemed to provide the necessary metatheoretical justification for the abandonment of the comparative method and efforts to map the social universe.

Since then, sociologists, with rare exceptions, have shown little interest in, much less awareness of the need for, a systematic, comprehensive, and adequately nuanced taxonomy of human societies and the kind of general theory of societies required by this kind of taxonomy. Yet such a taxonomy and such a theory are essential if our understanding of human societies is ever to advance beyond its present rudimentary and fragmented state. They provide the only basis on which we can hope to construct *a defensible system of interrelated special theories of the kind that will enable us to move beyond supposedly general theories based on observa-*

---

2. Everett Hughes referred to this unfortunate development as "ethnocentric sociology."

tions of a single society or handful of societies in a limited time period, and beyond the hodgepodge of unconnected case studies and common-sense propositions about those societies that have too long been our discipline's stock in trade. We need to recognize that one of the distinguishing features of a mature science is an integrated system of special theories established by covering principles that are grounded in a general theory.

Mapping the Social Universe: A Taxonomy of Societies

Because of the tremendous importance of subsistence technology, scholars since the eighteenth century have returned to it repeatedly whenever they have attempted to develop a comprehensive and systematic taxonomy of human societies. When one considers the entire range of societies, from the prehistoric past to the modern era, no other characteristic has greater predictive and explanatory power. Knowing a society's technological resources for obtaining energy and materials tells us more about the society and why it is as it is than any other single fact (Heise et al., 1976).[3]

Not surprisingly, the oldest and most widely used methods of societal classification focus on precisely those resources. One is based on the technology of *energy* production. As early as the middle of the eighteenth century, the French scholar and reformer Turgot differentiated among hunting, pastoral, and farming societies, and Montesquieu among savagery, barbarism, and civilization, which he linked directly to differences in modes of subsistence.

The other long-standing method is based on the technology of *materials*. Beginning in the nineteenth century, archaeologists differentiated among paleolithic, neolithic, chalcolithic, bronze-, iron-, and steel-age societies. More recently, however, as the techniques of archaeological research have grown more sophisticated and theoretical interests have increased, archaeologists have shifted the focus of their attention from materials to energy, so that today one reads with increasing frequency in their literature of food-collecting and food-producing societies. This shift was stimulated by the discovery that the distinction between paleolithic and neolithic societies closely approximates the distinction between food-collecting and food-producing societies (Childe, 1936).

The most satisfactory system of classifying societies currently available is a refinement of the eighteenth-century schema developed by Turgot and others. Modern research suggests the utility of differentiating among seven basic types of societies, plus subdivisions of the basic types and various hybrid types that combine substantial elements of two or more of the basic types.

---

3. Measures of technology always load heavily on the first factor in any broadly based factor analysis.

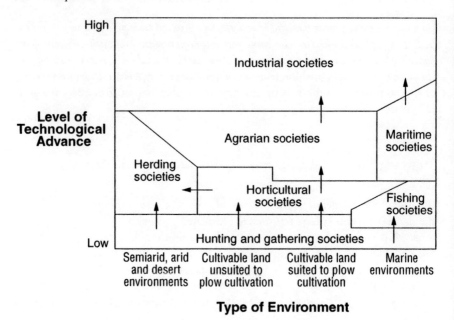

Figure 5.1 An ecological-evolutionary taxonomy of societies

Figure 5.1 indicates the two-dimensional nature of the modern taxonomy. In other words, the basic taxons are products of the interaction of the two most basic variables influencing societal development according to ecological-evolutionary theory—namely, the characteristics of the environments in which these societies are located and the level of technological resources available to them. The horizontal dimension reflects variations in the biophysical environment; and the vertical, variations in subsistence technology.

As the figure indicates, technologically advanced types of societies are capable of expanding into new and different kinds of environments from those in which they developed initially. Thus, modern industrial societies, while developing initially in areas suited to plow cultivation and/or areas favoring overseas trade and commerce, are now found in nearly all kinds of environments. Also, many horticultural and agrarian societies of the past annexed territories previously occupied by maritime or fishing societies. The important point, however, is that each of the basic societal types reflects a unique combination of environmental and technological characteristics and these determine what might be called their *operative* technology (i.e., those technological resources actually employed in their most essential economic activities). While other technologies may be known, environmental conditions render them less relevant and less important in the production of goods and services.[4]

Within the framework defined by the ecological-evolutionary taxonomy, one can easily add further specifications to achieve greater precision in explanation and prediction. For example, in contemporary societies, one can use GNP per capita or energy consumption per capita to obtain a much more precise measure of the overall level of technological development (Frisbee and Clarke, 1979). In preindustrial societies, one can often find important secondary technological criteria. Thus, agrarian societies can be subdivided on the basis of the presence or absence of iron tools and weapons; horticultural societies can be divided on the basis of the presence or absence of metallurgy and/or irrigation and fertilization; and herding societies can be divided on the basis of the presence or absence of large domesticates, such as cattle, horses, and camels.

One can also use nontechnological criteria to subdivide the basic taxons. For example, agrarian societies can be divided on the basis of their dominant religious tradition into Christian, Muslim, Buddhist, and so forth. Similarly, industrial societies of the last 100 years can be divided on the basis of the ideologies of their ruling elites into capitalist, democratic socialist, and revolutionary socialist societies.

Subsets such as these can be quite useful in the analysis of certain kinds of problems. Thus, if one wished to explain the differences between American and Soviet societies of the recent past, differences in the ideologies of the dominant elites would have to be taken into account. But these differences should never be allowed to obscure the underlying similarities between the two societies that reflected the influence of their shared technologies. For it was this—not their ideologies—which explained the high degree of urbanization and literacy, the extreme division of labor, the small nuclear-family systems, the changing role of women, and most of the other characteristics they shared (Jones, 1983), to say nothing of the gradual convergence of their polities (e.g., the declining reliance on political repression in the Soviet Union following Stalin's death).

At the risk of seeming fanciful, we may consider a hypothetical table that explains why advocates of ecological-evolutionary theory base their societal taxonomy on technology rather than ideology, despite the obvious importance of ideology for certain kinds of problems. As Row A of Table 5.1 indicates, information concerning ideology would have been as good a predictor of patterns of social organization in the United States and the USSR in 1975 as information about the level of development of subsistence technology in the two societies.[5] But this

---

4. For example, members of maritime societies and members of agrarian societies share most of the same technological information, but information concerning methods of utilizing marine resources is less relevant for members of agrarian societies and information concerning farming is less relevant for members of maritime societies.

5. The date chosen for the comparison in Table 5.1 was deliberately selected so as to maximize the ideological differences among the societies in the several comparisons. Following the deaths of

Table 5.1. Five Hypothetical Comparisons of the Relative Power of Subsistence
Technology and Ideology to Explain Basic Patterns of Social Organization

Societies Compared	Explanatory Power of:	
	Subsistence Technology	Ideology
A. U.S. and U.S.S.R., 1975	.4	.4
B. U.S., U.S.S.R., China, and India, 1975	.5	.3
C. All societies, 1975	.6	.2
D. All known societies, past and present	.7	.1
E. U.S.S.R., 1935 and 1975	.7	.4

Sources: Although Table 5.1 is hypothetical, it is not without empirical support. See, for example, Heise *et al.* (1976) and Sawyer (1967).

is true only because of the highly biased nature of the sample of societies being compared, a sample limited to two societies that shared a largely common industrial technology but differed enormously in terms of ideology.

The theoretical relevance and importance of this becomes more evident when we add two other societies to the analysis, China and India (Row B). Now we have two industrial societies and two industrializing agrarian societies and two Marxist-Leninist societies and two societies with democratic polities. As a result, the explanatory power of subsistence technology is increased, compared to the former example, and the explanatory power of ideology reduced.

Next, when we add all the other societies in the world of 1975 to the analysis (Row C), the predictive power of technology increases still further and the predictive power of ideology declines once again. Then, if we add to the comparison, *as any science of human societies must,* all known societies of the past as well as the present (Row D), the balance tips further still. Finally, it is important to note that were we to compare Soviet society in 1975 with Soviet society in 1935 (Row E), the relative importance of technology would again loom large, since the ideology of Soviet elites changed little in those forty years, while Soviet technology changed greatly. Row E, however, like Rows A, B, and C, is not the kind of comparison on which a *general* theory of human societies should be based. Instead, a truly general theory should be based on the most inclusive possible data set, or Row D.

Although the figures shown in Table 5.1 are hypothetical, they are not fanciful. A factor analysis limited to nation-states in the modern world found that per capita GNP and variables linked to it constituted the first factor, while ideology and related variables were only the third factor (Sawyer, 1967).[6] Another fac-

---

Mao and Chernenko, pragmatism began to transform the dominant ideologies in Marxist-Leninist societies everywhere far more than ever before.

6. Other studies, such as Frisbee and Clarke (1979), have shown that per capita GNP is an excellent measure of the overall level of technological development in contemporary societies.

tor analysis, using *preindustrial* societies (Heise et al., 1976), found that the first factor loaded most heavily on technological variables and that nothing that could be identified as an ideological factor was statistically significant. Equally important, however, the second factor in this study appeared to be an environmental factor of the kind that is incorporated into the ecological-evolutionary taxonomy of societies (see Figure 5.1). Thus, although the numbers in Table 5.1 are hypothetical, their relative sizes have an empirical foundation.

Individual Societies and the Taxons

Reification is always a temptation in the social sciences, and for this reason it needs to be emphasized that the taxons described in the pages that follow are *not* descriptions of actual societies. Rather, they are simplifying *abstractions* that draw attention to certain theoretically important constellations of variables that have been observed repeatedly in various sets of societies. Each individual society, however, when considered in its totality, is unique. Thus, the taxons are, in effect, like Weber's "ideal types" and should be judged on the basis of their ability to enhance our understanding of human societies, individually and collectively, and of the social and cultural processes that have shaped them.

The analysis of taxons should never be thought of as a substitute for the study of individual societies. But neither should the study of individual societies be regarded as a substitute for the study of taxons, as many historical sociologists, historians, and other humanists seem to believe.[7] *Properly understood, the analysis of individual societies and the analysis of societal taxons are complementary modes of inquiry, each enhancing the other.*

Turning to the societal taxons of contemporary ecological-evolutionary theory, we should note at the outset that the vertical dimension underlying the taxonomy (see Figure 5.1) is a continuum. In other words, the theory assumes that infinitely fine gradations are possible in levels of technological development, which means that individual societies at the lower end of a given taxon tend to have more in common with societies at the upper end of the next lower taxon than they have with societies at the upper end of their own taxon.

To illustrate this point, consider the category of hunting and gathering societies. This category, as defined, includes every society that obtains 50 percent or more of its food supply from these two interrelated modes of subsistence (except for those in the New World that obtained horses and guns from the Europeans).[8] As Table 5.2 indicates, the practice of slavery is virtually nonexistent among societies

---

7. Moreover, the study of individual societies benefits enormously, in most cases, if the taxonomic classification of these societies is clearly established at the outset. In this connection, see Chapters 8 and 9 in Part II of this volume.

8. See Lenski (1966: 95–96) for an explanation of the exclusion of the horse and gun tribes from the hunting and gathering taxon. See also the section on hybrid societies later in this chapter.

Table 5.2. Frequency of Slavery Among Hunting and Gathering Societies by Degree
of Dependence on Hunting and Gathering as Means of Subsistence

Degree of Dependence on Hunting and Gathering	Slavery Present	Hereditary Slavery Present	N
Highest	2%	0%	48
Second Highest	8%	0%	69
Lowest	43%	17%	94

Source: Patrick Nolan, based on machine-readable version of George Peter Murdock's *Ethnographic Atlas.*

that are most dependent on hunting and gathering as their means of subsistence. However, as dependence on hunting and gathering is reduced and reliance on other, technologically more advanced (i.e., more productive) means of subsistence increases, the incidence of slavery increases, and slavery sometimes even becomes hereditary. This more developed form of slavery appears for the first time only in hunting and gathering societies that are closest to the boundary separating this type of society from more advanced types. Collectively, societies on the two sides of this boundary resemble one another much more closely than marginal hunting and gathering societies (i.e., those that barely obtain 50 percent of their subsistence by means of hunting and gathering) resemble the purest instances of this type of society (i.e., those that obtain 90 percent or more of their subsistence in this way). The same is true of other comparisons involving other types of societies: Marginal cases on opposite sides of a taxonomic boundary usually have more in common with one another than with other societies at the opposite end of their own taxon.

In view of this, some may ask: Why use societal taxons? The chief reason is that the quality of the information available on the level of technological development of most societies is such that more precise measures are not sufficiently reliable. Table 5.2 illustrates the point: Estimates of the degree of dependence of societies on hunting and gathering are just that—*estimates*—and some of them are almost certainly flawed. The surprising thing about this table, and others like it, is that theoretically significant and meaningful patterns emerge in spite of this.

In many cases, however, it is impossible even to estimate percentage dependence on various modes of subsistence. This is especially true when archaeological data are the only source available. In such cases, societies can usually be classified in terms of the basic taxonomy, and, if greater precision is required, it is often possible to find reliable indicators of useful subdivisions within taxons. Thus, hunting and gathering societies can be divided into simple and advanced subtypes depending on the presence or absence of the bow and arrow; horticultural societies, on the presence or absence of metallurgy and/or irrigation and fertilization; agrarian societies, on the presence or absence of iron tools and weapons; and herding societies, on the presence or absence of large domesticates (i.e., camels, horses, or cattle).

Thus, when the costs and benefits of using a taxonomy of the kind described above are all taken into account, the benefits clearly outweigh the costs. The principal hazard seems to be the temptation to reify the taxons and treat them as something more than they actually are, but this is a hazard that can be avoided by drawing attention to it.

Hunting and Gathering Societies

As their name indicates, hunting and gathering societies depend on one or both of these technologies as their principal source, or sources, of subsistence. Some of these societies supplement these sources with fishing or horticulture, but these are always secondary for societies in this taxon. When hunting and gathering cease to be the principal sources of subsistence, a society ceases to be a hunting and gathering society.

Until the last 10,000 to 12,000 years, all human societies were hunting and gathering societies so far as we can judge today. Since then, however, the number of these societies has steadily dwindled and few, if any, still survive.

So long as a society depended on hunting and gathering as its primary modes of subsistence, its possibilities for development were severely constrained. Hunting and gathering produced very small yields in terms of food and energy per square mile. Hence, populations were necessarily small and densities low. Even in the most favorable environments, densities seldom reached 10 per square mile. Communities, therefore, were small, averaging 25 to 30 members in groups that depended entirely or almost entirely on hunting and gathering (Hassan, 1981: 53; Nolan and Lenski, 1999: table 5.3). In addition, since hunting and gathering groups never developed any means of transportation other than walking, it was virtually impossible for them to develop sustained ties among communities and thus establish multicommunity societies. As a result, each community was usually autonomous, and community and society were one and the same.[9]

Given the small size of these societies and their limited store of technological information, there was little opportunity for the division of labor to expand beyond the biologically based categories of age and sex. Some of these societies have had headmen and shamans, but these were never more than part time occupations and the individuals who filled them spent most of their waking hours performing the same tasks as others of their age and sex. And just as there has been little occupational specialization, so, too, for the same reasons, there has been little organizational specialization. With rare exceptions, the family served as an all-purpose organization, performing not only the domestic functions that families perform in all societies but also political, economic, religious, and educational functions.

---

9. On rare occasions, military threats have led a few hunting and gathering groups to form temporary multicommunity alliances and a few of these groups joined together briefly for ceremonial activities, but neither of these activities was sufficiently sustained to justify treating the groups that resulted as societies (i.e., autonomous political entities).

With few exceptions, hunting and gathering societies have been nomadic. The animals on which they have depended for meat were soon frightened away from the area around the campsite or were killed off by the hunters, and the women soon depleted the edible vegetable materials close to the campsite. Thus, within a matter of weeks or months, depending on the nature of the environment, it became more rewarding to move than to stay put.

Because these societies were usually nomadic, and because productivity was low, the accumulation of possessions was minimal. This, in combination with the small size of the group and the limited degree of occupational specialization, led to a system of minimal inequality. The principal form of inequality in hunting and gathering societies has been prestige, and differences in prestige have been closely linked to differences in skill in hunting, healing, and other qualities valued by the members.

Societies that have depended on hunting and gathering for subsistence have also had only a limited store of technological information overall. With respect to materials, for example, they have depended on wood, bone, stone, and other things that have been immediately available and do not require complex processing in order to become useful. Pottery and metals, two of the oldest types of more highly processed materials, did not appear on the human scene until societies were able to establish more permanent settlements.

Because of the limited store of technological information available to the members of hunting and gathering societies, and because of the small size of these groups, independent inventions and discoveries have been rare. In addition, the absence of anything more than the most rudimentary means of transportation and communication limited contact with other societies and all of these characteristics combined to foster ideological conservatism and to ensure a low rate of change, except when contact was established with more advanced societies. Not surprisingly, in view of the limited store of information available to hunting and gathering societies, animism was the prevailing ideology.

Although it is still not possible to specify with complete confidence all of the many linkages among the characteristics of this set of societies, Figure 5.2 provides a rough first approximation. Others will undoubtedly improve on this model in the years ahead, but even in its present form, it is useful for several reasons. First, it is an open-ended model that invites changes as the need for them is indicated by research. Second, it is relatively unambiguous and therefore cannot easily be falsified empirically. Third, the model is a valuable reminder of the diverse and varied ramifications of subsistence technology and its enormous importance in shaping the life of human societies. Finally, the model helps one appreciate the limiting and self-perpetuating nature of societal systems that depend on hunting and gathering; whatever changes are made in the future, as the model is refined and improved, these elements will almost certainly remain.

Before we leave this first, and most basic, set of societies, it may be well to consider one of the more important features of the model shown in Figure 5.2. If the model is correct in showing a system that tends to be self-perpetuating, one has to ask how change ever came about and why we do not still live in a world made up entirely of hunting and gathering societies.

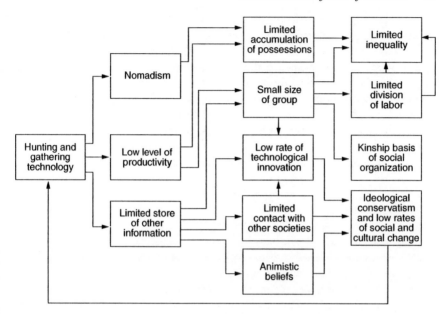

Figure 5.2 Model of relationships among the characteristics of hunting and gathering societies

To answer this question, we need to refer again to Figure 4.2. Comparing Figure 5.2 with this earlier figure, we find that the model of hunting and gathering societies is essentially a much more highly specified version of *a single part of the earlier model:* It is a model of the phenotypic properties of one kind of society. But as Figure 4.2 indicates, changes in these properties are ultimately due to influences originating outside the phenotype—that is, originating in the environment or in the genotypic properties of human populations, or both.

Over the years, various attempts have been made to explain why human societies made the shift from hunting and gathering to plant cultivation and animal domestication as their basic mode of subsistence. At one time this was regarded as an obvious matter and merely the result of the natural human desire for a better way of life. In recent decades, however, that view has been all but abandoned as scholars have gained a better appreciation of the attractions of the hunting and gathering way of life (*vide,* e.g., Lee and Devore, 1969) and the costs entailed by a shift to plant cultivation and animal domestication.

Even before this development, however, some scholars were looking elsewhere for an explanation. V. Gordon Childe (1936), for example, proposed an environmental explanation. He suggested that there had been a causal link between the end of the last Ice Age (which led to major changes in the flora and fauna on which human populations depended) and the adoption of newer modes of subsistence. Later, various scholars (e.g., Cohen, 1977) argued that population growth and the resulting pressures on food resources were the catalyst. Finally, Marvin Harris (1977) argued that all three elements of our basic model—genotype, phenotype, and environment—were involved. In other words, population growth combined with technological advance to produce an overkill of large-game animals on which human societies in many areas had become dependent. The loss of this vital resource compelled these societies to turn to farming and herding, making use of information about plants and animals that they already possessed, but which had previously been unimportant, because hunting and gathering were more rewarding and less onerous. Although it is still too early to say which of these explanations will eventually prove correct, it seems unlikely that future research on this problem will necessitate any substantial modification of ecological-evolutionary theory or the models developed to this point.

Fishing Societies

Fishing is the second oldest mode of subsistence. Already in the Upper Paleolithic, members of some societies were making harpoons and fish gorgets (Hawkes, 1963: 213), and by the Mesolithic era fishing appears to have replaced hunting as the primary source of animal protein in a number of societies.

Actually, it is something of a misnomer to call any group a "fishing" society, since it is doubtful that any society ever depended only on fishing for its food supply. Except in the Arctic, nearly all fishing peoples have obtained fruit and vegetables by foraging or cultivation, and many have supplemented their diet by hunting or horticulture or both. To classify a society as a fishing society, therefore, means simply that fishing has been its most important subsistence activity.

In some ways, fishing societies might be regarded as hunting and gathering societies that have adapted to aquatic rather than terrestrial environments. One might argue that the only difference is that fish, rather than land animals, are the object of the chase and that the technology of the group has been modified accordingly. But this ignores the fact that the shift from hunting to fishing has important social and cultural consequences: Above all, a fishing economy has the potential for supporting a larger, more sedentary, more affluent, and more differentiated population than a hunting and gathering economy.

The reason for this is that members of a fishing society are less likely to deplete the food resources of their environment than are hunters and gatherers. Fish have much higher reproductive rates than most larger land animals. Moreover, the tools available to members of most fishing societies do not allow them to utilize the surrounding waters as intensively as hunters utilize their hunting grounds. Hence, the supply of fish is constantly replenished and fishing peoples are freed from the necessity of relocating their settlements every few weeks or months.

Figure 5.3 provides a model of some of the more important consequences that result from the shift from hunting to fishing as the principal mode of subsistence. The first-order effects are greater permanence in settlements and greater population densities. Second- and third-order effects include an increase in possessions and wealth, greater social inequality, an increase in the probability of

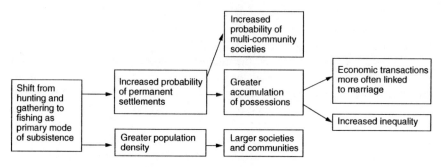

Figure 5.3 Some consequences of the shift from hunting and gathering to fishing as the primary mode of subsistence

economic transactions being linked to marriage (e.g., requirement of a bride price), and an increase in the average size of communities and societies.

The *potential* inherent in a fishing economy is best seen in the Indians of the Pacific Northwest—the Kwakiutl, the Haida, the Tlinglit, and others. Their sociocultural systems were larger, richer, and more complex than those of most hunters and gatherers. In harsher environments, such as the Arctic, however, there was not the same potential and the social systems and cultures of fishing peoples were quite limited.

From a developmental standpoint, fishing societies have had about as much in common with *simple* horticultural societies (but not with *advanced* horticultural societies) as with hunting and gathering societies. For example, when the three taxons are compared in terms of average size of *communities,* fishing societies, with an average size of 90, fall almost at the midpoint between the other two, averaging 40 and 138 respectively (Nolan and Lenski, 2004: 199). On the other hand, when comparison is based on the average size of the *societies as a whole,* fishing societies much more closely resemble hunting and gathering societies (ibid.). In still other respects, however, such as the incidence of slavery and other measures of inequality, they more closely resemble simple horticultural societies.

Horticultural Societies

Horticultural societies may be the least homogeneous of the basic taxons (Goldschmidt, 1959: 194). In size, for example, they have ranged from groups of a few dozen concentrated in a single village to empires with several million inhabitants. In part, these differences reflect the influence of variations in the environment, but to a much greater degree they reflect differences in level of technological development. Thus, if we divide horticultural societies into those that have practiced metallurgy and those that have not, we find that the former have been, on average, three-and-a-half times the size of the latter (Nolan and

Lenski, 2004: table 4.2). For this reason, it is often useful to differentiate between *simple* horticultural societies that have not practiced metallurgy and *advanced* horticultural societies that have.

Viewed as whole, however, the distinguishing mark of every horticultural society is the practice of gardening, or farming without the plow. The basic tools that horticulturalists employ are either the digging stick or the hoe. This type of farming is often referred to as swidden, or slash-and-burn, cultivation, reflecting the practice of periodic clearing of new gardens by killing off the natural vegetation and burning it, with the ashes providing fertilizer for subsequent crops. Except in rare circumstances, the gardens cultivated by horticulturalists have to be abandoned after a few years, partly because weeds take over the plot, and partly because the fertility of the soil is depleted to the point where the benefits of cultivation no longer justify the costs. At this point, it becomes more rewarding to abandon existing gardens and clear new ones.

Despite such moves, farming, like fishing, results in more permanent settlements than are possible in most hunting and gathering societies, and this, in turn, leads to a greater accumulation of possessions, greater social inequality, and other things. It is no coincidence that the presence of pottery in archaeological sites has long been recognized as one of the best indicators of the presence of neolithic horticulturalists rather than paleolithic hunters and gatherers. The weight and durability of pottery made it unsuitable for nomadic peoples who were compelled to relocate their settlements several times each year; but for more settled horticulturalists, the benefits outweighed the costs. And once pottery-making was established in horticultural societies, the foundation was laid for the development of metallurgy, since both technologies require higher temperatures than simple wood fires can produce (Aitchison, 1960; Forbes, 1964). In other words, the potter's kiln was an essential step on the road to smelting, casting, alloying, and all the other basic elements of metallurgy.

Organizationally, the most important development associated with the shift from hunting and gathering to horticulture was the emergence of a potential for *sustained economic surpluses.* For the first time in human history, societies became capable of producing, and storing for extended periods, more food than the producers required to feed themselves and their dependents.

It must be emphasized, however, that horticultural societies had only a *potential* for creating an economic surplus. That potential often failed to be realized because of population growth: When numbers increased as rapidly as production, there was no surplus—something that appears to have happened many times.

Sometimes, however, this did not occur and the potential became a reality, often with revolutionary consequences. Before considering these consequences, we should note that the initial motivation for the creation of the surplus seems to have been to provide for the needs of the group in periods when crops failed and current food supplies were inadequate. In effect, a portion of the harvest was given to the headman to hold in trust until it was needed, either by individual families or by the group as a whole. It also seems to have been a practice in many groups to turn over a portion of the harvest to religious leaders for sacrifices to the gods to ensure their continuing favor. In short, the new horticultural technology made it possible for some societies to implement, more effectively than previously, beliefs and values that had their origin in the older, now-vanishing, hunting and gathering way of life.

In time, however, new uses came to be found for economic surpluses. Political leaders used them sometimes to subsidize groups of retainers to do their bidding (Lenski, 1966: 164–168). Similarly, religious leaders sometimes used the resources made available to them to support artisans and craftsmen who produced artifacts for use in cultic activities. In short, economic surpluses gradually came to provide the foundation for a system of full-time occupational specialization.

These were merely the first steps in what eventually became a revolutionary transformation of human societies. For example, such developments paved the way for a substantial increase in social inequality. Those who controlled the economic surplus came to enjoy far more power than others. Moreover, as their control came to be institutionalized, it could be handed down from fathers to sons, making inequality hereditary.[10] Thus, the status of individuals within the group gradually became less a reward for services rendered to the community as a whole and more a privilege dependent on the accident of birth.

Closely linked to the growth of inequality was the growth of the state. As noted above, one of the uses to which the economic surplus was often put in horticultural societies was the support of retainers dependent on the headman. With the support of these retainers, an individual could sometimes gain power over an entire village—or more. Thus, it is no surprise that among horticultural societies one can observe the full range of political types from autonomous villages led by headmen lacking any real authority through chiefdoms with increasingly greater power over increasingly larger numbers of people and on to small states and even modest empires. From the standpoint of sheer size, the largest of the empires formed by horticulturalists (of which we have knowledge today) appear to have been the Incan Empire in South America and Songhay, a West African society, both of which, at the peak of their power, ruled over several million people.

As the growth of the state suggests, another of the consequences of the shift to horticulture and the creation of an economic surplus was an increase in warfare. For the first time in history, warfare could be economically profitable: By conquering other horticulturalists, a ruler could gain control over their surplus and thereby increase the quantity of goods and services at his own disposal. It is no surprise, therefore, to find that present evidence indicates that the incidence of warfare was far greater in advanced horticultural societies than in simple horticultural societies, and greater, too, in simple horticultural societies than in hunting and gathering (see Table 5.3).

---

10. The office of headman has often been hereditary in hunting and gathering societies, but holders of the office have had little or no more power than other males. Typically, the most influential individuals in these societies have been the best hunters and wise old men and women, but even they enjoyed influence rather than authority or the power to command (Lenski, 1966: ch. 5).

Table 5.3. Incidence of Warfare, by Societal Type (in percentages)

Type of Society	Perpetual	Common	Rare or Absent	Total	N
Hunting and gathering	0	27	73	100	22
Simple horticultural	5	55	41	100	22
Advanced horticultural	34	48	17	100	29

Source: Adapted from data in Leavitt, Appendix B.

Another of the important innovations associated with horticultural societies is the appearance of urban communities. This, too, was a by-product of the formation of the economic surplus. Because urban communities are, by definition, communities in which the majority of the population is freed from the necessity of producing its own food and fibers, they can develop only where at least some surplus is produced. Urban communities are normally the most convenient place of residence for the majority of the occupational specialists (i.e., nonfarmers), since urban settlements usually develop around the places of residence of the political and religious elites who support these specialists.

Figure 5.4 offers a tentative model of the more important developments that seem to occur in response to the shift from hunting and gathering to horticulture. As is obvious, these constitute a radical transformation in the nature of human societies. To appreciate the magnitude of the changes involved, one need only compare Incan society or Songhay at the height of their powers (Davidson and Buah, 1966; von Hagen, 1961) with the most advanced societies of hunters and gatherers of which we have knowledge. With respect to population size, for example, one is comparing societies of several million members with societies of several hundred, at most. Alternatively, if we compare the *median* size of advanced horticultural societies in Murdock's (1967) data set with the median size of hunting and gathering societies, this is a comparison of 5,250 with 40. In thinking about horticultural societies, we need to remember, however, that most of the developments shown in Figure 5.4 occurred only after societies developed the institutional arrangements that were needed to extract the surplus on a *sustained* basis. When this failed to happen, as was often the case, the shift to horticulture meant little more than an increase in food production, growth in population, more permanent settlements, a modest increase in possessions, and probably the spread of ancestor worship.[11]

Agrarian Societies

Agrarian societies, like horticultural, are farming societies. The difference between them is that agrarian societies employ some kind of plow in the work of cultivation whereas horticulturalists rely on the hoe or the digging stick.

---

11. As Figure 5.4 suggests, the spread of ancestor worship in horticultural societies appears to be the result of the establishment of more permanent settlements, which force populations to live in

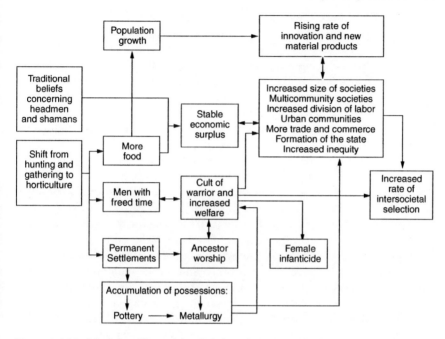

Figure 5.4 Model of the effects of the shift from hunting and gathering to horticulture

This distinction may not seem the stuff of which social revolutions are made, yet this is how prehistorians and archaeologists have come to view the matter. For example, V. Gordon Childe once wrote:

> The plow heralded an agricultural revolution. Plowing stirs up those fertile elements in the soil that in semi-arid regions are liable to sink down beyond the reach of plant roots. With two oxen and a plow a man could cultivate in a day a far larger area than can a woman with a hoe. The plot (or garden) gives place to the field, and agriculture (from Latin *ager*, "a field") really begins. And all that means larger crops, more food, and expanding populations. (1936: 100)

As Figure 5.1 indicates, not all cultivable land is suitable for plow agriculture. Especially in the tropics, vast territories have proven unsuitable. Partly this has been a matter of soils, partly a matter of terrain, and partly a matter of micropredators that attack and kill oxen and other draft animals needed to pull the plow. As a result, there are still large areas—especially, sub-Saharan Africa and much of the hill country in southeast Asia and Latin America—where horticulture, rather than agriculture, remains the dominant mode of farming.

closer proximity to their buried dead. This seems to have led to greater mindfulness of the ancestors and to the development of ceremonies designed to obtain their support and favor.

In parts of the northern hemisphere, in contrast, especially in the temperate zone, plow agriculture replaced horticulture, fields replaced gardens, and productivity increased tremendously. These developments had far-reaching consequences for the societies that adopted agriculture. The best single measure of the magnitude of the change that could result is provided by the upper limits of the range of size achieved by the two types of societies. Previously, we noted that early sixteenth-century Incan society and Songhay were the largest horticultural societies of which we presently have knowledge, and each of these had several million inhabitants at the peak of its power. In contrast, mid-nineteenth-century China—before the beginnings of industrialization—was the largest *agrarian* society in history and it had a population of several hundred million (Chang, 1955: 102).

This hundred-fold difference in size was due partly to the greater density of population that plow agriculture is able to sustain, and partly to the greater scale of organization that is possible in an agrarian society. One reason for the greater density of population is that much more of the land can be cultivated at any given time. In slash-and-burn horticultural systems, gardens must be allowed to revert to wilderness after a few years of cultivation and it takes many years before that land can be used again. Thus, only a limited fraction of the cultivable land in a horticultural society is under cultivation at any given time (often as little as 10 percent). And, while it is true that agriculturalists have usually been compelled to leave a part of their land fallow in any given year, the fallow is seldom more than a quarter or a third of the total. Thus, the shift from horticulture to agriculture often increased the amount of cultivable land five-fold or more. In addition, the use of fertilizer, the practice of irrigation, the harnessing of animal energy, and the more efficient control of weeds all led to greater yields on the cultivated land and substantially greater economic surpluses.

From the standpoint of *territory* controlled, early-sixteenth-century Songhay appears to have been the largest horticultural society that ever developed. At the peak of its power, its empire spread over more than 500,000 square miles—an area comparable to the state of Alaska today. In contrast, mid-nineteenth-century Russia's empire covered nearly 8 million square miles (Blum, 1961: 278), or roughly fifteen times the area of Songhay. In part, this difference was due to advances in the technologies of transportation and communication that made it easier for rulers to control distant territories. The development of literacy was especially important in this regard, since it facilitated the shift from the more limited and constrained kinship-based polities of horticultural societies to the more flexible and expandable bureaucratic systems of agrarian societies. The growth of the state apparatus in agrarian societies seems to have been both consequence and cause of the growth of the economic surplus. Larger surpluses made it possible for rulers to support larger numbers of officials and retainers, and this, in turn, made it possible for them to extract more in taxes and tribute from producers.

Not surprisingly, the growth of the economic surplus that usually resulted from the shift to agriculture had the effect of extending many of the trends associated with the beginnings of horticulture. Thus, in agrarian societies there was a greater division of labor, larger urban populations (and a larger percentage of the population residing in them), greater accumulations of wealth, increased inequality, and increased trade and commerce. There were also a number of new developments, such as the emergence of the first supranational religions, such as Buddhism, Christianity, and Islam; the invention of writing[12] and money; and, interestingly, a slowdown, at least temporarily, in the rate of technological innovation.

The last of these developments is important because it illustrates the role of feedback in the process of societal change. V. Gordon Childe first called attention to this slowdown, which he attributed in part to the increasingly exploitative nature of the polities of agrarian societies. Carrying his analysis a step further, one may argue that the new agrarian societies came dangerously close to separating technological expertise and knowledge from incentive. Peasants and artisans had the expertise and knowledge that were essential to technological innovation, but the governing class controlled the benefits. In addition, the ideologies of agrarian societies increasingly justified this exploitative social system. Also, for members of the governing class, warfare became an increasingly attractive shortcut to wealth. And, finally, there was the added consideration that warfare, unlike work, was viewed as one of the few activities appropriate for the male members of that class. Thus, increasingly agrarian elites turned from the conquest of nature to the conquest of man.

Overall, the shift from horticulture to agriculture has meant a substantial transformation for the societies that made the shift. Although the difference between agrarian societies and horticultural is not as great as the difference between horticultural and hunting and gathering, it is still substantial. Figure 5.5 provides a model of some of the more important changes that have followed in the wake of the adoption of the plow, and it indicates the ways in which these changes seem to have been linked to one another and to the initial change. It should be kept in mind, however, that the sequence of developments shown in the model were not possible everywhere and the biophysical environment, as noted previously, often prevented societies from taking even the first step in the sequence.

Maritime Societies

Maritime societies have been the rarest of the basic societal types. These are societies that have relied on intersocietal trade and commerce as their primary mode of subsistence and their chief source of income. Technologically, they have had much in common with agrarian societies. What differentiated them was the way they used their technological information to take advantage of the opportunities afforded by their environmental situation. Located on large bodies of water, in an

---

12. In a very few instances, precursors of what we would recognize as full-fledged systems of writing developed in advanced horticultural societies (Schmandt-Bessert, 1978; von Hagen, 1961). This is not surprising for the reasons outlined earlier, under "Individual Societies and the Taxons."

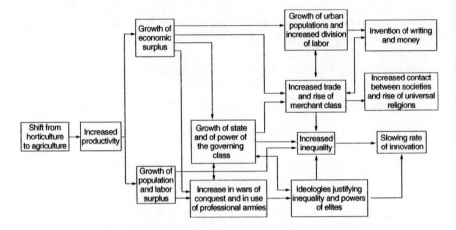

Figure 5.5 Model of the effects of the shift from horticulture to agriculture

era when it was cheaper to move goods by water than by land, these societies found international trade and commerce far more profitable than either fishing or the cultivation of their limited land resources.

The first maritime society in history of which we have knowledge today was developed by the Minoans on the island of Crete, late in the third millennium B.C. Other well-known maritime societies included the Phoenician city-states; Carthage; some of the Greek city-states; Venice; Genoa; Danzig, Luebeck, and other members of the Hanseatic League; and Holland.

Maritime societies resembled agrarian societies in many ways, especially the urban centers of those societies. But there were important differences. Maritime societies were much smaller, often containing only a single city and its hinterland. Only two maritime societies, Carthage and Holland, ever developed empires worthy of the name, and, significantly, both were *overseas* empires. In each case, the empire was created more as an adjunct to commercial activity than as a purely militaristic venture. This feature was linked with another, more basic peculiarity: In a largely agrarian world in which monarchy was the normal—almost universal—form of government, maritime societies were usually republics. Although there were a few monarchies in these societies, they usually occurred early in their history, suggesting that they were carryovers from a premaritime past. The explanation for the republican tendency in maritime societies seems to be that commerce, rather than warfare and the exploitation of vast peasant masses, was the primary concern of the governing class. Being less concerned than elites in agrarian societies with the conquest and control of large peasant populations, these nations had less need for a strong, centralized hierarchical government. An oligarchy of wealthy merchants could do the job, since their primary responsibilities would be to regulate commercial competition and to provide naval forces to defend their access to foreign ports. Navies, rather than armies, were the chief military resource of maritime societies—unlike agrarian societies, which depended more on armies.

Another peculiarity of maritime societies was their unusual system of values and incentives. In agrarian societies, the governing class usually viewed work of any kind as degrading, and since this was the class that all others envied and emulated, its views rubbed off on the rest. This was especially evident in the case of merchants in agrarian societies, who, when they became wealthy, often gave up their commercial activities. This anti–work ethic undoubtedly contributed to the slowdown in the rate of technological innovation in these societies.

In maritime societies, in contrast, merchants were the dominant class, and a very different view of economic activity prevailed. Though more research is needed on the subject, there is reason to believe that the rate of technological advance was considerably greater in maritime societies than in agrarian, especially when one takes into account their much smaller size. There is also good reason to believe that even in agrarian societies the rate of technological advance was correlated with the social and political strength of the merchant class.[13]

Herding Societies

Herding societies, like fishing and maritime societies, have been adaptations to distinctive environmental conditions. Although animal domestication preceded plant cultivation, a number of scholars believe that herding societies were an off-shoot of simple agrarian societies—an adaptation to environmental conditions that precluded farming (Goldschmidt, 1959: 210). As Figure 5.1 suggests, their overall level of technological development has been comparable to that of horti-cultural and simple agrarian societies.

A pastoral economy has usually necessitated a nomadic or seminomadic way of life (Krader, 1968). In fact, our word "nomad" comes from an early Greek word meaning "herder of cattle." Among the herding societies coded by Murdock (1967), more than 90 percent were wholly or partly nomadic. In this respect, they closely resemble hunting and gathering societies.

Herding societies are also like hunting and gathering societies in size of communities. On average, their communities appear to be even smaller than those of simple horticulturalists, judging from the data coded by Murdock (Nolan and Lenski, 2004: 184):

Hunting and gathering communities	40
Herding communities	72
Simple horticultural communities	138

---

13. Compare, for example, the status of merchants and the rate of innovation in Europe during the sixteenth, seventeenth, and eighteenth centuries with the situation in India and China. Both status and rate were higher in Europe, and while this could be coincidence, the evidence suggests a causal link.

Given the sparse resources of their territories, large and dense concentrations of population have been impossible. Despite the small size of their communities, herding societies themselves have been, on average, huge compared to the typical hunting and gathering or simple horticultural society. This is because the average herding society has consisted of approximately eighty communities, whereas the average hunting and gathering society has had only one. Hence, the median size of herding societies has far surpassed the others (ibid.):

Hunting and gathering societies	40
Simple horticultural societies	1,500
Herding societies	5,750

The size of herding societies has been a product of both environment and technology. Open grasslands, where most herders have lived, present few obstacles to movement and, therefore, to political expansion. Moreover, since early in the second millennium B.C., many herding peoples have possessed the technology required for harnessing and riding horses and camels, and this greatly facilitated military conquest and political expansion.

The basic resource in these societies has been livestock, and the size of its herd has been the measure of a family's status. Large herds have signified not only wealth but power, for only a strong man, or the head of a strong family, could defend such vulnerable property against rivals and enemies. Thus, in most of these societies, and especially in advanced herding societies (i.e., those with horses or camels and herds of larger animals, such as cattle), marked social inequality has been the rule. Hereditary slavery, for example, has been far more common in herding societies than in any other type (it is present in 61 percent of herding societies compared to 2–35 percent in other sets of societies). Other kinds of inequality have also been very common, especially inequality based on wealth.

With respect to kinship, herding societies have been noteworthy on at least two counts. First, they have been more likely than any other type of society to require the payment of a bride price or bride service (required in 88 percent versus 37–82 percent in other types of societies). Second, they have been more likely to require newly married couples to live with the husband's kinsmen (97 percent versus 72–87 percent). These strong patriarchal tendencies have several sources. They reflect, for example, the highly mobile and often militant nature of advanced herding societies. Raiding and warfare have been frequent activities, and these activities promoted the development of male authority structures. Moreover, the basic economic activities in these societies have been men's work. In this respect, they stand in sharp contrast to horticultural societies, where women have so often played the dominant role in subsistence activities. It is hardly coincidence that horticultural societies have been noteworthy because of their frequent female-oriented kinship patterns (e.g., matrilineality), while herding societies have been noted for the opposite (Nolan and Lenski, 1999: 200).

As early as the eighteenth century B.C., some herding societies had developed the technology required to harness horses to chariots. This gave them an important military advantage over their less mobile agrarian neighbors and enabled them to win control of much of the Middle East—at least until the new technology was adopted by the more populous agrarian societies. Later, herders invented the gear and tackle needed to ride horses and camels, and this led to a new wave of conquests beginning in the ninth century B.C. (McNeill, 1963). During the next 2,500 years, a succession of herding societies attacked agrarian societies from China to Europe, often conquering them. The empires and dynasties they established include some of the largest in history. The Mongol Empire, founded by Genghis Khan, once stretched from eastern Europe to the shores of the Pacific and launched attacks against places as far apart as Austria and Japan. Other famous empires and dynasties founded by herding societies include the Mogul Empire, established in India by a branch of the Mongols, the Manchu dynasty in China, the Ottoman Empire in the Middle East, and the early Islamic states.

Despite frequent military victories, herding societies were never able to displace agrarian societies. In the end, it was always the conquering pastoralists who changed their mode of life. There were a number of reasons for this, but it was primarily because the economic surplus that could be produced by agriculture was so much greater than that which could be produced by herding. After a few early conquerors tried to turn fields into pastures, they realized that they were, in effect, killing the goose that laid the golden eggs, and they chose to give up their traditional way of life in order to preserve their economic gains. Thus, despite impressive military victories, the limits of the herding world were never permanently enlarged, and in more recent centuries many of the territories controlled by herding societies have come under the sway of agriculturalists.

The repeated failures of herding societies to convert agrarian populations into populations of pastoralists is a fact of considerable theoretical importance. It is one of the clearest indications we have of the constraints that material factors set on societal development. Given the nature of human nature and the constraints of the environment, decisionmakers (in this case, the leaders of herding societies) appear more inclined to sacrifice cherished institutional arrangements and customary practices rooted in traditional beliefs and values than to give up substantial material benefits that would otherwise be theirs. As we will see in several of the case studies in the second part of this volume, the experience of herding societies is not an isolated or aberrant case. On the contrary, when push has come to shove, most people in positions of power have made the same basic kind of decision, which suggests that the social construction of reality is not nearly as unfettered a process as many sociologists today seem to believe.

Industrial Societies

Industrial societies are the newest set of societies. Early in the nineteenth century, Britain became the first society in which industrial technology—that is, machines powered by inanimate energy sources—became the leading source of income and wealth. Today, there are more than twenty industrial societies in Europe, North America, and Japan. Although the causes of the Industrial Revolution are still a subject of debate, the consequences, by and large, are not. It is generally recognized that industrialization has led to massive increases in productivity and this, in turn, has led both to higher standards of living in the societies most affected and to substantial population growth throughout the world. In Britain, the gross national product (GNP) has increased about a hundred-fold since the beginning of the nineteenth century and population has increased three-fold. During this period, per capita income has multiplied approximately thirty-fold and life expectancy at birth has tripled. Comparable changes are evident in other advanced industrial societies.

These changes have led to countless other changes. Women in most industrial societies today, for example, give birth during their lifetime to only about a quarter as many children as women in preindustrial societies of the recent past, and the age structures of these societies have been transformed dramatically. Children make up a much smaller proportion of the population and elderly people are far more numerous than in any type of nonindustrial society.

For the first time in history, the family is no longer the most important productive unit in the economy, and the vast majority of men and a growing majority of women are employed outside the household. Young people, too, no longer spend most of their time in household activities; school has replaced the family, and peer-group ties have replaced family ties as the center of their lives.

Money has become far more important in the daily lives of people than ever before. Subsistence economies have been replaced by cash economies, and the flow of trade and commerce is vastly greater than in preindustrial societies. Because of the new technology and the magnitude of the economic surplus, only a small minority of workers remain in farming and the division of labor has become far more complex. In the United States, the Department of Labor counts more than 20,000 distinct, full-time occupational specialties. Communities, too, are much more specialized than in the past, and industrialization has stimulated a tremendous proliferation of specialized associations. Increased specialization, in turn, had led to increased economic interdependence.

Politically, the most striking change resulting from industrialization has been the decline and disappearance of hereditary monarchies. Most industrial societies are now republics, and even where the institution of hereditary monarchy still survives, the monarch has almost no power. A majority of advanced industrial societies are not only republican but democratic as well, with mass political parties vying for voter support. Even in the relatively small minority of nondemocratic industrial societies of the recent past (e.g., the Soviet Union and Nazi Germany), governments claimed to rule in the name of the people as a whole and maintained some of the formal elements of a democratic system (e.g., elections).

The members of modern industrial societies have far more information available to them than members of any other set of societies have ever had. These societies are, in effect, the intellectual heirs of all their predecessors. No single individual, of course, can possibly master all of the vast informational resources these societies possess, but public educational systems, the mass media, libraries, data banks, the Internet, ease of travel, and programs of continuing education make it possible for the average member of these societies to know far more about the world than members of any other type of society.

Advances in the technologies of communications and of information-processing and storage have greatly increased the accessibility of information, and this in combination with the wealth of these societies (which enables them to support large numbers of full-time scientists and engineers) has led to a fantastic increase in the rate of scientific discovery and technological advance. In fact, more scientific knowledge was acquired in the industrial societies of the twentieth century than in all other societies combined and in all previous centuries.

These developments have had a profound impact on the basic belief systems of members of industrial societies. In preindustrial societies, supernaturalistic belief systems exercised a powerful influence over the masses of people and often over elites as well. But these ideologies have steadily lost influence in industrial societies as the naturalistic worldview of modern science has been spread both by educational institutions and by the mass media (Catton, 1966). As the older ideologies have declined, newer ones have gradually replaced them. Some of these, such as Marxism, have been as broadly comprehensive as the older religious ideologies, while others, such as democratism, capitalism, liberalism, nationalism, and democratic socialism, are more limited in the claims they make on both individuals and societies. But all of the newer ideologies have one thing in common: They are all predicated on the belief that humans can, to a substantial degree, shape and control their destiny. This is in striking contrast to the older ideologies and their insistence that human life depended on forces beyond human control—fate, destiny, God, the gods—and that the best way to cope with this world's ills was either by passive acceptance of them or by reliance on magic, ritual, prayer, sacrifice to the gods, and/or respect for tradition.

Finally, it should be noted that industrial societies, as a set, are unique because of the impact they have had on other societies beyond their own boundaries. Because of their technological resources and wealth, no society, however remote, has escaped their influence. The agents of this influence have been extraordinarily diverse: businesspeople, politicians, scholars, missionaries, tourists, and others have all contributed and the mass media have been especially potent. As a result, there has been a remarkable tendency throughout the entire global system toward cultural convergence around the norms and practices of industrial societies, even in societies where the process of industrialization has barely begun (cf., e.g., Inkeles and Sirowy, 1983).

Postindustrial Societies?

During the 1970s, Daniel Bell published *The Coming of Post-Industrial Society: A Venture in Social Forecasting*, a volume that became extraordinarily influential. In it he argued that a new type of society was emerging that would differ in fundamental ways from industrial societies. In these new societies, the labor force would be employed increasingly in nonmanual occupations, jobs that would require primarily intellectual skills.

Bell was obviously correct in his analysis. No one can quarrel with it. One can, however, question the appropriateness of the label "post-industrial" society, which he popularized. It seems to suggest that advanced societies are no longer dependent on industrial technology. Clearly, this is not the case, nor is it likely to be at any time in the near future. If anything, advanced societies today are even more dependent on industrial technology (i.e., machines powered by inanimate energy sources) than their predecessors of the eighteenth-, nineteenth-, and twentieth centuries.

This is why it seems preferable to think in terms of an ongoing Industrial Revolution with multiple phases (Lenski, 1970: 313–326). *Every* new phase in the Industrial Revolution—not just the current one—has meant important changes in the lives of people and in the nature of societies. In fact, rapid and continuous innovation and change are so striking a feature of technologically advanced contemporary societies that we soon would find it necessary to talk about "post-post-industrial societies" and, later still, "post-post-post-industrial societies" as further important changes occurred. Faced with this possibility, I believe it preferable to think of the societies that Bell labeled "post-industrial" as a subset of industrial societies—namely, those in the latest (to date) phase of an ongoing social and cultural revolution generated by further advances in industrial technology.

Hybrid Societies

Not all societies fit readily into any one of the various taxons. Many have combined two or more of the basic modes of subsistence in ways that make it impossible to say that one was dominant. Many, for example, have combined hunting and gathering with horticulture, fishing, or herding. Others have combined agriculture with maritime activities or herding. Still others have combined modern industrial production with various pre-industrial modes of subsistence. When no one technology is dominant, it is best to recognize societies as the hybrids they actually are.

Usually, hybrid societies have combined elements of the technologies of adjacent taxons in unsurprising ways. Typically, they have occupied intermediate positions in most respects, standing somewhere between the modal patterns of the types of societies whose characteristics they combine. Occasionally, however, more unusual patterns emerge, as when the Plains Indians of the United States acquired the horse and gun from Europeans. In this case, two elements of the cultures of advanced agrarian societies were "grafted" onto the cultures of hunting and gathering or simple horticultural societies—societies at very different levels of development. The introduction of these new elements of technology drastically altered the patterns of life for nearly all of the tribes that were affected. Among other things, the introduction of the horse and gun led to greatly increased spatial mobility, wealth, inequality, warfare, and numbers (Ewers, 1955; Lewis, 1942;

Mishkin, 1940). In a few cases, the adoption of the horse and gun even led societies on the horticultural level to adopt hunting as their chief means of subsistence.

From the standpoint of theory and its development, hybrid societies are quite important. As in the case of the Plains Indians, they provide unique opportunities to observe the impact of specific technological innovations on societies. In the contemporary world, there are two sets of societal hybrids of special theoretical interest and importance: the industrializing agrarian societies of Asia, the Middle East, North Africa, and Latin America, and the industrializing horticultural societies of sub-Saharan Africa, Papua New Guinea, and Haiti (see Lenski and Nolan, 1984; Nolan and Lenski, 1985).

Special Theories in Retrospect

One of the attractive features of ecological-evolutionary theory is its ability to generate a series of interrelated special theories, each of which is grounded in the general theory. Too often, sociological theories have lacked the kind of special theories that would enable one to bridge the gap between the propositions of general theory that apply to all societies throughout history and the system-specific propositions that emerge from the study of individual societies.

Ecological-evolutionary theory offers students of human societies more than a general theory, and more than system-specific propositions (e.g., propositions that apply only to industrial societies). Building on the foundation of its general theory, it divides the universe of human societies into its most basic subdivisions and then provides a series of testable—and falsifiable—models concerning their characteristics. The transition from general theory to the various special theories is accomplished by specifying the nature of the subsistence technology on which each of the various sets of societies depend. By increasing the degree of specification in this way, we end up with a reduced number of societies to which a given analysis is applicable, but our ability to predict is increased. Instead of asserting merely that subsistence technology exercises an influence on patterns of social organization and ideology, as shown in Figure 5.3, we are enabled to say that a specific form of subsistence technology, such as hunting and gathering, increases or decreases the probability of the occurrence of specific organizational and ideological elements, as shown in Figure 5.2 or Figure 5.4. Furthermore, if we wish, we can increase the specification of either the technological variable or one or more of its effects, thereby increasing the precision of our predictions. For example, if we specify that a subset of horticultural societies practices metallurgy or produces an economic surplus, we are able to explain and predict more of the other characteristics of these societies and with greater precision and accuracy.

So long as the sets and subsets of societies are defined on the basis of criteria derived from the general theory, relations among the sets and subsets combine to form a coherent whole. This is tremendously important in the development of a science, but it is something that sociologists have been slow to recognize or acknowledge. Neither the study of individual societies nor the study of societies in general is an adequate substitute for the study of sets and subsets of societies that have been defined by and grounded in a general theory.

This line of thought will be extended in the next chapter as the temporal dimension is introduced, enabling us to deal in a more systematic manner with one of the most important sets of variables that affect human societies—namely, the sociocultural environment to which they are exposed and to which they must adapt.

Excursus: Testing Ecological-Evolutionary Theory

Before theories can be accepted in the world of science, even tentatively, they must be tested over and over again and in as many ways as possible. No theory is ever considered to be unqualifiedly true, but a few come close, having survived repeated testing. At the other extreme, countless theories have been abandoned because of tests that failed to produce predicted results.

Testing can also lead to the *modification* of theories. This is especially likely in the study of phenomena involving complex interactions among large numbers of variables, as in the social sciences. This is why theory construction in the social sciences requires frequent and repeated alternation between the processes of induction and deduction and why such theories must be open-ended.

Social scientists have been slow to recognize the importance of these principles or to appreciate their potential benefits. For various reasons there is a fairly widespread tendency to "rush to judgment" and to make premature claims of having proven or disproven theories. Careerism, for example, can lead to exaggerated claims for test results, since claims to have "proven" or "disproven" an important theory bring instant recognition. Intellectual and ideological commitments may also lead to exaggerated claims, and insufficient appreciation of the distinction between probabilism and determinism can lead to mistaken conclusions about the significance and implications of "deviant" cases.

The last of these is especially important from the standpoint of ecological-evolutionary theory. If theories are couched in deterministic terms, a single deviant case is enough to falsify them. This is not so, however, when theories are stated in probabilistic terms: Propositions stated in probabilistic terms can be falsified only when *the total distribution of cases* violates assertions about that distribution. Thus, the existence of a small minority of sedentary hunting and gathering societies does not falsify the causal model shown in Figure 5.2. The model would be falsified only if the majority, or a substantial minority, of hunting and gathering societies were sedentary.[14]

---

14. Even then, it would not necessarily follow that the larger theory on which the model was based was invalid. This might be true, but, also, it might not. Other possibilities that would have to be considered include (1) flawed data, (2) flawed analysis of the data, (3) errors in the specification of the model, and (4) errors in the derivation of the model from the general theory.

Unfortunately, many of the critics of evolutionary theory have failed to grasp this important principle. In their eagerness to debunk evolutionary theory, they have often focused on a small number of unrepresentative and deviant cases to "prove" their point, while ignoring the overall distribution. In this connection, one is reminded of Robert Nisbet's (1969: 293–294) use of the 1951 pennant race as grounds for rejecting the evolutionary thesis that major social and cultural changes have often been the result of cumulative processes of change.

Although Nisbet's argument is exceptional for its irrelevance and triviality, it is not exceptional in other ways. Many otherwise competent macrosociologists and macroanthropologists still seem unable to grasp the fundamental distinction between determinism and probabilism. The seriousness of this is unquestionable because it places an enormous obstacle in the path of any effort to construct probabilistic macrosociological theory.[15]

---

15. The problem is far more serious in macrosociology than in most other branches of sociology, because macrosociology tends to attract individuals with limited interest in quantitative analysis. Thus, for many in macrosociology, probabilism seems an alien concept.

6

CHARACTERISTICS OF THE GLOBAL SYSTEM OF SOCIETIES

During the nineteenth and early twentieth centuries, evolutionary theory suffered because of the failure of evolutionists to differentiate clearly between propositions that applied to the global system of societies and those that applied to individual societies. Too often it was assumed by proponents and critics alike, that the same propositions applied, or were meant to apply, on both levels.

Today, we know better. Patterns of continuity and change in individual societies are not always paralleled by those in the global system. Sometimes they are, but often they are not, and it is dangerous to assume that they are. Even when similar patterns can be observed on both levels, there may be exceptions among individual societies that are theoretically important.

Marshall Sahlins was the first to address this problem directly. In an important essay published in 1960, he advanced the thesis that there are two kinds of evolution and they operate on different levels of social organization (Sahlins and Service, 1960). *Specific evolution,* according to Sahlins, is the process of change whereby each individual society adapts to its own unique environment, and it is this kind of evolution that is responsible for the diversity of social and cultural patterns that have intrigued anthropologists for so long. *General evolution,* in contrast, refers to the directional changes that have occurred in the universe of human societies, such as the long-run growth of world population, the long-run growth in world economic output or GWP, and the long-run increase in the global division of labor.

Many of the problems associated with evolutionary theory in the past were the result of overly facile attempts to explain the characteristics of individual societies using principles derived from analyses of the evolution of the global system. When evolutionists did this, their ideas were often vulnerable to easy falsification.

Sahlins's "solution" to the problem was an important step forward, but it left something to be desired, since directional change has not been entirely lacking in individual societies, nor is the process of adaptive radiation entirely absent in the universe of societies. Despite this difficulty, Sahlins's distinction between general and specific evolution sensitizes us to the necessity of specifying the level, or levels, of organization to which propositions apply.

During the 1970s, and later, the importance of Sahlins's distinction became even more apparent thanks to the work of Immanuel Wallerstein and his followers. Wallerstein's world-system theory brought home to sociologists and others the fact that the processes of change operating at the global level are more than the sum of the processes operating within individual societies. The universe of contemporary societies is, indeed, a system composed of interdependent and interacting parts and not simply an aggregation of independent and unrelated entities.

It is easy to conclude from the writings of Wallerstein and his followers, however, that the formation of a social system of global dimensions is a relatively recent development in history, a product of the modern era. For, while Wallerstein has written about earlier "world" systems, none of them was close to global in scope; none of them ever included more than a small minority of the societies of their day.

There is another sense, however, in which the concept of a global system of societies predates the modern era and extends far back into the past. For hundreds of thousands of years, human societies have interacted with one another and have exchanged important elements of *information*. Although *direct* contacts and exchanges, prior to the modern era, were limited to societies that were neighbors, or at least in close proximity to one another, many elements of culture (e.g., the spread of various technologies and religions) diffused more widely. Sometimes this was the result of migrations of entire populations (e.g., the Germanic peoples and the Mongols), sometimes because of the movement of individuals (e.g., missionaries and merchants). And sometimes it was the result of the operation of extended chains of communication that linked societies whose members never came in direct contact with one another.

Because of mechanisms such as these, one is forced to recognize that the process of information-cumulation has been operating on a global basis for thousands of years. Already during the Lower Paleolithic, the Acheulean toolmaking tradition was shared by societies throughout all of Africa and Europe and much of southern Asia—in other words, throughout virtually all of the then-occupied world (Hawkes, 1963: 117ff.). Later, the Indo-European family of languages spread from India to Ireland, and Islam spread from Spain to China. If we could trace the diffusion of all the many elements of culture, we would almost certainly find that no fully human society ever failed to participate to some extent, however spasmodically, in this global system and to enjoy at least some of its benefits.

Clearly, then, the existence of the global system is not new. What is new is the nature of the system. Because of advances in transportation and communication technologies, contacts between societies have become far more frequent and far more sustained than in the past. In addition, societies that are far distant from one another geographically are now able to maintain direct and continuous contacts. And, finally, the exchanges between distant societies are no longer limited to information: They often involve exchanges of goods and services and the exercise of political influence (as illustrated by the recent exercise of American power in the Middle East in the wars with Iraq). Thus, the global system of societies has become far more important today than it ever was in the past.

An Ecological-Evolutionary Model of the Global System

The model that ecological-evolutionary theory proposes for explaining the characteristics of the global system of societies (see Figure 6.1) is a modified version of the model presented earlier in Figure 4.2 to explain the characteristics of individual societies. The only differences are that (1) the unit of analysis is the global system, rather than an individual society, and (2) the model for the global system makes no allowance for a sociocultural environment, since humanity has yet to encounter any other symbol-using, culture-possessing population.

One of the most important characteristics of the global system is the dramatic change that has occurred in its technology in the last 10,000 to 20,000 years. Prior to this time, the store of technological information available to humans was extremely meager by contemporary standards. If it were possible to measure such things, we would probably find that substantially less than 1 percent of the current store of technological information was available before 20,000 B.P.

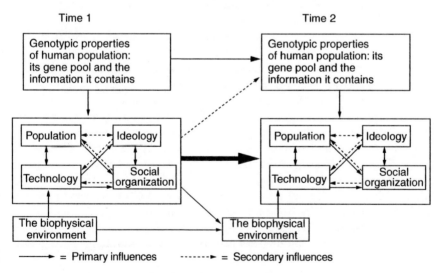

Figure 6.1 Tentative ecological-evolutionary model of the determinants of the characteristics of the global system of societies

This dramatic expansion in the store of technological information has transformed the global system of societies, as noted earlier in Chapter 2. Population has increased a thousand-fold in just the last 10,000 years, and energy consumption by humans has increased approximately ten thousand-fold. In this same period, the human population has all but abandoned its historic pursuits of hunting and gathering and turned first to farming and more recently to other increasingly more specialized occupations. During this period, the first towns and cities were established, the principles of metallurgy discovered, writing invented, monetary systems created, the first supranational religions established, and the modern world, as we know it today, brought into being.

Not all societies, however, adopted these changes. Many clung to older, traditional ways of life for thousands of years after the first societies made the transition from hunting and gathering to horticulture. A few of these societies even managed to survive into the last century. As a result, until recently, societies became increasingly diversified.

At the end of the Old Stone Age, variation in human societies was limited largely to the kinds of differences that arise from the necessity of adapting to different biophysical environments. Thus, societies in the tropics differed technologically from societies in temperate regions and in arctic regions. This meant differences in clothing, housing, tools, food, and related vocabularies, but these differences offered no competitive advantage, since every society in a given environment was constrained to adopt more or less the same social and cultural patterns. What they did not invent or discover for themselves, they copied from their neighbors. There were probably also differences in morals and customs, but we have no direct evidence of this today.[1] One also supposes that societies that were more successful in minimizing intragroup conflict and in maximizing cooperation fared better than their neighbors.

Throughout the vast span of time we call the Paleolithic, or Old Stone Age, variations in size and organizational complexity were limited. The constraints on growth that are inevitable in foraging societies held differences to a minimum. Every society was tiny and this precluded any significant development of the division of labor and other forms of organizational complexity. Societal survival depended primarily on the quantity and quality of the information their members possessed concerning the resources of their own immediate environment and on the skill with which these resources were used to satisfy the members' needs.

The situation changed dramatically, however, once a few societies began to make the transition from hunting and gathering to horticulture. Now, for the first time, variations in size and complexity became a significant factor in the process of intersocietal selection. In fact, they soon became the *dominant factor.*

Horticulture, as we have seen, produces higher yields in terms of food per unit of land than does hunting and gathering, and agriculture produces greater

---

1. This statement is based on the assumption that technology limits, but does not determine, morals and customs.

yields than horticulture. Given the genetically based propensity of human populations to expand, unless constrained by environmental or cultural forces, societies that shifted from hunting and gathering to horticulture, and from horticulture
to agriculture, usually grew larger than societies that clung to the older technologies. Thus, when conflicts developed between a society adhering to the older technology and one that had adopted the newer, the latter was likely to have more
fighting men at its disposal.

In addition, the newer subsistence technologies paved the way for other
kinds of technological advances, some of which had important military applications. Horticulture facilitated the discovery of the principles of metallurgy, and
bronze weapons gave horticultural societies another important military advantage
over hunting and gathering societies. Later, agrarian societies discovered the techniques of smelting iron and manufacturing iron weapons, which gave them an
important advantage over their horticultural neighbors (since tin was scarce and,
therefore, bronze was in short supply).

Finally, the new subsistence technologies contributed to organizational advances that proved of military value. The emergence of the state, with its centralized authority structure, enabled technologically advanced societies to mobilize
resources more effectively and in ways that gave them a military edge. Not only
could the actions of fighting men be coordinated more effectively, there was a
mechanism in place to facilitate the transfer of food and other resources from
farmers to fighters. Thus, societies that adopted the newer subsistence technologies enjoyed a substantial military advantage over those that did not. Figure 6.2
illustrates the nature of the mechanisms that seem to have been involved. While
the advantages may not have been great enough to ensure victory each and every
time two such societies came into conflict, they were more than sufficient to ensure the eventual triumph of the horticulturalists over hunters and gatherers, and
agriculturalists over horticulturalists, in contested territories. In the long run, societies with the simpler technologies could survive only in two kinds of locations:
(1) those that were unsuited to the more advanced technologies (e.g., mountains,
deserts), and (2) those that were sufficiently remote that distance or other geographical obstacles provided the necessary protection, as in the case of Australia
prior to the eighteenth century.

Looking back over the last 5,000 to 10,000 years, it is clear that the chief
threat to the survival of individual societies has come from other human societies
(McNeill, 1976). In effect, human societies have been engaged in a deadly game
of musical chairs in which the vast majority have been eliminated by losing their
territorial base and its resources to their more powerful neighbors.[2] The critical
resource required for success in this game has been military might, and this, in
turn, has depended on a society's level of subsistence technology. Thus, *societal*

---

2. The individual members of conquered societies have often been spared so that they might
serve their conquerors. Thus, "only" their society was destroyed. This has been especially true since
the beginnings of farming and the formation of the first economic surplus.

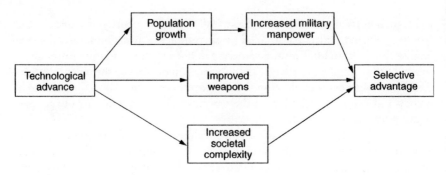

Figure 6.2 Model of the effects of technological advance on the process of intersocietal selection in the last 10,000 years

survival has been largely a function of a society's level of technological advance relative to the societies with which it has been in competition.

The Great Paradox Revisited

Earlier I said that one of the important challenges confronting ecological-evolutionary theory, and other macrosocial theories, is to explain how the forces of change could be dominant in a global system that is made up of individual societies in the vast majority of which the forces of continuity have been dominant. By now, it should be clear that the paradox is an illusion created by the implicit assumption that processes operative on one level of social organization have to be operative on other levels as well. Obviously, this is not true: Processes can work quite differently on different levels.

Within individual societies, there is a continuous process of selection at work: The members constantly choose between alternative ways of doing things. This is true even in simpler societies, though the number of such choices in them is far less than in more complex societies. In the light of existing values, members select one option rather than another, and the high value that most place on preserving the *status quo* ensures a substantial degree of social and cultural continuity. Preserving the *status quo* is usually the best strategy for minimizing risks in societies in which risk-taking can be a costly luxury, and preserving the *status quo* also promises to preserve the privileges of the more powerful members of the group. Thus, appeals to tradition usually win out in simpler societies, and from a numerical standpoint, these societies have far outnumbered more complex societies.

Intersocietal selection is a very different process. Its outcome, as we have seen, is determined, over the long run, by the level of technological advance of the competing societies, not by any rational process of decisionmaking. No human mind ever determines, in God-like fashion, that stronger and technologically more advanced societies are preferable and more worthy of survival. The outcome of this process has been as blind and purposeless as the outcome of the process of natural selection in the biotic world, and just as indifferent to human beliefs and values—except for the genetically based instinct of self-preservation and self-enhancement that humans share with other animals. If technologically advanced societies tend to survive while less advanced societies are eliminated, it is not because the former are superior in anything except their possession of survival-relevant resources.

This can be an unsettling thought, for it suggests that the basic engine of change that has shaped the course of human history has been totally indifferent to the values civilized peoples profess to cherish most—one possible reason why many social scientists find it hard to accept ecological-evolutionary theory. Unlike most competing theories, it draws attention to forces that lie beyond human control, and, unlike classical Marxian theory, which shares this characteristic, it offers no assurance of a happy ending.

Within the global system of societies, ecological-evolutionary theory sees variation arising among societies as they respond to the challenges that confront them and struggle to adapt to the varying circumstances they encounter. Because human populations, like other populations, are capable of producing more offspring than are needed merely to sustain their numbers, societies tend to expand and competition for territories and other scarce resources tends to develop. In the struggles that have ensued, technologically advanced societies have enjoyed a substantially greater probability of survival than less advanced societies, with the result that the characteristics of the global system have changed enormously even while the majority of individual societies resisted change.

Figure 6.3 provides a model of the evolutionary process as it has operated in the global system of societies during the last 10,000 years. As the figure indicates, the genetically based tendency of societies to expand, interacting with the environmentally based process of societal variation, has led to the process of intersocietal selection. This, in turn, has led to the basic trends of human history as we have come to know them—the growth of human population, the increasing complexity of social systems, the increasing impact of the human population on the biophysical environment, and all the rest. Until quite recently, these trends have been largely unintended consequences of impersonal forces and processes beyond human comprehension and control. The greatest challenge that lies ahead is to begin to employ our growing understanding of these processes to achieve some measure of control over the forces that shape human destiny. Whether that can be achieved in time to avert catastrophe is still an open question, but to ignore what has been learned is to court disaster.

Historical Eras

Because of the magnitude and importance of the changes that have occurred over the course of human history, historically oriented social scientists have found it helpful to think of it in terms of various segments. Archaeologists have been at the

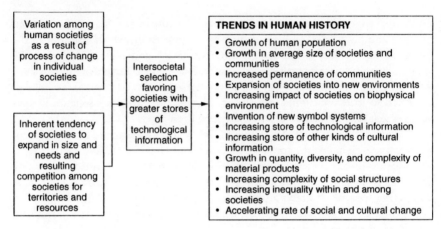

Figure 6.3 Model of sociocultural evolution in the global system of societies in the last 10,000 years

forefront of efforts to define meaningful and useful segments. Already in the early decades of the nineteenth century, Christian Jurgensen Thomsen, a Danish museum curator, proposed the division of the prehistoric past into Stone, Bronze, and Iron Ages. Later generations of archaeologists have refined his categories to the point where now they differentiate among Lower Paleolithic, Middle Paleolithic, Upper Paleolithic, Mesolithic, Neolithic, Chalcolithic, Copper, Early Bronze, Late Bronze, Iron, and Steel Ages. Depending on the analysis involved, these segments may involve the global system as a whole or some limited geographical region. When discussing the global system as a whole, the system of classification is based on the highest level of technological development found anywhere; when dealing with more limited areas, classification is based on the level of development within that area. Thus, at a time when the global system had entered the Iron Age, large areas of the world remained in the Neolithic or even the Mesolithic.

In response to the work of V. Gordon Childe in the years before World War II, a growing number of archaeologists adopted a system of classification based on subsistence technology. For example, Robert Braidwood proposed a three-fold division of prehistory into (1) a food-gathering stage, (2) a food-collecting stage, and (3) a food-producing stage. Each of these, he argued, could be subdivided into two or three eras. As with the older system of classification, stages and eras would vary from one region to another, depending on their level of technological development.

Ecological-evolutionary theory offers yet another way of dividing history, whether in the world system as a whole or in specific regions. This method of classification emerges out of the societal typology described in Chapter 5. Building on its typology of societies, ecological-evolutionary theory divides the vast span of human history into four major eras: (1) the hunting and gathering era, (2) the horticultural era, (3) the agrarian era, and (4) the industrial era. Each era is defined by the type of society that has been politically and militarily dominant in it and therefore has enjoyed a selective advantage over other societies in competition for territories and other essential resources.

This way of classifying history can be easily translated into or combined with the older schemes. As Childe (1936) made clear, and archaeologists today acknowledge, the beginning of the Neolithic era corresponded to the beginning of the food-producing stage and the beginning of the horticultural era. Similarly, the beginning of the true Bronze Age (as distinguished from the Copper Age) roughly coincides with the beginning of the agrarian era, and the beginning of the Iron Age with the beginning of the advanced agrarian era (if one wishes to adopt a more precise system of classification).

For the present, it seems preferable to refer to the various segments of the historical continuum as "eras," rather than as "stages," since the latter suggests a stair-step model of development, which is misleading. Despite Sanderson's advocacy of a sociological analogue to Stephen Jay Gould's (1976) thesis of evolution as a process of "punctuated equilibrium," there seems little reason to believe that growth and development, whether at the global or regional level, have been concentrated wholly or largely in a few brief years. Clearly, this has not been true in the recent past, and there is considerable evidence that it was not true in a number of earlier periods. Thus, it seems more appropriate and less misleading to refer to the industrial era rather than to the industrial stage.

Refining the Special Theories

In Chapter 5 we saw how a series of special theories can be generated from a more general theory by increasing the specification of one of the independent variables. By specifying the nature of the subsistence technology of a set of societies, we were able to predict and explain many of their other characteristics. We also saw how this process of specification can be extended by adding information about other independent variables or about important intervening variables.

One of the most important variables that can be added in this way is information about the historical era involved. By taking this into account, as well as information about the mode of subsistence, we greatly increase our powers of prediction and explanation. For example, when we specify that a set of hunting and gathering societies exists in a world dominated by industrial societies, many predictions can be made that otherwise couldn't be. What we have done, in effect, is to introduce vital information concerning the *sociocultural environment* in which this set of societies operates.

Figure 6.4 illustrates how the concept of historical eras can be combined with the concept of societal types to produce a set of special theories that are more powerful than any that could be generated by either of the concepts alone. As the

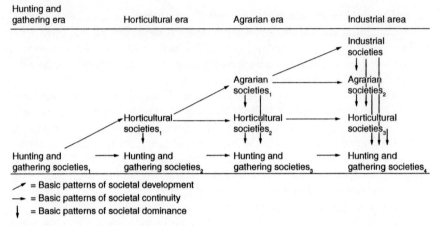

Figure 6.4 Societal types by historical eras

figure indicates, the relation of a particular type of society to its environment changes dramatically from one era to the next. A type that is politically and militarily dominant in one era can be seriously threatened in subsequent eras. Thus, even though the internal forces acting on a set of societies remain largely the same from one era to the next, the external forces acting on it vary greatly and must be taken into account if we hope to understand the changes that occur.

If the model shown in Figure 6.4 is correct, we should not expect hunting and gathering societies[4] to be the same as hunting and gathering societies[1]. On the contrary, because of the presence of industrial societies with their enormous technological and other resources, we should expect hunting and gathering societies[4] to be subject to environmental influences unlike anything experienced by hunting and gathering societies[1]. In fact, we should expect to find them engaged in a losing struggle for survival.

Similarly, we would expect the situation of agrarian societies[2] to be significantly different from the situation of agrarian societies[1]. While their chances of survival are far better than those of hunting and gathering societies[4], the pressures for change within them should be enormous. The technological resources of industrial societies and their wealth provide these societies with both the cultural and the technical means of penetrating and transforming traditional cultures everywhere. Sometimes, as the Islamic Revolution in Iran demonstrated, individual societies can halt or even reverse the trend for a time, but the long-term prospects seem dim for revolutions that seek a return to the *status quo ante*. At best, they are likely to delay the process of change and perhaps preserve a bit more of their society's traditional culture.

Building on the taxonomy shown in Figure 6.4, one would also predict that horticultural societies[3] would have substantially greater difficulty adapting to the demands of the industrial era than would agrarian societies[2]. The latter have at their command many social and cultural resources that the former lack, such as a tradition of at least limited literacy, a partially monetized economy, and experience with bureaucracy and urbanization.[3] This is a subject to which I will return in the second part of this volume (see Chapter 10). It is an especially important subject, since it brings ecological-evolutionary theory into conflict with another important macrosociological theory, world-system theory. Indeed, the analysis of data relevant to this issue provides a valuable opportunity to compare the predictive power of the two theories.

The Evolution of the Evolutionary Process

One of the popular misconceptions concerning evolution is the belief that the process itself is fixed and stable and that only its products—be they species or societies—change. The fact of the matter is that while there are certain enduring aspects of the evolutionary process, *the process itself has evolved.* Emergence characterizes the process of evolution as well as its products. This is why we have today a family of evolutionary theories (see Chapter 1) and not a single all-purpose theory to cover the spectrum of the sciences from cosmology to sociology.

The taxonomy of historical eras is a valuable reminder that what is true of the evolutionary process as a whole is also true of sociocultural evolution. The process of sociocultural evolution has evolved and the concept of emergence applies to it no less than to its products. We have already noted an important instance of this associated with the transition from the hunting and gathering era to the horticultural era. Prior to the horticultural era, intersocietal selection appears to have been based on the quantity and quality of technological information that societies possessed concerning the challenges and resources of their own particular niche in the biophysical environment. Beginning with the horticultural era, however, the quantity and quality of technological information relevant to military matters became crucial and this gave rise to dramatic and revolutionary changes in the global system of societies.

This was not the end of the matter, however. There is good reason to believe that certain technological advances of the modern era are altering the historic relationship between technology and ideology. As noted earlier, ideological factors are able to influence societal characteristics only within limits set by technology. Moreover, technology not only defines the limits of the possible, it has also determined the economic costs of the various options available within those limits. But when technological advances (e.g., contraceptive technology) slow the rate of population growth, and thereby increase the economic surplus, then the quantity of resources that can be allocated on the basis of ideological considerations is greatly increased and the importance of the ideological factor is enhanced. This has already happened in advanced industrial societies.

---

3. A few horticultural societies have had some literacy and some urbanization, though usually much less than the average agrarian society.

Conversely, technological advance appears to reduce the influence of a society's biophysical environment relative to other determinants of its characteristics. Improved methods of transportation make it possible to import resources that are lacking in a particular territory. Thus, modern industrial technology makes it possible for substantial populations to reside in desert areas, such as the American Southwest, or in subarctic regions, such as Alaska (though, again, one must beware of exaggerating the magnitude of the change). Meanwhile, this same new industrial technology has greatly enhanced the importance of the sociocultural environment and made societies more dependent than ever before on other societies.

As these examples suggest, the relative importance of the various determinants of the characteristics of individual societies changes from one historical era to the next. If it were possible to deal with this problem quantitatively, we would see that the coefficients associated with each of the variables in our regression equations were changing from era to era. Figure 6.5 indicates the kinds of changes that have occurred because of the evolution of the sociocultural evolutionary process.

During the hunting and gathering era, the most important variable from the standpoint of explaining differences among the universe of societies was almost certainly the biophysical environment. Societies were obliged to adapt to the peculiarities of the challenges and resources of their own immediate territories, with the result that significant differences developed between those in the tropics and those in temperate, subarctic, and arctic regions. Similarly, differences developed between societies in arid regions and those in well-watered regions, and between societies in mountainous regions and those on the plains.

With the emergence of the horticultural era, technological differences gradually became the most important determinant of societal characteristics within the universe of societies. The technological differences among horticultural, herding, fishing, and hunting and gathering societies became better predictors of more of the sociologically relevant characteristics of societies (though not of each and every individual characteristic). Differences in subsistence technologies predicted

	Hunting and gathering era	Horticultural era	Agrarian era	Industrial era
First-order differences	Biophysical environment	Technology	Technology	Technology
Second-order differences		Biophysical environment	Biophysical environment	Ideology
Third-order differences			Ideology	Biophysical environment

Figure 6.5 Effects of the evolution of the evolutionary process on the relative importance of major determinants of the characteristics of individual societies

and explained the increasing differences in the size of societies, their modes of governance, the appearance of the first urban communities, the beginnings of full-time occupational specialization, increasing inequality, and more. In short, differences in subsistence technologies predicted and explained which societies retained the traditional patterns of societal organization, and which adopted the newer and more complex patterns.

The emergence of agrarian societies and the beginning of the agrarian era meant further change in the relative strength of the various determinants of the characteristics of individual societies. With the shift to plow agriculture, the potential for production of an economic surplus was substantially increased and this, in turn, increased the potential for the formation and growth of new occupations and new social classes, and it also facilitated the growth of urban communities and the expansion of empires. Thus, the relative importance of the technological factor was again substantially enhanced, since the differences between agrarian societies and hunting and gathering societies were substantially greater than the differences between horticultural societies and hunting and gathering societies.

The agrarian era is also associated with the growing importance of ideology. This was the era in which the first supraethnic religions (Buddhism, Christianity, Islam) made their appearance, and, indeed, the contrasts between these new religions of agrarian societies and those of earlier societies are substantial. Their impact on daily life was not nearly as great, however, as the impact of the ideologies that emerged in the industrial era. With the onset of the industrial era, the relative strength of the major determinants shifted once more, with technological advances reducing the impact of the environmental factor on individual societies and increasing the impact of ideology.

Looking to the future, one can imagine that advances in technology will lead to modifications in human genetics that will have significant social consequences in technologically advanced societies. If the genetic bases of major diseases can be identified and eliminated, life expectancy could be substantially extended with both obvious and not so obvious consequences for societies.

Implications for Research

If the analysis up to this point has been correct, studies of individual societies or sets of societies should always specify the historical era, just as they should always specify the type or types of societies. In effect, research should always begin by locating the society or societies in question in terms of the theoretical grid shown in Figure 6.4.

Similarly, in drawing conclusions from empirical studies, investigators ought always to keep in mind the segment of the universe of societies to which their conclusions apply. Overgeneralization is one of the great temptations in science, and this temptation is especially serious in disciplines such as sociology, anthropology, and archaeology, each of which often works with only a small part of a larger universe of interrelated materials. The problem is especially acute in sociology, where the subset of societies studied has tended for half a century or more to be extraordinarily limited and anything but representative of the universe of human societies.

In the second half of this volume, the focus of concern will shift from the development of ecological-evolutionary theory itself to illustrations of its applicability to studies of individual societies and to comparative studies of sets of societies. In these studies I hope to show how ecological-evolutionary theory can guide empirical research and provide insights that would otherwise be missed. Before undertaking that, however, we should consider the major theoretical alternatives to ecological-evolutionary theory and assess their relative strengths and weaknesses. To this task we now turn in Chapter 7.

7

ECOLOGICAL-EVOLUTIONARY THEORY AND ITS ALTERNATIVES: A COMPARISON

There is no shortage of theories and theoretical perspectives in the social sciences today. They run the gamut from phenomenology and deconstructionism to sociobiology and from functionalism to critical theory. In addition, as Marvin Harris (1979) once observed, many social scientists are content to be eclectic, patching together bits and pieces of various theories. Given the surfeit of options, one may well ask whether we really need yet another theory and whether ecological-evolutionary theory can possibly add anything of significance to what is already available.

The best way to answer these questions is to compare ecological-evolutionary theory with the alternatives, noting how they resemble one another and how they differ. In the first part of this chapter, ecological-evolutionary theory is compared with a broad range of other theories in terms of a number of basic criteria. After that, more detailed comparisons are made with a smaller number of theories that most resemble, and most compete with, ecological-evolutionary theory.

Time Frame and Basic Unit(s) of Analysis

Social science theories differ enormously with respect to both the time frames they employ and the basic units of analysis on which they focus. Some theories and theoretical perspectives are largely synchronic, either ignoring the time dimension or relegating it to a minor role. This has been especially true of functionalism. Its perspective is built on the foundation laid down by Emile Durkheim

125

and expressed so well in the last of his major works, *The Elementary Forms of the Religious Life* (1912). According to Durkheim, one does not need to trace the evolution of religion over time or be overly concerned with its changing manifestations. These are secondary matters: One can construct a satisfactory theory of religion—and, presumably, of anything else—merely by studying synchronically functional relationships within a single society or set of societies.[1]

Modern functionalists have followed Durkheim faithfully in this respect. One finds the same synchronic approach in Davis and Moore's (1945) formulation of the basic principles of stratification and in Parsons's (1951) theory of the social system. Although the latter contains a chapter on social change, the chapter is singularly ahistorical. This may seem a contradiction in terms, but actually is not, since Parsons does not consider the possibility that the process of change may, itself, evolve over time or that there can be an evolution of the evolutionary process. Even in his treatment of change, Parsons, the functionalist, was more concerned with eternal verities than with contingent propositions.[2]

Even when contemporary theories and theorists have adopted a diachronic perspective, the time frames employed have been much more limited than that employed by ecological-evolutionary theory. Most social psychological theories employ time frames of very short duration, seldom extending beyond the life span of individuals and often much briefer. Even in organizational theories the time frame seldom extends beyond a few decades at most. The chief exception among contemporary theories is Wallerstein's world-system theory, which employs a time frame of 500 years. In contrast, ecological-evolutionary theory employs a time frame of thousands of years.

Figure 7.1 illustrates the differences among theories and theoretical perspectives in the social sciences today. As the figure indicates, none of the other theories concerns itself with quite the same comprehensive data set as ecological-evolutionary theory. Most focus on smaller units of analysis and employ much more limited time frames, or none at all. The chief exceptions are modernization theory, Wallerstein's world-system theory, Parsons's evolutionism, and Marvin Harris's cultural materialism. Modernization theory and world-system theory, however, are microevolutionary theories, since their time frames are limited to only a few centuries. Parsonsian evolutionism and cultural materialism share the macrochronic time frame of ecological-evolutionary theory, but tend to ignore the important global system of societies.

---

1. See especially Durkheim's development of the thesis in the concluding chapter of *The Elementary Forms,* where he writes that "there is something eternal in religion which is destined to survive all of the particular symbols in which religious thought has enveloped itself" (p. 427).

2. Later in his career, Parsons (1966, 1971) recognized his mistake and adopted an evolutionary perspective. This differed, however, in fundamental ways from ecological-evolutionary theory, as will be explained later in this chapter.

Unit(s) of analysis	Time frame					
	Millennia	Centuries	Decades	Years	Lesser interals	Synchronic analyses
The global system and total societies	Ecological-evolutionary theory					
		World-system theory				
		Modernization theory				
Total societies	Parsonsian evolutionism ----------					
	Cultural materialism -------------					
Regions and communities				Human ecology ---------------------		
Associations and institutions					Various microorganizational theories ---------	
				Functionalism -------------------------------------		
					Symbolic interactionism ------------------	
Individuals						Ethnomethodology -----
						Exchange theories ------

Figure 7.1 Time frames and units of analysis in selected social science theories

Independent Variables

Social science theories and theoretical perspectives differ not only in the data sets they seek to explain but also in the variables they deem important for explanatory purposes. Explanatory concepts of great importance in some theories are of secondary importance in others, or ignored altogether.

Figure 7.2 provides a summary comparison of a number of theories and theoretical perspectives viewed from the standpoint of the kinds of variables their proponents consider important in shaping basic societal patterns. Although a summary such as this captures only a few of the more important features of the theories involved, it helps one to see more clearly some of the significant ways in which ecological-evolutionary theory differs from other theories and theoretical perspectives in sociology today.

In the first place, it should be noted that in the row for ecological-evolutionary theory there are no minuses or zeros. In other words, ecological-evolutionary theory does not ignore or minimize the importance of any of the six sets of determinants indicated. In this respect, it seems unique. Not surprisingly, Parsons's idealist version of evolutionism comes closest in this regard, since it, too, takes account of all six sets of determinants. It gives scant attention, however, to

Relative strength of determinants
of social system characteristics:

Theories and theoretical perspectives	Biological constants	Biophysical environment	Sociocultural environment	Technology	Social organization	Ideology
Ecological-evolutionary theory	•	•	•	•	+	+
Idealist evolutionism (Parsons)	0/+	0	+	0	+	•
Human ecology (Hawley)	0/+	•	•	•	•	−
World-system theory (Wallerstein)	−	+	•	+	+	+
Classical Marxism	−	0	+	•	•	+
Idealist Marxism (critical theory, Maoism)	−	−	0/+	−	+	•
Weber	−	0	+	0	•	•
Durkheim	−	−	0/+	0	•	+
Functionalism (Parsons, Merton, K. Davis)	−/0	−	0/+	0	•	•
Social psychological reductionism	−	−	0	−	+	•
Sociobiology	•	+	+	−	−	−

• =	major determinant
0 =	minor determinant
+ =	other important determinant
− =	influence not recognized or explicitly denied

Figure 7.2 A comparison of theories and theoretical perspectives with respect to hypothesized strength of determinants of social system characteristics

the biological constants, the biophysical environment, and technology. Human ecology and world-system theory are two other theories that offer a broadly inclusive *explanans*.

A second characteristic of ecological-evolutionary theory that can be seen in Figure 7.2 is the relative importance it attaches to exogenous variables. With the exception of human ecology, world-system theory, and sociobiology, other theories explain the characteristics of social systems largely or entirely in terms of other social-system characteristics. At most, some acknowledge the importance of the sociocultural environment and the influence of other societies.

The attention that ecological-evolutionary theory gives to exogenous determinants—especially to the biological constants and the biophysical environment—and to technology, which is the interface between the biophysical environment and the rest of the sociocultural system, makes it a more materialist theory than most. Ecological-evolutionary theory does not, however, deny the importance of social organizational and ideological variables (as other theories often deny the importance of the material determinants). On the contrary, it recognizes their substantial importance, but sees this influence constrained by other, even more basic, influences. In this respect, ecological-evolutionary theory parts company with the utopian strain in contemporary sociology and with the often-exaggerated view of reality as a social construct.

Methodology and Epistemology

Finally, theories and theoretical perspectives differ in terms of methodology and epistemology. Earlier, in Chapter 2, a number of the methodological and epistemological characteristics of ecological-evolutionary theory were identified and discussed. Before concluding this part of the comparison of ecological-evolutionary theory and its alternatives, we would do well to consider differences on this level.

One of the most important characteristics of any social science theory is the stance it assumes relative to the biological sciences. Basically, there are three options. First, theories may adopt a reductionist stance and attempt to explain social and cultural phenomena in biological terms. This has been the approach of most sociobiologists. Second, at the opposite pole, theories may deny that biological forces contribute to the social and cultural characteristics of human groups in any significant way. This has been the dominant stance in the social sciences since early in the last century, though there has been some pulling back from the more extreme and more dogmatic versions of this position in recent years. Third, theories may assume that explanations of social and cultural phenomena must take account of constraints that our species' genetic heritage imposes on social systems and that humans are not entirely free to shape societies as they might wish, despite the enormous behavioral flexibility that culture allows. This is the position of ecological-evolutionary theory and, to some extent, at least implicitly, of Parsonsian evolutionism and human ecology as developed by Amos Hawley. There is also evidence that Marvin Harris moved cautiously in this direction in later years.

Another important methodological difference among social science theories and theorists involves their use, or avoidance, of special theories. Once again, there are three basic options. First, some have concentrated on the development of universal propositions that apply everywhere, regardless of time or place. Sociobiologists provide a classic instance of this, though Durkheim and the functionalists tend to do so also.[3] Second, some have made use of special theories without properly grounding them in general theory. Robert Merton even made a virtue of this in his advocacy of middle-range theories. Third, and finally, some have made use of special theories, but have endeavored to ground them in a more general theory of society. Marx did this, though most of his special theories (e.g., his theories of prefeudal types of societies) never got beyond the embryonic state. Among contemporary sociological theories, world-system theory, Parsons's evolutionism, and ecological-evolutionary theory all offer special theories that are grounded in a more general theory.

---

3. It is true, of course, that Durkheim, in *The Division of Labor in Society* (1893) and *Suicide* (1897), developed a number of propositions of more limited scope, as have many functionalists since his day; however, his later work reveals a growing concern with universal principles, and modern functionalists have largely shared this concern.

Theories differ also in the degree to which they rely on induction, deduction, or a combination of the two. A small number of social science theories are primarily deductive: Blau's theory of social structure is a good example, and Parsons's (1951) theory of the social system is another. Far more social science theories are primarily inductive: Status attainment theory and demographic transition theory are familiar examples. Finally, many theories strive to achieve something of a balance between induction and deduction. These theories typically start with a general idea formulated on the basis of observations, and then strive to refine the idea in light of further observations. This has been true of Hawley's human ecology, and it is also true of ecological-evolutionary theory.

Reliance on inductive logic, as opposed to deductive, tends to be linked with the flexibility of theories and their openness to new ideas and new information. The greater the dependence on deductive reasoning, the more resistant to change theories tend to be. Some theories are relatively open and flexible in the early stages of their development, but become closed later as their proponents come increasingly to value orthodoxy. This was the fate of classical Marxian theory: Already in Marx's own lifetime, conformity to his views became a prime virtue and, after his death, deviation from the party line became unforgivable. What little flexibility classical Marxism has retained has been due almost entirely to the semantic skills of Marxists and their ability to restate, as circumstances dictated, the "real meaning" of Marxist theory. Although this may be good politics, it is hardly good science.

Some theories are relatively open and flexible with respect to a broad range of issues, but are closed and inflexible with respect to certain others. This is true, for example, of Hawley's position with respect to the role of values and ideology in social systems. His reluctance to treat them as anything more than epiphenomena has clearly limited the appeal of human ecology. Many others have been unwilling to acknowledge the influence of our species' genetic heritage on social systems, though this has not appreciably limited the appeal of these theories, thanks to the biases that most social scientists bring to their work.

At the opposite extreme from theories that exaggerate the role of deductive logic, overreliance on induction can easily lead to a kind of unprofitable eclecticism. Functionalism has long had a tendency in this direction: Because everything has a function for someone, everything is important. This easily creates the impression that nothing is any more important for explanatory purposes than anything else.[4]

Ecological-evolutionary theory strives to avoid both the Scylla of deductive rigidity and the Charybdis of inductive flexibility by taking the demands of both seriously. Its basic assumptions provide a viable framework for thought and analysis, but within the limits set by those assumptions substantial flexibility is pos-

---

4. The same has not been true of the work of Talcott Parsons, whose commitment to general theory helped him to avoid this impression. The writings of many lesser functionalists, however, are often hard to distinguish from the writings of avowed eclectics.

sible. As noted earlier, ecological-evolutionary theory encourages a continuous testing of theory in the light of available evidence and a modification of theory whenever that is indicated.

Parsonsian Evolutionism

Over the years, a number of sociologists (e.g., Granovetter, 1979; Nisbet, 1969) have apparently had great difficulty in differentiating between ecological-evolutionary theory and the kind of evolutionary theory developed by Talcott Parsons in his later years. While it is true that both theories are concerned with a process of cumulative change in human societies and both acknowledge the influence of the same inclusive set of determinants (see Figure 7.2), they differ greatly in the relative weights they assign to the various determinants and in the social and cultural mechanisms they see as operative.

Parsonsian evolutionism stands firmly in the idealist tradition stemming from the work of Kant and Hegel. Parsons (1966) made his position patently clear when he wrote:

> I am a cultural determinist, rather than a social determinist. Similarly, I believe that, within the social system, the normative elements are more important for social change than the "material interests" of constitutive units. The longer the time perspective, and the broader the system involved, the greater is [their] *relative* importance. (p. 113)

He then went on to say that

> the present analysis has been couched on the level of the longest time-perspective and broadest comparative scope. Therefore, in this study, the emphasis in accounting for the main patterns and processes of change has been placed at the highest cybernetic level. This level is cultural rather than social and, within the cultural category, religious rather than secular. Within the social category, values and norms, especially legal norms, stand higher than political and economic interests. (pp. 113–114)

Thus, for him ideology was the most powerful influence on social systems, especially *religious* beliefs and values. And, while Parsons softened these assertions a bit by acknowledging that priorities may be different when more limited processes or time frames are involved and that every cultural development depends on prior developments of other kinds, his commitment to the fundamental power of ideology in long-term processes of change is clear.

Ecological-evolutionary theory, in contrast, takes a more materialist view of human societies and their development. Genetics, the biophysical environment, and technology are seen as exercising the greatest influence over long-term processes of societal development and the more important social and cultural patterns that result. Beliefs and values are not treated as autonomous forces; on the contrary, they are seen as arising out of the daily life experiences of people, experiences that necessarily reflect to a great degree the possibilities and limitations of the material resources they control, the genetic heritage they possess, and the nature of the biophysical environment to which they are exposed and on which they depend. This is not to suggest that all the countless variations in the content of specific ideologies can be predicted or explained in this way,[5] but ecological-evolutionary theory does assert that the most basic transformations in ideology, such as the rise of secular humanist ideologies in the industrial era, or the kinds of changes that occurred during the early history of ancient Israel (see Chapter 8), cannot be adequately explained without reference to changes in the material conditions of the life of the peoples involved. Moreover, as we have noted, ecological-evolutionary theory does not deny that the influence of material factors on ideology is mediated by social organization or that ideologies, once developed, can exercise an influence on technological development. But these are secondary according to ecological-evolutionary theory: Ideologies such as Marxism or market capitalism, for example, could emerge only in technologically advanced societies, and ideologies such as animism and ancestor worship can flourish only in technologically limited societies.

Despite this critical difference between the two versions of neoevolutionary theory, there is an important area of agreement concerning the determinants of societal patterns. Both theories recognize that material factors limit the possibilities for development of social organization and ideology. Parsons assumes, however, that the limits are so broad and unconstraining that they are of little theoretical interest or importance. Ecological-evolutionary theory, in contrast, sees the limits as much narrower and therefore much more interesting and important. More than that, it asserts that material factors also influence the choices that societies make among the options available to them by influencing the relative costs and benefits of possible options. Thus, when members of a society adopt a more costly solution to one of their problems (e.g., because of ideological considerations), they reduce the range of choices available to them with respect to other problems.

A second important difference between Parsonsian evolutionism and ecological-evolutionary theory is that the former largely ignores the global system of societies. Its concern is limited to individual societies and sets of societies. As a result, it fails to address the important phenomenon of intersocietal selection and its consequences. This neglect is one reason why Parsons and his followers have been able to minimize the role of material factors in societal development as suc-

---

5. As noted earlier (see Figure 4.2), ecological-evolutionary theory assumes that the cultures of societies at any given time are influenced greatly by their social and cultural heritages. In other words, the ideology of a group at any given time is powerfully influenced by inherited patterns of social organization and inherited beliefs and values.

cessfully as they have, since greater attention to external threats to the survival and well-being of societies would almost certainly direct attention to the influence of technological innovation on military power.

One other important difference between Parsonsian evolutionism and ecological-evolutionary theory is that the latter sees the process of sociocultural evolution itself as evolving and sees relations among the various determinants of societal characteristics as not immutably fixed. Instead, technological advance increases the potential for an economic surplus, and this, in turn, increases the range of available options and thereby provides greater scope for ideological influence on the characteristics of social systems (see "Excursus: Further Notes on Technology and Ideology" at the end of the chapter). Because of this, the degree of disagreement between the two theories is less in the case of more advanced societies than in the case of simpler ones.

Culturalism Materialism

Culturalism materialism, as developed by Marvin Harris (1968, 1974, 1977, 1979), is closer than any other contemporary theory to ecological-evolutionary theory. It, too, provides an ecological and evolutionary explanation of continuity and change in human societies and, as its name indicates, views material factors as exercising greater influence than beliefs and values on social-system patterns. Harris's work on the sources of Hinduism's doctrine of the sacred cow (Harris, 1974; see also Vaidyanathan, 1982) is an especially impressive application of principles shared by cultural materialism and ecological-evolutionary theory. In it, he mobilized a substantial body of evidence to support the thesis that this doctrine, which has often been cited by idealists as evidence of the independence of beliefs and values from material considerations, is a strikingly adaptive response to the material conditions of Indian society. He showed it to be a doctrine that has been surprisingly successful in protecting a vital capital resource during periods of famine, when pressures to consume this resource would otherwise have been overwhelming.

Despite the great similarity between cultural materialism and ecological-evolutionary theory, there is one important area of divergence. Marvin Harris has been reluctant to acknowledge the influence of genetic factors on sociocultural systems. His sharp attacks on sociobiology have sometimes made it seem as though he shared the view that human nature is entirely a product of environmental influences.

Later writings by Harris suggest, however, that he was having second thoughts on the matter and that the differences between cultural materialism and ecological-evolutionary theory may not be as great as they once appeared. Over the years, he increasingly invoked population pressures as an explanatory factor in analyses of a number of problems, and such pressures imply a genetic propensity for human populations to produce offspring in greater numbers than environments can sustain. And, while it is possible for societies to avoid the most unpleasant consequences of this by some combination of infanticide, abortion, contraception, celibacy, and advances in productive technology, the fact remains that these social and cultural responses have been necessitated by the genetic factor. Explicit acknowledgment of this in the formulation of the general theory, however, would be preferable to the practice of introducing the principle in analyses of specific problems.

In his volume *Cultural Materialism,* Harris took a further step in a brief discussion titled "Bio-Psychological Constants" (1979: 62–64). Here, he cautiously suggested four such constraints: (1) a need for food and a preference for higher, rather than lower, intake of calories, proteins, and other nutrients; (2) an aversion to inactivity, but a preference for economizing in the expenditure of energy in the performance of tasks; (3) a desire for sexual intercourse and a preference for heterosexual intercourse; (4) a need for love and affection. While acknowledging that this list is probably too limited, he cautions against the temptation "to reduce all sociocultural similarities to an imaginary genetic 'biogram.'" (p. 62)

One cannot help but suspect that Harris's list of bio-psychological constants might have been somewhat longer if he had studied the many varied social experiments of the last hundred years that have been predicated on the assumption that human nature is environmentally determined. Had he compared the dazzling promises and high expectations of these efforts with the subsequent results, he might have gone further than he did in acknowledging the existence of genetic constraints on societal organization and development. One cannot study the efforts to create the "new socialist man" in the Soviet Union, China, or Cuba, or the attempts to reduce crime and elevate morals through systems of free public education in western societies, without coming to recognize the bias toward self-centeredness and self-aggrandizement that humans inherit as part of their mammalian-primate heritage—a bias that becomes especially important in larger and more complex societies in which the members are compelled to interact continuously with large numbers of others in secondary group relationships. Although it would be foolhardy to assert that no society can ever overcome these inherited tendencies, it is equally foolhardy to ignore them. This is especially true in an era in which new evidence of genetic predispositions to various kinds of diseases, including some with important behavioral consequences (e.g., schizophrenia), is constantly being reported.

World-System Theory

World-system theory is another theory with which ecological-evolutionary theory has much in common. Both share an interest in networks of societies as well as in individual societies. Both employ relatively long time frames, though ecological-evolutionary theory's, as noted earlier, is much longer.

Both theories also view the sociocultural environment as a major influence on the development of individual societies. For world-system theory, it is the preeminent influence; ecological-evolutionary theory, in contrast, hypothesizes more of a balance between this exogenous influence on societal development and various internal forces, especially the technoeconomic heritage of a society that results from the centuries-long struggle of its members to wrest a livelihood from the environment. In the second part of this volume, the chapter titled "Trajectories of Development Among Societies" provides a test of ecological-evolutionary theory and world-system theory on this important issue.

The two theories also differ in their assessment of the role of biological factors in human life. World-system theory ignores the influence of genetics, with its proponents adopting the traditional Marxist view of the nature/nurture issue. Belief in the environmental determination of human nature has always been a basic article of faith for Marxists and neo-Marxists. This is essential if one is to have much hope for the emergence of an egalitarian social order in large and complex societies, to say nothing of the world as a whole. Unfortunately, however, the evidence to date indicates that humans have either been unwilling or unable to construct this kind of social order. Thus, those who dream of an egalitarian social order have been compelled to postulate either a dramatic transformation in our species' genetic heritage or the elimination of some important obstacle in the social and cultural heritage of societies. Since the former has seemed unlikely, hopes have been pinned on the latter.

Eighteenth-century revolutionaries pinned their hopes on the overthrow of monarchy and state church. This was to usher in a new era of liberty, equality, and fraternity. Instead, it brought conflict, the Terror, and, finally, Napoleon. In the nineteenth century, a new diagnosis provided egalitarians with a new explanation for inequality and injustice. Marx and Engels identified the institution of private property as the ultimate corrupting influence in human life and argued that when it was eliminated, societies would soon come to enjoy freedom, justice, and equality.

Once again, however, the diagnosis proved faulty. Private ownership of the means of production was abolished in the Soviet Union nearly a century ago, but long before the Soviet Union came to an end, thoughtful Marxists had already abandoned hope for the emergence of either the new man or the new society (Huberman and Sweezy, 1967). To make matters worse, the experience of the People's Republic of China, Cuba, North Korea, Vietnam, Kampuchea, and the other newer Marxist states only seemed to confirm conclusions based on Soviet experience.

Drawing on ideas of Lenin, world-system theorists offer yet another diagnosis and prescription. For them, the capitalist world-economy is the ultimate source of evil, and the cure must take the form of worldwide socialist revolution. Thus, despite repeated failures of past diagnoses and past prescriptions, world-system theorists cling to the belief that the evils of human life are merely products of social institutions, and not of any inherent features of our species' genetic heritage.[6]

---

6. It is tempting to suggest that if Marx and other utopians had been more familiar with modern biology they would have been far less inclined to imagine that a primate species, such as *Homo sapiens,* could successfully create a system of social organization like that of the social insects.

As the foregoing indicates, world-system theory has a strong normative component that often influences the analytical component, causing the theory to emphasize certain explanatory concepts and ignore or minimize others (e.g., the genetic component). In this respect, world-system theory differs not only from ecological-evolutionary theory but from most other contemporary theories as well.

The analytical principles of world-system theory are not necessarily invalid because of this linkage to normative principles, though the risk of error due to wishful thinking is greatly increased. Support for the theory, however, can come only from empirical evidence. To date, such evidence indicates that the capitalist world-economy does exert considerable influence on the social and cultural characteristics of individual societies, though not nearly as much as world-system theory might lead one to expect (Lenski and Nolan, 1984; Nolan, 1988).

Modernization Theory

The last of the macroorganizational theories with which ecological-evolutionary theory competes is modernization theory. Modernization theory, like world-system theory, is a microevolutionary theory with a time frame limited to the last several centuries. Like Parsonsian evolutionism and cultural materialism, the units of analysis on which modernization theorists have focused have usually been individual societies, but modernization theory has always had at least an implicit concept of a global system of interacting societies that exchange information and influence one another in a variety of ways.

Apart from the more limited time frame and less explicit treatment of the global system of societies, the chief difference between modernization theory and ecological-evolutionary theory is the way in which they explain the characteristics of societies. As an offshoot of functionalism and close kin to Parsonsian evolutionism, modernization theory attaches great importance to the role of beliefs and values in shaping the other characteristics of societies. As Alex Inkeles (1966) expressed it at one point, before people can escape traditional institutions, they must

> become modern in spirit, adopt and incorporate into their personalities the attitudes, values and modes of acting . . . identified with modern man. Without this ingredient neither foreign aid nor domestic revolution can hope successfully to bring an underdeveloped nation into the ranks of those capable of self-sustained growth. (p. 315)

To explain the source of this modern spirit, modernization theorists have variously invoked religion (Bellah, 1957), the mass media (Lerner, 1958), educational systems (Inkeles and Smith, 1974), and modern work organizations (Inkeles and Smith, 1974). Except for religion, these are usually seen as imports from, and extensions of, societies that are, themselves, already modern. Thus, in modernization theory the issue of where the antitraditional spirit comes from in the first place either tends to be ignored or is resolved by invoking Max Weber's thesis of the Protestant ethic and its contribution to the spirit of capitalism. Crasser material factors, such as the cumulation of technological information and its consequences, or the interplay of human nature and the biophysical environment, have much less appeal to most modernization theorists.

Historical Particularism

Before concluding this brief survey of alternatives to ecological-evolutionary theory, there is one other that should be considered—historical particularism. As its name suggests, this approach to the study of human societies and other phenomena employs the historical method and emphasizes the idiosyncratic nature of social phenomena, including societies. Historical particularists share the humanistic antipathy to the search for significant regularities in the realm of human affairs. Each society is unique and the goal of historical particularists is to document and explicate this fact.

Ecological-evolutionary theory has no quarrel with the assertion that every society is unique, at least when judged by the totality of its characteristics. But it denies that this is all that can or should be said about human societies. For while it is true that each is unique in the totality of its characteristics, it is also true that many of the same forces impinge on societies and influence their development, with the result that societies, when viewed in all their diversity, can be fruitfully compared with one another. To neglect this aspect of human societies, or to denigrate its importance, is, from the standpoint of ecological-evolutionary theory, to neglect or denigrate something that is essential to an adequate understanding of human societies.

In many ways, the bias of historical particularists with regard to idiosyncratic analysis seems to be linked to their preference for idealist explanations of social phenomena. It is the exceptional particularist, such as Fernand Braudel (1973), who finds much explanatory merit in material factors of any kind. Like functionalists, most particularists are greatly impressed by beliefs and values and by social institutions. The closest that most of them come to focusing on material factors is in analyses of the state and of the various interest groups that struggle for its control. While ecological-evolutionary theorists applaud the skill and sensitivity with which much of the work of the particularists is carried out (e.g., Moore, 1963; Skocpol, 1979; Tilly, 1964), they are disturbed by the pervasive neglect of forces they judge to be important in shaping the nature of societies and they are not persuaded that the overall strategy of the particularists is capable of fulfilling the potential of the social sciences.[7]

---

7. I believe that the special mission of the social sciences is distinct from that of the humanities, and that historical particularists in the social sciences have ignored that mission. That mission is to construct an empirically falsifiable general theory of human societies that can provide the grounding

Retrospect and Prospect

By now it should be clear that ecological-evolutionary theory seeks to identify and explain, as far as possible, the most basic characteristics of the most inclusive possible data set in the social sciences—all human societies, viewed both individually and collectively, throughout the total span of human history. It seeks to do this by taking account of both the cultural and noncultural forces that impinge on humans in their daily lives. In its efforts at explanation, it strives to identify principles that apply to all societies, others that apply to specific sets of societies, and still others that apply only to individual societies. Its ultimate goal is a theory that is grounded in the biological sciences, *but is not reductionist in nature*. Its goal is a parsimonious theory that does equal justice to the uniformities and the diversities present in the data sets it seeks to explain. And, finally, its goal is a theory that is sufficiently open and flexible that the products of new research can be incorporated into it without destroying it, and yet sufficiently structured that it does not degenerate into a mushy, formless eclecticism.

To be accepted by the scholarly community, a scientific theory must be able to pass three basic tests. First, its principles must be consistent with existing evidence and must not be demonstrably false. Second, it should be capable of generating new insights into the processes at work within the area of its concern. Third, it should provide better explanations of the phenomena with which it deals than do its competitors.

In Part II of this volume, I propose to test some of the basic assumptions of ecological-evolutionary theory by posing a series of problems of interest to social scientists and others to see what contribution the theory can make to our understanding of them. The problems that I have selected are highly diverse in nature. They range from a problem that has been primarily of concern to a highly specialized group of biblical scholars to one that should be of concern to the majority of social scientists. The diversity of the problems is intentional, since I believe that one of the primary appeals of ecological-evolutionary theory is its capacity for dealing effectively with an extraordinarily broad range of issues and problems. But readers must decide for themselves whether they share my optimism.

---

for special theories and for more fruitful studies of individual societies. In contrast, the special mission of the humanities is to explore the uniqueness of every individual and every social system. In effect, as I see it, the mission of the social sciences complements the mission of the humanities, and *vice versa;* the efforts of *both* are essential to an adequate understanding of human life. A problem arises only when enthusiasts of one approach deny the other's legitimacy, which, unfortunately, humanists and their allies within the social sciences too often tend to do. While it may be true that the task of constructing a valid theory of human societies is vastly more difficult, and entails far greater risks of error, than analyses of a single society or even a comparison of two or three societies, this does not negate the need for the theory nor does it mean that efforts to construct such a theory are inevitably doomed to failure.

Excursus: Further Notes on Technology and Ideology

To understand the changing relationship between technology and ideology, we need to keep in mind that as the technology of a society advances, its economic resources increase. These, in turn, open up new possibilities and new opportunities for solving problems. As Figure 7.3 indicates, the technologically least developed societies have the fewest options available to them. In Figure 7.3, the least developed society has only two options open to it for solving a particular problem, either M or N. In contrast, a more developed society has a wider range of options available, I through P, and the most developed society has the widest range available to it, E through V.

These differences are important, because the more choices a society has, the more opportunity there is for ideology to influence outcomes.

But this is not the whole story. Because of technology and the environment, all of the various alternative solutions to a given problem that fall within the range

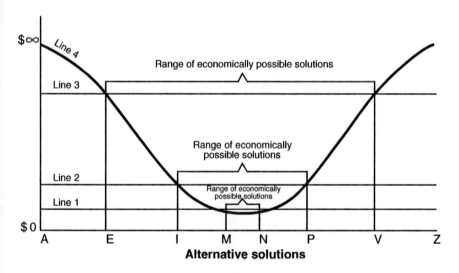

Line 1: Resources available in
technologically primitive society
Line 2: Resources available in
technologically intermediate
society
Line 3: Resources available in
technologically advanced society
Line 4: Costs of alternative solutions

Figure 7.3 Influence of technological advance on the range of possible solutions to problems

of the possible in a society are not likely to cost the same. Some are more expensive than others, and in a world in which economic resources are finite and human needs and desires infinitely expandable, economizing is unavoidable. Thus, technology not only limits the range of possibilities available to a society, it also influences the choices that come to be made within those limits by determining or greatly influencing the relative costs of the different options. Thus, once again technology constrains the implementation of ideologically based efforts, and technological constraints, acting in concert with human genetics, seem likely to remain a more powerful determinant of societal development than ideology, much as we might wish otherwise.

To say this, however, is not to affirm technological determinism as I have emphasized elsewhere (Lenski, 1970: 139–142; Nolan and Lenski, 2004: 74–76). On the contrary, it is an explicit assertion that other variables, notably including ideology, usually come into play in societal decisionmaking.

PART II

Applications

INTRODUCTION TO PART II

Treatises on theory normally end once the theory has been presented and its basic principles explicated. In the present instance, however, I believe that something more is needed, namely, a demonstration of the relevance of the theory for substantive problems.

The need for such a demonstration has become evident to me over the years as I have observed the reactions of students and fellow sociologists to presentations of the theory. I have found that while ecological-evolutionary theory seems plausible to many, most have difficulty in seeing how it can be tested and otherwise applied in research.

These reactions reflect, I believe, the drastic changes that occurred in the discipline of sociology in the twentieth century, especially in the United States, though not here alone. When the foundations of the discipline were being laid in Europe in the eighteenth and nineteenth centuries, the primary concern of the founders was to create a science of human societies that could explain the tremendous social and cultural diversity that Europeans had discovered in their recently established contacts with the peoples of Asia, Africa, the Americas, and the islands of the Pacific. All of the newly emerging social sciences were challenged by the growing recognition that many of these recently discovered societies bore fascinating resemblance in significant ways to societies of the past, known to Europeans through history and archaeology. Therefore, the founders of sociology (and most of the other social sciences) sought, above all, to understand the circumstances and forces that had enabled their own ancestors to move from what was then referred to as the states of savagery and barbarism to a state of civilization. This interest in societal development was intensified in the nineteenth century as the impact of the new industrial technology became more pronounced, and as scholars became aware that the historic process of societal transformation was

143

continuing in their own day, and even accelerating. For a discipline in which such concerns were central, the relevance of evolutionary theory was obvious.

Now, however, most sociologists focus on far more limited problems and work within a narrowly restricted time perspective. As Everett Hughes observed more than forty years ago, American sociology had become highly ethnocentric, concerned largely with American phenomena. And, he could have added, it had also lost the historical vision of its founders and become concerned much too narrowly with the contemporary scene. Related to this, it had been seduced by synchronic theories that omitted the temporal dimension altogether.

When sociologists do explore the past, as a number have again begun to do in recent years, it is usually in a manner that imitates, more than it complements, the work of historians. When such studies are at all comparative, they are on such a limited scale that the larger questions that once gave rise to the social sciences and to sociology are commonly ignored. Efforts to understand the universe of human societies, past as well as present, are rarely undertaken.

Many would say that this is all to the good: the larger questions posed by that universe cannot be answered by science. Others (e.g., Merton) have taken the view that while it may be possible to answer them at some time in the distant future, this will only be possible if sociologists first accumulate a vast store of detailed information and "middle range theories" about more limited processes. Only then should we even begin to think about the larger issues.

In my opinion, the latter view rests on a profound misunderstanding of the relationship between theory and research. For theory and research to be fruitful, they must interact. Theory must generate research and research must generate theory and this interaction must be sustained and continuous. Unless it is, theory degenerates into stale orthodoxies and research becomes fragmented, empiricist, and loses much of its value (except, perhaps, as a vehicle for advancing academic careers).

For all these reasons, then, it seems imperative to me to move beyond the presentation of the principles of ecological-evolutionary theory to demonstrations of its testability and its relevance for research. Because the theory incorporates many different propositions that are relevant to many different data sets, no single definitive test of the theory is possible. Instead, what is needed are many varying tests involving differing combinations of variables.

If these yield consistently negative results, the theory has to be abandoned. If, as is more likely, the results are mixed, they can contribute to modifications and refinements of the theory.

As noted previously (p. 138), the problems to which the theory will be applied in the chapters that follow have been deliberately chosen with an eye to their diversity and variability. They have also been chosen because of their relevance to ongoing controversies. For example, the chapter that follows (on the rise and early development of ancient Israel) is included because many historical sociologists in recent years have denied that general theories, such as ecological-evolutionary theory, are relevant or useful in studies of individual societies. I believe that this chapter suggests that a good theory can sometimes provide important insights that otherwise elude even those who have devoted a lifetime to the study of a particular society.

In addition, there is one other reason why I feel it is imperative to include a series of research applications in this volume on ecological-evolutionary theory. The study of specific problems provides a unique opportunity to deal with certain misunderstandings concerning the theory itself. Above all, applying the theory to the analysis of a varied set of problems makes it possible to demonstrate the nondeterministic and complex nature of the theory's explantory system, thereby helping, I hope, to correct a misunderstanding that has been fostered by some, despite many explicit statements to the contrary. And, related to this, these applications provide numerous opportunities to explore in greater detail and with greater specificity the fascinating and complex nature of the interrelations between extra- and intra-societal phenomena and, among the latter, the equally fascinating and complex interrelations between technology, population, social organization, and ideology.

Finally, for those who desire additional tests of ecological-evolutionary theory, I strongly recommend Jared Diamond's excellent volume, *Guns, Germs, and Steel: The Fates of Human Societies*. Although Diamond does not label his analysis as ecological and evolutionary, and though there are some differences in his perspective, these differences are not major. Thus, most of the chapters in *Guns, Germs, and Steel* provide valuable further tests of the principles on which ecological-evolutionary theory is based.

8

THE ORIGINS AND EARLY DEVELOPMENT OF ANCIENT ISRAEL

Over the years, biblical scholars have carried on a lively debate concerning the origins of ancient Israel. Who were the people who first called themselves Israelites? Where did they come from? What manner of people were they, and what were the circumstances that led to the formation of this new society?

Unfortunately, questions such as these hold little interest for most contemporary sociologists, the majority of whom have little interest in anything that occurred before the twentieth century. This is in sharp contrast to the interests of most of the founders of the discipline in the eighteenth and nineteenth centuries. The latter drew much of their inspiration from the historical record and the picture it presented of societal change and development. Their interest was, of course, both cause and consequence of their evolutionary perspectives. As they recognized, and contemporary sociologists too often forget, a true science of human societies cannot safely neglect any significant part of the total societal record, and, as the work of functionalists has demonstrated, synchronic analysis and theory are no substitute for a diachronic perspective.

One of the greatest satisfactions I have derived from my work with neoevolutionary theory has come about as a result of interest shown in the theory by a number of biblical scholars and by the seemingly fruitful application of certain of its principles to several of the more recalcitrant problems in their discipline. In this time of extreme scholarly specialization, opportunities for involvement in, and contributions to, debates outside one's own field are rare. This is especially true in fields such as biblical studies where the mastery of esoteric technical skills, such as the ability to read texts in obscure ancient languages (e.g., Ugaritic) and extensive specialized substantive knowledge are usually prerequisites to participation.

147

Some years ago, however, ecological-evolutionary theory provided me with just such an opportunity. This came about initially as a by-product of a decision by a biblical scholar, Marvin Chaney, to take his sabbatical leave in my department. Chaney's decision was a result of his interest in certain newer ideas emerging among biblical scholars concerning ancient Israel's origins and early development. He came to Chapel Hill because of work that one of my colleagues and I had done that he believed was relevant to questions on which he was working.

During Chaney's year in Chapel Hill, he introduced me to various aspects of his own research and more especially to a relatively new and controversial theory concerning Israel's origins that he found attractive. Over a period of months, as we discussed this theory and the relevant evidence from archaeology and from biblical and other ancient texts, this theory, when viewed from the perspective of ecological-evolutionary theory, seemed to me to raise a number of interesting questions. As a consequence, I queried Chaney extensively about the relevant evidence and this led me eventually to propose a modification in the theory or model with which he and several other scholars were working.

Subsequently, Chaney arranged for me to have an opportunity to present my ideas at a meeting of the Religious Studies Association at which a major statement of the new theory (Gottwald, 1979) was to be discussed. Later, my remarks at this meeting were published as a review essay (Lenski, 1980). These activities led to an exchange of correspondence with the author of the monograph and, subsequently, to the publication of a paper by him (Gottwald, 1983) in which he modified his original thesis somewhat to take account of my critique. More recently, while working with another biblical scholar, Charles Carter, I decided to push my critique further.

What will finally result from this small incursion into biblical studies by a sociologist armed only with a theory remains to be seen. The majority of biblical scholars view the social sciences with great skepticism and are reluctant to believe that they can provide anything useful to the understanding of the problems with which they are dealing. For the moment, however, this venture provides a rare and unusual test of the relevance and utility of ecological-evolutionary theory, and early results suggest that the theory may be capable of going beyond the elaboration of the obvious (i.e., the systematization of well-established relationships) and is able to provide novel insights concerning societies and their development, even societies that are well outside the scope of conventional sociological concern. It also provides a useful illustration of how the general theory presented in Part I of this volume can be applied to the analysis of individual societies and how this kind of activity can contribute to the development of the theory itself.

Early Efforts to Explain Israel's Origins

The earliest account of the origins of ancient Israel is found in the bible, and, more specifically, in the books of the Pentateuch and in Joshua, Judges, and I and II Samuel. There we read the famous story of the Exodus from Egypt and the subsequent conquest of the land of Canaan that began under the leadership of Joshua and was completed several centuries later under David and Solomon.

For centuries, this account was accepted unquestioningly as Holy Writ. But with the growth of religious skepticism in the eighteenth and nineteenth centuries, challenges to biblical authority began to appear. It is not my purpose here (nor am I qualified) to trace the development of thought concerning Israel's origins, except to note that, on the basis of modern textual analysis and archaeological research, no major biblical scholar today accepts the biblical account as a complete or adequate account of what actually transpired more than thirty centuries ago.

At the point at which I became interested in the question, biblical scholars were divided into three schools of thought, each committed to a different explanatory theory or model of Israel's origins (Gottwald, 1979: pt. V). Two of these shared the view that the Israelites were originally a nomadic or seminomadic pastoral people who had migrated into the land of Canaan (or Palestine) from desert regions east of the Jordan River, and had gradually won control over the land and its original inhabitants.

According to proponents of the first of these models (e.g., Albright, 1956; Bright, 1972; Lapp, 1969; Wright, 1957), control of Canaan was achieved by an extended process of military conquest, not unlike that recorded in the bible, though differing in certain significant details. For example, because of indisputable archaeological evidence that Jericho had not been inhabited for several centuries prior to the beginnings of Israel, this aspect of the biblical account is rejected as unhistorical.

Proponents of the second model (Alt, 1966; Noth, 1960; Weippert, 1971), referred to either as the "immigration" or "nomadic infiltration" model, argue that the early Israelites were land-hungry nomads and seminomads from the trans-Jordan region who gradually adopted a more sedentary way of life following migration to the sparsely settled hill country of eastern Palestine (Gottwald, 1979: ch. 21). According to proponents of this model, these migrants, joined perhaps by a small band of ex-slaves from Egypt, the Exodus people of the biblical account, eventually won control over the land largely by peaceful means—through population growth and the conversion of many of the older inhabitants to Israel's new religion. Military conquest played only a minor role in Israel's origins in this second model.

These older theories, or models, although still accepted by the majority of biblical scholars, have been undermined in recent years by a number of criticisms that have been summarized succinctly by Chaney in a paper titled "Ancient Palestinian Peasant Movements and the Formation of Premonarchic Israel" (1983). For sociologists, the most powerful of these criticisms is the demographic. Both of the older theories, or models, are predicated on the assumption that there was a large surplus population in the desert region beyond the Jordan River to the east of Palestine. But as Chaney (1983: 43) observes, "The romantic image of the Syro-Arabian desert as a vast womb, producing wave upon wave of Proto-Semites, is as demographically fallacious as it is long-lived in historiography." Not only is there no evidence for the existence of a sufficient population of desert dwellers to justify theories of conquest or mass immigration from that source at the time of Israel's founding, but archaeological evidence indicates that the number of pastoralists in the Syro-Arabian desert at that time was negligible.

Another major flaw in both the conquest and immigration models is the absence of archaeological evidence to support the thesis of the intrusion into Palestine of a new people with a new culture. Normally, when one ethnic group is displaced by another, either by conquest or by migration, the demographic discontinuity is manifested archaeologically by changes in material culture (e.g., new designs on pottery, new tools, and/or new modes of construction). In Palestine, in the thirteenth and twelfth centuries B.C.E., when Israel first appears in the highlands of Palestine, none of these things is evident. Once again, Chaney (1983: 46) provides a succinct summary:

> While insisting that the material culture of Israel's earliest settlements must be intrusive, proponents have been totally unable to find antecedents outside Palestine in a manner parallel to that of, for instance, the Philistines [a people who migrated into Palestine in roughly the same period in which the Israelites supposedly entered the land].

On the contrary, the evidence from all the earliest Israelite settlements reflects a remarkable continuity with the material culture of the older, pre-Israelite, or Canaanite, settlements (Carter, n.d.; Fritz, 1987).

The Peasant Revolt Model

Owing to the inability of proponents of the older models to produce evidence to support their thesis of an external source for early Israel, some scholars have turned to developments within Palestine (or Canaan) itself for an explanation of Israel's origins. These efforts led to the formulation of a striking new line of theory propounded first by George Mendenhall of the University of Michigan. In what has been described as a "landmark essay," he argued that

> there was no statistically important invasion of Palestine at the beginning of the twelve tribe system of Israel. There was no radical displacement of population, there was no genocide, there was no large scale driving out of population. . . . [W]hat happened instead may be termed, from the point of view of the secular historian interested only in socio-political processes, a *peasants' revolt* against the network of interlocking Canaanite city-states. (1962: 107; emphasis added)

Mendenhall argued that leadership for this revolt was provided by a small but ideologically dedicated and zealous group of ex-slaves who, as reported in the book of Exodus, had fled Egypt. This group "polarized the existing population all over the land" (Mendenhall, 1962: 113). Some joined the new movement led by the ex-slaves, while others, primarily the kings of the Canaanitish city-states and their supporters, fought it. Thus, what had originally been a single ethnic and cultural community divided along religious and political lines, with the opposing groups coming to be known as Israelites and Canaanites. But these labels were applied to members of a single ethnic group (not unlike the Reds and Whites in early postrevolutionary Russia), not to different ethnic groups, as biblical scholars had always assumed.

One feature of the peasant revolt model that makes it of special interest to sociologists is its advocates' claim that Israel was a radically new kind of society, a major social mutant in the ancient world. Mendenhall (1973: 12) drew attention to this when he wrote:

> A formative period is by definition one which is concerned to break with the contemporary and recent past, partly because it is intolerable or unsatisfactory, but more importantly because there comes about a vision and conviction that something much more excellent is not only possible but necessary. Discontent movements are a constant, as the history of revolt, war, and rebellion indicates. But rare indeed are those movements in history that result in such creative breaks with the past that they survive for centuries and expand over large population areas to create some sort of social unity or unified tradition that did not exist before. The first such movement to survive was the biblical one [i.e., the movement that gave birth to the new society of Israel].

Not only did Israel worship a new kind of deity—the monotheistic Yahweh, as contrasted with the polytheistic deities of the Canaanites—but it possessed a new kind of moral order based on laws derived from Yahweh. This included, among other things, strikingly new and egalitarian patterns of land tenure, the abolition of monarchical government and all its trappings, and its replacement by a much more egalitarian, much less exploitative, and much less oppressive, decentralized, theocratic republic.

Although Mendenhall's peasant revolt model solved a number of serious problems associated with the older conquest and immigration models, it did not eliminate all of them, and it introduced some new problems of its own. For example, Martin Buss (1980, 274) argued that Mendenhall's view of Israel in the premonarchic period is "unduly idealized"—a tendency that is as old as the biblical account itself (see, for example, the writings of the prophets who viewed this earliest period of Israel's history as the standard against which later periods were judged and invariably found wanting). And Chaney (1983: 49) argued that Mendenhall's "heavy, almost exclusive emphasis upon religious ideology as the explanation of premonarchic Israel's social mutations has tended to obscure other important [causal] factors."

These problems led others, including Chaney, to develop alternative versions of the peasant revolt model. The most influential and powerful of these has been the work of Norman Gottwald and is stated most fully in his monograph titled *The Tribes of Yahweh: A Sociology of the Religion of Liberated Israel 1250–1050 B.C.* In this volume, Gottwald leveled a vigorous attack against his fellow biblical scholars for overreliance on the humanistic tradition of textual analysis and for neglect of sociological methodology and theory. He argued

> that when we take the significant results of literary, historical, and religious study of the Bible and present them within the framework of a social scientific approach, new and illuminating patterns of interpretation emerge. While social science cannot resolve the impasse into which particular lines of literary, historical, and religious inquiry have fallen by producing new data out of whole cloth, it can set the tentative and fragmentary results of what the humanities have to say about the origins of biblical religion in an entirely new contextual light. Furthermore, it can sometimes call attention to data which do not appear pertinent to a humanistic formulation of biblical problems but which become pertinent to a social formulation of biblical problems. (1979: 16)

Building on this foundation, Gottwald developed an impressive analysis of both the data and their earlier explanations. In the final sections of his monograph, however, he offered a much less idealistic version of peasant revolt theory than that provided by Mendenhall. In it, he drew heavily on the work of Marx, Weber, Durkheim, and, among contemporary social scientists, Marvin Harris. For Gottwald (1979: 700), the new religion of Israel was "the symbolic expression of the Israelite socioeconomic revolution," rather than the reverse, as Mendenhall saw it. And where Mendenhall tended to equate early Israel's rejection of the forms of power typically exercised by agrarian societies with the outright repudiation of sociopolitical power, Gottwald (1979: 94) asserted that "Israel challenged one form of power [political] by means of another form of power [religious or ideological]," and that "Israel consciously exercised power even as it attributed the source of all power to its deity."

Although Mendenhall and Gottwald have been the most important contributors to the development of the peasant revolt model, there have been others. Chaney (1983, 1986), for example, extended Gottwald's use of social science concepts and perspectives (e.g., by introducing the concept of agrarian societies and their attributes) and argued persuasively for the relevance of the Amarna letters, a file of correspondence to the Egyptian court from writers describing widespread political unrest in Palestine in the century prior to the founding of Israel.

Questions Raised by Ecological-Evolutionary Theory

Viewed from a sociological perspective, the peasant revolt model of Israel's origins is much more persuasive than either of its rivals. The apparent lack of any substantial human population in the Syro-Arabian desert at the time when Israel came into being is a major barrier to the acceptance of both the conquest and immigration models. In addition, there is a growing body of evidence that links the culture of the early Israelites to older Canaanite culture, as the peasant revolt model would lead one to expect. This is especially evident in the material culture of the earliest Israelite settlements, and there is also evidence that some of the oldest and most important names in the Hebrew tradition (e.g., Abram) have Canaanite origins. These are not what one would expect if the earliest Israelites were from alien ethnic stock and had previously employed a radically different mode of subsistence (pastoralism rather than agriculture), as both the conquest and immigration models assume.

Although the peasant revolt model is compatible with these important aspects of the empirical record, the model is not without problems of its own. While its claim of a peasant revolt is hardly surprising to anyone familiar with agrarian societies (Lenski, 1966: 274–275), and while there is also substantial evidence of widespread peasant unrest and revolts in the century preceding the emergence of Israel (Chaney, 1983, 1986), there is no record of such revolts in the thirteenth century when the highland communities that became Israel were first settled. This could, of course, be due merely to the failure of relevant evidence to survive, but the lack of evidence on such a crucial point is troubling.

More troubling still is the assertion that the revolt was successful. Most peasant revolts in agrarian societies of the preindustrial era were hopeless affairs from the start. Sometimes, minor victories were won in isolated village struggles, but revolts that spread more widely had little chance of success, since they quickly ran up against the well-armed and better-organized forces of the governing class. Of all the many peasant revolts in China's long history, for example, only three were successful prior to the twentieth century (Eberhard, 1952: 52), and it is difficult to find comparable successes elsewhere (see, for example, the ruthless suppression of the English peasants' revolt in the thirteenth century, and the German peasants' revolt in the sixteenth century).

But even this is not the end of the problems raised by the peasant revolt model when viewed from a broadly comparative historical perspective. Even in those rare, rare instances when peasants succeeded in overthrowing the political establishment, they were never able to follow this up with a radical reconstitution of society of the kind that Gottwald, Mendenhall, and other proponents of the revolt model claim occurred in early Israel. Even when an emperor was deposed in China, and a peasant replaced him on the imperial throne, there were almost no changes in the basic institutional structure of society. While a few of the peasant rebels gained enormous power and wealth for themselves and their families, the oppressive and exploitative imperial system that caused the revolt continued much as it always had. Thus, if Mendenhall, Gottwald, Chaney, and other revolt theorists are correct, and peasant uprisings in Palestine in the thirteenth and twelfth centuries B.C.E. gave rise to the formation of a radically new kind of society, this development would probably have been *unique and totally without parallel in all the long history of the agrarian era.*

This suggests that one should view the hypothesized model with almost as much skepticism as the older conquest and immigration models. In short, before one can accept the peasant revolt model of the origin of Israel, there must be a satisfactory explanation of how it was possible for the peasants of ancient Canaan to achieve what, to the best of our knowledge, no other group of peasants anywhere in the preindustrial world was able to achieve.

The existence of grinding oppression and widespread peasant grievances are not enough to explain the striking institutional differences between premonarchic Israel (i.e., from about 1250–1000 B.C.E.) and the princely city-states of Canaan. Comparable conditions existed in almost every agrarian society of the past. Nor is the presence of a powerful new ideology (i.e., the new Yahwist faith of Israel) an adequate explanation: The peasant revolts in thirteenth-century England and sixteenth-century Germany both possessed powerful and compelling egalitarian ideologies—and both ended in total failure!

Another, less serious problem raised by the peasant revolt model involves the question of timing and location. Why did the revolt occur when and where it did? Why in the thirteenth century? Why not the fifteenth or the eighteenth century? Or, why not the tenth or the fifth? What was special about the thirteenth century? And why did Israel get its start in the hill country? Why not in the lowlands or along the coastal plain where conditions were probably more oppressive?

Finally, there is the important problem of why Israel was unable to preserve the unique social system it had created. Why was it that after a few brief centuries Israel abandoned its egalitarian social institutions and reverted to the patterns of a typical agrarian society? Why did it abandon its republican form of government and adopt the monarchical form that its founders had rejected? And why did it allow the reintroduction of oppressive and exploitative institutions and the growth of gross political and economic inequality, especially if Mendenhall and Gottwald are correct in their assertions about the conscious intentionality and purposiveness of the institutional innovations that characterized early Israel? These are all questions that are not satisfactorily answered by either version of the peasant revolt model.

Biophysical Environment and Technology: Bases for a New Model of Israel's Origins

Viewed from the perspective of ecological-evolutionary theory, there are three facts of importance on which everyone who has studied the question of Israel's origins agrees (Hopkins, 1987: 181). First, Israel had its beginnings in the hill country of Palestine; none of its earliest settlements were in the fertile lowlands to the west, the historic centers of human settlement in Palestine. Second, prior to the thirteenth century B.C.E., the hill country of Palestine was very sparsely settled; by recent count, only twenty-nine hill country sites have been identified that predate the mid-thirteenth century. Third, beginning at this time, there was an explosive growth in the number of settlements in the area and in the size of the human population (according to one recent survey, ninety-seven new settlements were established and the rate of population growth appears to have averaged nearly 2 percent per year between 1200 and 1150 B.C.E. (Stager, 1985: 3).

Compared to the lowlands to the west, the hill country had few natural resources. The hilly terrain, thin rocky soil, and tough scrub forest all presented obstacles to permanent settlement. In addition, water was scarce during the long summer months (Hopkins, 1987: 184). Because of Palestine's Mediterranean-type climate, rainfall occurred almost entirely in the winter months. As a result, most springs and streams in the highlands dried up in the summer months, and without an adequate water supply, it was impossible for farmers and their live-stock to survive. The few small settlements prior to the thirteenth century were all located adjacent to the handful of springs in the area that flowed continuously throughout the year.

Beginning in the thirteenth century, however, several important new technologies were introduced into the hill country that made it possible for people gradually to overcome these historic environmental constraints and thus laid the foundation for a substantial growth in human population over the course of the next several centuries (Gottwald, 1979: 655–660). First, the Hittite monopoly over the production and manufacture of iron and iron implements came to an end, and with the sharp reduction in price that followed, iron became available for the first time for the manufacture of the various tools required by peasant farmers (Chaney, 1986: 64–66). Iron axes and plow tips, even though few in number for a long time, greatly facilitated the clearing of the tough scrub forest and plowing of the land, thus opening large areas of the highlands to cultivation for the first time.

Iron tools may also have facilitated the construction of cisterns for storing water in the soft and permeable rock of the highlands. In addition, a relatively new technique for lining the porous walls of cisterns was introduced into the highlands. The use of a burnt-lime plaster lining effectively prevented leakage through the porous rock walls of cisterns in the region. Thus, substantial quantities of water could be stored during the winter to sustain human populations and their flocks through the long, dry summer months.

Finally, rock terracing was introduced—a practice that enabled hill country farmers to conserve water, control erosion, and minimize the loss of precious top soil on hilly slopes (Anderson, 1987: 22–23). The introduction of rock terracing in combination with the introduction of iron tools was probably responsible for another important innovation in much of the hill country, the cultivation of cereal crops (Gottwald, 1979: 657; Chaney, 1986: 63). Previously, hill country farmers in most areas had been restricted to vine, olive, and nut cultivation and were dependent on others for basic staples. In short, the more or less simultaneous introduction in the hill country of several important new technologies seems to have laid the foundation for a substantial growth in the region's population beginning in the thirteenth century.

One may ask, of course, where the migrants who first settled the hill country came from. Advocates of the peasant revolt model argue that they were peasant rebels fleeing to the hills for safety. That is certainly a plausible explanation, but it is contingent on the still-missing evidence of peasant revolts during the century when Israel was founded.

Ecological-evolutionary theory offers as an alternative the normal tendency of human populations in the preindustrial past to expand as new resources became available. This pattern is amply evident in both prehistoric and historic times. Prior to the recent past, whenever new resources have become available, whether through settlement of new territories or through the development of new technologies, human populations have increased. In agrarian societies, peasants have always produced more offspring than their meager farms could support. Thus, there has always been outmigration from long-settled rural areas (except in the aftermath of wars, famines, and pestilence). Typically, these migrants have moved to cities and towns where most of them entered the class of wretched expendables (Lenski, 1966: 281–284). When, however, there were new territories to be occupied and new frontiers to be settled, some part of the flow of migration would be diverted, as happened during the settlement of the European colonies in the New World. On a much smaller scale, this is what would have happened when new technologies created new opportunities for settlement in the highlands of Palestine in the thirteenth century B.C.E. The normal tendency to migrate to frontiers may well have been intensified in ancient Palestine by the invasion of the coastal region by the so-called sea peoples—an invasion that coincided with the early expansion of population in the hill country (Carter, n.d.).

The opening up of the hill country to more substantial migration and new settlements may also explain one other piece of the puzzle that gives the peasant revolt model trouble—namely, the apparent *decline* in the incidence of peasant revolts following the fourteenth century. As noted above, the record shows widespread peasant unrest in the fourteenth century, but little or none in the thirteenth. While this may be nothing more than a reflection of limitations in the evidence available, it could also be a reflection of changing social conditions resulting from the application of new technologies in the hill country. In other words, given a choice between fighting a well-entrenched and powerful governing class and migrating to new territories where they could carve out farms of their own, free from the control of elites, it would hardly be surprising if oppressed peasants chose the latter.

In any case, when the hill country was first settled, the governing class in Canaan apparently took little interest in it. This was not the kind of land that could be expected to produce an economic surplus worthy of the governing class's attention (Hopkins, 1987: 185). The costs of establishing and maintaining control of it (i.e., equipping an army and supporting the necessary staff of resident officials) would almost certainly have exceeded the benefits that could be expected for many years. Moreover, the hill country may even have been viewed by members of the governing class as a relatively safe outlet for excess population, especially for troublemakers and malcontents who were unwilling or unable to adapt to the demands made of them in an established agrarian society. Only later would the governing class discover to its dismay that the buildup of population in the hill country and the new society that had taken root there had become a threat to its control of the lowlands and to its established position of power and privilege.

Premonarchic Israel as a Frontier Society

Viewed from the perspective of ecological-evolutionary theory, premonarchic Israel, with its small highland farms, largely subsistence economy, decentralized republican government, and highly egalitarian social system, occupying what had been largely uninhabited territories, looked to me, as Chaney described it, remarkably like an interesting and familiar variant on the more basic model of agrarian society—namely, a frontier society (Lenski and Lenski, 1974: 261–262; Lenski and Lenski, 1987: 205–207). This has been a short-lived type of society that has appeared briefly from time to time when members of an agrarian society have migrated to previously uninhabited territory or to territory thinly inhabited by horticulturalists, hunters and gatherers, or other technologically less advanced peoples.

There are a number of instances of this type of society scattered throughout the historical record. The Norwegian-Irish settlement of Iceland (Thomssen, 1980) is one of the earliest of which we have a clear record. Others include the Cossack settlement of the Russian steppes, the Boer settlement of southern Africa, and the European settlements in the Americas, New Zealand, and Australia.

The idea of the frontier as the source from which a distinctive kind of socio-cultural system arises owes much to the work of Frederick Jackson Turner (1894, 1920), the American historian. His studies led him to the conclusion that the values and institutions American society had inherited from Europe had been profoundly transformed by the frontier experience. According to Turner (e.g., 1920: 35), the frontier had promoted the emergence of new and distinctive qualities such as individualism, democracy, and nationalism. It also produced antipathy to governmental control (ibid.: 30).

Although Turner believed that the western frontier had made an indelible impression on the life of American society, he recognized that the values and institutions created by frontier conditions could not survive unchanged once frontier conditions no longer prevailed. In a number of his essays he wrote of the decline and/or transformation of older frontier values as the new more settled mode of life became dominant.

Although Turner's writings were subjected to sharp attack beginning in the 1930s, and flaws have been found in his methods of analysis and some of his conclusions, his basic thesis that the frontier environment had generated new values and led to significant changes in American society in the eighteenth and nineteenth centuries seems unarguable (see, e.g., Billington, 1973). The same is true of his thesis that the closing of the frontier led to a reversal in the direction of the process of change in a number of important respects.

It also came to be recognized by at least some scholars that Turner's concept of the frontier and the kinds of effects it produces has an applicability that extends well beyond the limits of American society. James G. Leyburn's 1936 volume, *Frontier Folkways,* is an especially valuable example of this. In this volume, Leyburn examined a number of cases in which agrarian societies invaded territories previously occupied by technologically less advanced peoples. He concluded that the nature of the new society that resulted depended largely on the circumstances of its formation. If the formation of the new society was effectively controlled and directed by members of the governing class in the old society, the result tended to be a plantation system (or colony) in which many, or most, of the sociocultural patterns of the old society were preserved—especially the patterns of gross inequality, exploitation, and oppression. But if the new society emerged from the actions of numerous small farmers, and the governing authorities in the old society were not in firm control, the result was the kind of frontier society that Turner argued had emerged in the course of American history.

Leyburn's work, though neglected, is important for comparative sociologists. It specifies the limits of the applicability of Turner's model of a frontier society, and it focuses attention on a key element in the causal process—namely, the presence or absence of the governing class and traditional governmental authority in the critical early stages of societal formation.

While working with Chaney during his year in Chapel Hill, I was not yet inclined to question the assumption that a peasant revolt, or series of revolts, had been the primary cause of the formation of the new society of Israel. The apparent alternatives, the conquest and immigration models, were clearly unsatisfactory, and the Amarna letters from the fourteenth century, together with biblical and archaeological evidence of fighting between Israelites and Canaanites in the premonarchic period, made the peasant revolt model seem quite plausible.

At the same time, however, the concept of the frontier seemed relevant and potentially useful as a way of answering a number of questions that were not adequately addressed by the peasant revolt model (see "Premonarchic Israel as a Frontier Society" above). As a result, I proposed, in my review (1980) of Gottwald's volume, that a combined peasant revolt–frontier society model might explain more than a pure peasant revolt model.

Later, however, while working with Charles Carter, another biblical scholar who developed an interest in ecological-evolutionary theory, I became more aware of the seriousness with which many biblical scholars view the lack of direct evidence of peasant revolts in Palestine in the premonarchic era. I also became more aware of other relevant evidence concerning this phase of Palestinian history.

These new understandings, combined with further reflection, have led me to conclude that the opening of the new frontier in the highlands beginning in the thirteenth century was probably the principal cause of the developments that followed, and that the concept of a peasant revolt should be thought of as a possible (though unproven and nonessential) contributory influence. In short, it now seems to me that the frontier society model handles more of the basic issues more successfully than does the peasant revolt model. In fact, by itself, and standing alone, it appears to account for most of the existing evidence.

The Frontier Society and Peasant Revolt Models Compared

As noted previously, the peasant revolt model hypothesizes a pattern of development that appears to be without precedent in the agrarian era. Despite thousands of peasant risings in preindustrial Europe and Asia, only a handful succeeded in toppling an established government, and none of those—except, presumably, Israel—followed this up with a social and cultural revolution. Thus, the absence of any historical precedent indicates, at a minimum, a need for great caution when considering this model.

In contrast, the frontier society model hypothesizes a pattern of development that, as Turner, Leyburn, Thomssen, and others have shown, has occurred a number of times in the past. In fact, it has been the typical pattern of development whenever new territories have been settled by small farmers acting on their own initiative, rather than under the direction and control of elites based in more settled areas (Leyburn, 1936: ch. 11).

Second, as noted earlier, there is no evidence of significant peasant revolts in Palestine in the thirteenth, twelfth, or eleventh centuries: They have to be assumed. In contrast, there is ample evidence of the settlement of new territories and the rapid growth of population in the Palestinian highlands in this period. Furthermore, archaeological evidence indicates that these new settlements were poor and relatively backward culturally compared to the older, established settlements in the lowlands (Fritz, 1987). This, of course, is exactly what a frontier society model would lead one to expect.

Third, the frontier society model provides an answer to the question of why Israel got its start in the thirteenth century and not some other, and in the hill country and not in the lowlands or along the coastal plain. It was not until that century that the application of new technologies (iron, rock terracing, slake-limed cisterns) made widespread human settlement in the highlands possible. In contrast, the peasant revolt model provides no answer to the question of why peasant revolts in the thirteenth century should have been able to accomplish what similar revolts in the fourteenth and other centuries did not. And if the latter model is at least able to provide a plausible explanation of the locational aspect of Israel's origins, it is no more plausible than that provided by the frontier society model.

Fourth, and perhaps most important of all, the frontier society model provides an explanation, rooted in the experience of other frontier societies, of why Israel so quickly abandoned the distinctive institutional system it initially created (e.g., why it abandoned republican government and adopted a monarchical form of government; why it abandoned the militia system and adopted a professional army; and why it shifted from a decentralized religious system involving many scattered local shrines, each with its own resident priests, to one increasingly dominated by a single royal temple and a high priest.

Frontiers, frontier values, and frontier institutions are transitory phenomena, as Turner and others have observed. Once the wilderness is conquered and population and wealth increase, the foundations of the libertarian and egalitarian spirit are slowly eroded, more conventional values take their place, and institutional changes become likely.

Norman Gottwald, the leading proponent of the peasant revolt model, responded to my earlier challenge on this point (Lenski, 1980) by suggesting that Israel's social and cultural reversion following the establishment of the monarchy under David was due to the incorporation of large numbers of Canaanites into the population of Israel following Israel's conquest of the lowlands. These people, Gottwald (1983: 17) argued, lacked "the social revolutionary history that the highland Israelites experienced" and thus were not in a position to "comprehend the meaning of joining the social body of Israel as an intertribal movement toward social equality." He went on to say that "it is by no means clear that David and his monarchic successors were interested in acculturating these newcomers to old Israelite consciousness, since their main agenda was to strengthen the centralized power of the new Israelite state."

The problem with this argument, as I see it, is that the move away from egalitarian social institutions began at a time when the highland population was still demographically and politically dominant in Israel (i.e., before the conquest of the lowlands). Moreover, the first kings in Israel, Saul and David, were both of pure highland stock. Thus, it seems unfair—and, more important, incorrect—to shift the "blame" for the social and cultural reversion of Israel onto the conquered Canaanites.

But the problem for the peasant revolt model is even more serious. If, as Gottwald (1983: 18–19) argued, Israel's egalitarian social system was a conscious and deliberate collective response to the highly stratified, oppressive, and exploitative systems of its Canaanitish neighbors, one would surely expect that the new system would be defended with extraordinary zeal. At a minimum, one would expect a prolonged and bitter civil war between defenders of the old order and proponents of the new. Yet there is little in the biblical account to suggest this: David seems to have encountered remarkably little resistance to his new policies, and even the excesses of his son and heir, Solomon, did not generate the kind or degree of resistance during his extended reign that one would expect if Israel's egalitarian social system was as intentional as Gottwald believes. But this is exactly what the frontier society model would predict in a geographically expanded state that had by now incorporated the more productive, wealth-producing lowlands, and where frontier settlements had become increasingly marginal economically.

Finally, there is the question of Israel's new faith and its relation to the competing models of Israel's origins. At the outset, it needs to be recognized and kept firmly in mind that our knowledge of this important aspect of Israel's culture is derived entirely from accounts that were not set down in writing until many centuries after the period in question. Most biblical scholars today agree that our view of this early period, therefore, necessarily reflects to a substantial degree the needs, biases, interests, and experiences of a much later generation of Israel's religious elite.

Keeping this in mind, we then need to ask what were the distinctive features of Israel's new religion as reported by later generations of priests and scholars. First, and foremost, there was Israel's monotheism, which they contrasted with the polytheism of Israel's neighbors. Second, Israel was described as having established a unique covenant, or contractual relationship, with its deity: In return for obedience to his laws, Yahweh would provide for the safety and welfare of Israel. These laws included both ritual and ethical elements.

Proponents of the peasant revolt model argue that the religion of early Israel provides strong support for their thesis that Canaanite society, its values, beliefs, and institutions, served as a *negative* model for the early Israelites, and there appears to be much truth in this view. However, a frontier society model leads to the same conclusion, especially for the earlier phase of frontier experience. Thus, when one compares the two models in this respect, the result appears to be a standoff.

But this is not the whole story. In the centuries following the establishment of the monarchy, the people of Israel repeatedly failed to honor the covenant established with Yahweh. The biblical account reports frequent backsliding, even reversion to Canaanitish beliefs and practices (see, for example, the dramatic account of Elijah's contest with the priests of the baal). In addition, the new political and economic elites in Israel engaged in a variety of ruthless, greedy, and dishonest actions that led to harsh condemnations by a succession of preachers, known to history as the prophets. These preachers, or prophets—Amos, Micah, Hosea, and others—proclaimed that Yahweh would exact a terrible vengeance if Israel continued to violate its sacred covenant obligations. Although the lines were not always clearly drawn, there is reason to see in Israel, during the period of the monarchy, a chronic religious and/or ideological struggle between the new political, economic, and religious elites (i.e., the priests associated with the royal temple cultus) on the one hand and the masses of ordinary citizens and the prophets on the other.[1]

A Further Link in the Causal Chain

There is yet another problem that needs to be addressed. How can we explain the fact that so many of the elements of the faith of early Israel loom so large in

---

1. Chaney (1986: 68ff.) has suggested that this struggle divided Israel along geographical and environmental lines as well as along more obvious class lines. Specifically, he suggested that the older system of values that developed when Israel was still a frontier society continued to enjoy their greatest support in the communities of small, freeholding farmers that survived for an extended period in the hill country. Once again, this is what a frontier society model would lead one to expect.

modern Judaism? If frontier conditions ceased to be decisive in Israel's experience by the time of David and Solomon, how can we explain the continuing importance of ethical and ritual norms that appear to have had their origin in the premonarchic period and in response to conditions that prevailed at that time?

Here, ecological-evolutionary theory invokes again Dubos's (1968: 270) important principle that the past is not dead history but living material, much of which exercises an influence for extended periods. It is clear from the biblical account that, during the years of the monarchy, there was a continuing struggle between two segments of the population, as we have just seen. One invoked a newer ideology that reflected the more complex and more cosmopolitan social experience of Israel's new political and religious elites and that served their interests. The other invoked an older, egalitarian ideology that was rooted in Israel's past—an ideology that had been dominant when Israel was still a society of frontiersmen scratching out a meager living in the hill country of Palestine. But this was an ideology that continued to serve the interests of the lower classes in society.

This older ideology would almost certainly never have become the dominant element in Jewish culture except for a remarkable set of circumstances, which, in their totality, have rarely occurred in human history. The key to these developments was the declining fortunes of the kingdom of Israel. Less than a hundred years after the establishment of the monarchy under David, Israel split into a northern and a southern kingdom. A century later, the powerful Assyrian Empire became increasingly active in the west and by 721 B.C. the northern kingdom was conquered. Not only was the kingdom destroyed, its elites were scattered throughout the Assyrian Empire and foreigners were settled in much of what had once been the land of Israel. As a result, ten of the original twelve tribes of Israel disappeared forever from the stage of history.

And this was not the end of disasters. Less than 150 years later, the southern kingdom was conquered by the Babylonians and its leaders sent off into exile. Thus, in effect, the message of the prophets was fulfilled and they were vindicated. The people of Israel had broken the covenant their forebears had made with Yahweh and now Yahweh had wreaked vengeance on the nation. With much of the old leadership dead or discredited, a new and reconstituted religious elite emerged that took the teachings of the prophets more seriously. This meant, among other things, that an ethical code and a religious tradition that had evolved centuries earlier in response to the harsh and egalitarian conditions of frontier life gained new respect, but under a completely different set of circumstances.

During the period that has come to be known as the Babylonian Captivity, several critical institutional changes occurred. For example, the temple at Jerusalem, which had been the focal point of Jewish religious practice since David's day, was destroyed. The religious system that was based on, and had developed around, the rituals of temple worship was no longer viable. To fill the institutional vacuum that had been created, new institutions began to take shape. The study of scripture became increasingly important, as did a new class of religious leaders, men learned in scripture and in religious tradition. Thus, when the Captivity ended, and the leaders of the Jewish people were allowed to return to Palestine, the priestly elite and their tradition no longer possessed the same degree of authority and influence it had enjoyed earlier. Even after the temple was rebuilt and the temple cultus reestablished, religious leadership had to be shared with a new class of leaders, the forerunners of what was to become the rabbinate.

For a number of centuries following the Babylonian Captivity, there seems to have been an ongoing struggle or competition for religious dominance within Judaism. Evidence of this can be seen in the period when Christianity got its start. The Gospels speak often of differences between the Pharisees and the Saducees, and modern scholarship has uncovered evidence of a more populist and radical group known as the Essenes. This diversity reflected not only the influence of class differences and the effects of increasing exposure to foreign (especially Greek) influences, but also the lack of an independent monarchy that could support, with both money and coercive authority, an official state cult.

The last major transformation of the Jewish religious system came with the second destruction of the temple in Jerusalem in 70 C.E.—an event that marked the end of priestly power and authority and led to the dominance of the rabbinical class. This meant that scriptures and their interpretation replaced the temple cultus at the center of Jewish religious life. And this, in turn, meant that those elements of the early frontier faith that had been preserved and transmitted by the prophets during the period of the monarchy and the divided kingdom became central in the Jewish religious tradition. For believing Jews, and for believing Christians as well, the radical claims of the prophets had been vindicated by the unhappy fate of the religious and political elites who, in the days of the monarchy, had ignored the covenant that their forefathers had established with the King of Kings and Lord of Lords.

Ideology and the Exodus People

Finally, we come to the fascinating question of the relation of the frontier society model of Israel's origins to the account found in the bible itself. Above all, what are we to make of the biblical account of Moses and the Exodus from Egypt? Should all of that be dismissed as mere legend and without basis in fact? If not, how does it relate to the frontier society model?

At the outset it should be noted that most biblical scholars today, even while questioning many of the details of the Exodus story, regard the story as grounded ultimately in actual historical experience. In other words, at least *some* of Israel's early inhabitants were refugees who had fled from bondage in Egypt.

If we accept, then, the view that the new society of Israel included not only Canaanite peasants from the nearby lowlands but also a very different group of migrants, or refugees, from Egypt, several elements in the biblical account take on a new and sociologically interesting meaning. Above all, this view suggests an intriguing explanation of an otherwise puzzling element in premonarchic Israel—

namely, the Levites. According to the biblical account, premonarchic Israel was composed of twelve social units that have been rendered in English rather mis-leadingly as "tribes." In the biblical account, these were lineage groups, each de-scended from a common ancestor. Eleven of them were also geographically de-fined groups, each with a distinctive territory of its own. The tribe of Levi, however, unlike the rest, had no territory of its own. Instead, it was designated by the Lord to live in "cities" (i.e., tiny emergent urban centers) located within the territories of the other eleven tribes.

The Levites were also a religious elite, set apart by Yahweh from the rest of the people, with special duties and responsibilities. The bible explains this as their reward for loyalty to Moses and Yahweh at the time when, in Moses' absence (while on Mt. Sinai), the people created the infamous golden calf as an object of worship. According to the biblical account (Exodus, ch. 32), when Moses re-turned and discovered this he confronted the people and demanded to know who was on the Lord's side. Only the sons of Levi responded. Moses then commanded them to slay the idolators, which the sons of Levi did, killing 3,000 men. Because of their loyalty at this critical juncture, Moses said to the Levites, "Today you have ordained yourselves for the service of the Lord."

This tradition concerning the Levites and their special history is repeated and elaborated in various ways in other parts of the bible. In the Book of Num-bers (ch. 18), for example, we are told that Yahweh commanded members of the other eleven tribes to support the Levites by giving them a tenth of their income. Thus, in some of the oldest traditions of Israel a record is preserved of an impor-tant social and religious cleavage or distinction within the population dating to the premonarchic period. A small minority of the people were different from the rest, both socially and spiritually. Not only were they linked in a special way to Israel's new faith, they were also a privileged group of early urbanites who were supported economically by the rest of the population.

This picture of the tribe of Levi and its distinctive and privileged status in early Israel is what we might expect if the Levites were, in fact, descended from a small group of refugees from a highly advanced society, such as Egypt, who had migrated to a newly settled frontier region otherwise inhabited by poor and illit-erate subsistence farmers. In a society of independent-minded frontiersmen, a privileged status, such as the Levites enjoyed, would, in the absence of coercive force, require some rationale, such as a legitimizing myth, and no myth could be more compelling than one involving a divine injunction. Moreover, no group in such a society was in a better position to foster such a myth than refugees from one of the most advanced societies of its day.

This is not to suggest that the Egyptian refugees engaged in a calculated or deliberate effort to deceive and take advantage of their less well-educated neigh-bors any more than one would assume such intent on the part of the founders of other religious groups in the preindustrial past. We need only assume that the refugees brought with them, in addition to their cultural skills, a distinctive reli-gious faith and a distinctive history in which they took pride. Under the circumstances, it would hardly be surprising if the culturally more advanced minority settled in the emerging urban centers and came to dominate their less sophisticated peasant neighbors culturally (including religiously). Thus, a group like the Levites might well become the principal bearers of the new society's religious and historical tradition. And if, over time, the humble and less dramatic history of their peasant neighbors was gradually forgotten, that, too, would hardly be surprising. By the time the oral traditions of Israel's origins were written down many centuries later, memory of the Canaanite peasant origins of the majority of the original settlers may have been all but forgotten. By this time, memory of their origins may even have become confused with that of those other Canaanites who were incorporated into the kingdom much later through the conquests of David and Solomon (and whose presence in the expanded kingdom is clearly recognized in the biblical account). Thus, in the end the special traditions of a small, dominant elite may eventually have been transformed into the official and only surviving account of the origins of the nation as a whole.

On first consideration, it may seem strange that a cultured group of refugees from a highly advanced society, such as Egypt, would migrate to a recently settled and primitive frontier region. On reflection, however, this is not so surprising. There they would have their best chance of escaping the long arm of Egyptian authority, which still extended into Palestine. There they would also avoid the risk of falling under the control of the princes of Canaan. In short, despite its obvious disadvantages, the newly settled Palestinian frontier probably offered better prospects than any alternative.

If I am correct up to this point in this admittedly speculative reconstruction,[2] it would appear that the refugees provided early Israel with a vital ingredient that the peasant settlers from Canaan were not nearly as likely to provide—namely, a compelling myth capable of forging a strong sense of collective national identity and destiny. This myth gave the members of the new society a powerful motivation—beyond mere economic self-interest—for resisting the efforts of Canaanite elites to bring the new highland settlements under their political control once these settlements became more prosperous and productive. Thus, the Exodus people, the Levites, and their faith appear to have made a contribution to Israel's early survival and later brief success that was out of all proportion to their numbers in the population. In a fully nuanced ecological-evolutionary model of the early development of ancient Israel, therefore, ideology—while not the prime mover or *deus ex machina*, as some would have it—obviously played an important part.

Before we leave the Exodus people and their hypothesized role in early Israel, there is one other matter that merits comment—namely, the question of whether a group of ex-slaves would be capable of doing all that is attributed to

---

2. Although this reconstruction of the role of the Exodus people is speculative, it is not without precedent. On the contrary, I am following here the basic outlines of an analysis developed by both Mendenhall and Gottwald.

them here. In most western minds today, the term "slaves" conjures up the image of a badly demoralized, downtrodden, and uneducated group of people. This image is based largely on the early modern forms of slavery that developed in the New World. But even in the New World, and to a much greater extent in many other agrarian societies in which slavery was practiced, some slaves occupied a very privileged status. The Janissaries in the Ottoman Empire are a classic example. In many agrarian societies of the preindustrial past, some slaves were well-educated people, and if the biblical accounts of Joseph in Egypt, and of Moses later, have any basis in fact, the society from which the Exodus people fled was just such a society. Thus, it is not as unreasonable as it may at first seem to suppose that at least some of the Exodus people had enjoyed significant educational advantages in Egypt and were more inclined by training and experience to become religious leaders than to become subsistence farmers. In short, their experience in Egypt may well have prepared them for the role they were to assume in Israel.

A Concluding Note

Marvin Harris, the noted and controversial anthropologist, long insisted (e.g., 1968, 1979) that theories should define research strategies. In particular, theories should establish priorities for researchers, suggesting where they should begin to look for answers to the problems confronting them. This does not mean that researchers should force facts to fit some preconceived pattern. Rather, it means that research should not be conducted like blind man's bluff on a hit-and-miss basis; and, equally important, solutions should not be accepted as final or definitive when fundamental questions posed by relevant theories have not been explored and when all the relevant data have not been taken adequately into account.

For those who subscribe to ecological-evolutionary theory, this means that one should not attempt to draw conclusions about a specific society and its development unless and until one has examined fully the impact of the society's environment, its sociocultural heritage, our species' genetic heritage, and the interplay of all of these factors on one another. It also means that one should be skeptical of explanations that focus on ideological and social organizational variables to the neglect of these even more basic factors.

When these principles are applied to the study of ancient Israel, it would appear that new insights and understandings can be gained. Elements that have not seemed of great importance to most biblical scholars, such as the time and place of Israel's origin, seem, in the light of ecological-evolutionary theory and relevant comparative research, to be extremely important. Similarly, other elements, such as the transformation of Israel under David and Solomon, or the peculiar status of the Levites in the premonarchic period, and even the survival of certain religious traditions for more than 3,000 years, become more meaningful. In short, armed with a good theory, one may sometimes discover things that are otherwise overlooked or underestimated.

I do not want to claim too much for the present attempt to explain ancient Israel's origin and certain aspects of its subsequent development, but neither do I want to claim too little. Like any other model, the model of Israel's origin and subsequent development summarized above has to be tested over and over again against all available evidence—archaeological, literary-historical, and sociological. But the latter should also include the evidence of comparative research— studies of other societies that have, in certain key respects, resembled Israel at various stages of its development. It follows that, in evaluating the relative merits of this and competing models, we should take into account all that we know about other agrarian societies and especially what we know about new societies that have been established from time to time by small farmers moving into and occupying previously undeveloped or underdeveloped regions on the frontiers of agrarian societies, beyond the reach of traditional authorities.

As one who believes that societies that share similar basic attributes and are exposed to similar basic external forces tend to develop in a similar manner, I also believe that models of the development of individual societies that are based on, and grounded in, a broader theory of societal development are preferable to ones that are not. This does not mean, of course, that such models are preferable even when they fly in the face of relevant evidence. Nor does it mean that such models can explain all the varied twists and turns of any given society's history and development. It does mean, however, that a model grounded in a general theory that itself enjoys substantial empirical support from varied sources cannot lightly be brushed aside when it conforms to existing evidence as well as, or better than, alternative models, especially ones that have been fashioned to fit the facts of a single specific case.

How well the model of early Israel developed here will stand up to close scrutiny by biblical scholars remains to be seen. Only a few precincts have been heard from as yet, though I find these early returns encouraging. In any case, regardless of the ultimate fate of this particular model, I believe that tests in which a model based on principles derived from a general theory developed in one discipline competes with models constructed by specialists in another discipline provide one of the sternest assessments to which any theory can be subjected. If such a model is able to advance, in any significant way, our understanding of the data and causal processes involved, there would seem to be reason to believe that the general theory on which the model is based is not entirely without merit.

Excursus: A Related Development

To my surprise and pleasure, I have learned in recent years that two competing groups of New Testament scholars—The Context Group and the Jesus Seminar—have both found merit in certain aspects of ecological-evolutionary theory, especially the model of agrarian societies developed in *Power and Privilege* and in *Human Societies.* I first became aware of this while reading reviews of the work of

John Dominic Crossan, a leader in recent efforts to understand the historical Jesus. Through Crossan's work I became aware of the Jesus Seminar, of which he is a leading member, and this, in turn, led me to an awareness of The Context Group, a group of scholars who seek to apply the perspectives of the social sciences to the understanding of the New Testament.

In describing its aims and activities, the website of The Context Group states, "Perhaps the social-scientific perspective that has spread most broadly is the so-called Lenski-Kautsky model of agrarian societies. Combining the perspectives of sociologist Gerhard Lenski and [political scientist] John Kautsky, this schema describes the economic and social stratification of the Roman Empire along with its dependencies and provinces such as Galilee and Judea. . . . John Dominic Crossan popularized the model citing it in his influential 1998 work, *The Birth of Christianity.* But he was hardly the only scholar, much less the first, to do so."

In a similar vein, Jerome H. Nagrey has written, "Many recent scholars have begun to use the work of Gerhard Lenski as a useful tool for gaining a sense of the radical stratification of the world of antiquity. The part of Lenski's work pertinent to this study [of St. Paul and St. Luke] is the [model] of advanced agrarian societies, which adequately describes at a macro level the Roman empire of the time of Paul and Luke."

Needless to say, not all New Testament scholars take such a positive view of my model of agrarian societies. In fact, as in the field of Hebrew bible or Old Testament studies, many reject completely any effort to apply social science methods or theories to biblical analysis and interpretation. For such scholars, ecological-evolutionary theory is no better and no worse than any other theory coming out of the social sciences. It is simply irrelevant.

Despite this, I am encouraged by the response of scholars such as Crossan, Nagrey, and others. When scholars trained in disciplines in which I have absolutely no expertise find merit in some of the important elements of ecological-evolutionary theory, it gives me somewhat greater confidence that the theory as a whole has merit. But the final word has yet to be written, and a considerable measure of caution is certainly appropriate.

9

THE RISE OF THE WEST

The rise of western European societies in recent centuries has been one of the more surprising developments in human history. As recently as the fourteenth or fifteenth century, almost no one anticipated the degree of political, economic, and cultural dominance that these societies would come to enjoy on the world scene.

If the case of ancient Israel tests ecological-evolutionary theory's ability to contribute to our understanding of a society far removed in almost every way from the modern world and far outside the area of interest and concern of most contemporary sociologists, the rise of the West offers a different kind of challenge. It is the challenge of a problem much closer to home and one that has long been of interest to sociologists and others. It is also a problem of relevance for policymakers. Hence, the question: Is there anything that ecological-evolutionary theory can contribute to our understanding of a problem such as this?

Historical Perspective

Following the collapse of Roman rule early in the fifth century, western Europe entered a period that historians long referred to as "the dark ages." For the next thousand years, the societies of western Europe were small, weak, and backward compared to the great empires and civilizations of Asia and the Middle East: China, Byzantium, Persia, and the Ummayad and Abbasid Empires, for example.

During this period, Europe was so weak that much of it was overrun by a succession of invaders: the Moors in Spain and southern France, the Arabs in the Mediterranean (Sicily, Malta, Crete, Cyprus), the Avars and the Mongols in Russia and much of eastern Europe, and the Turks in southeastern and central Europe.

These invaders controlled large portions of Europe for centuries before they were finally expelled; and while it is true that most of western Europe was never conquered and that western Europeans even mounted attacks against the Muslims and Byzantines in the eastern Mediterranean during the Crusades, these attacks were eventually repulsed in a manner that afforded no hint of what the political future held in store.

A similar picture emerges when we compare western European societies of this period with those of Asia and the Middle East in *economic* terms: While western Europe's disadvantage in this respect may have been somewhat less pronounced than that in terms of military power, comparisons were hardly flattering. Early European visitors to the great urban centers and to the courts of rulers of the larger and more powerful societies of Asia and the Middle East were generally awed by the wealth they encountered. Once again, throughout most of the period from the fifth to the fifteenth centuries it would have been all but impossible to predict what lay ahead.

In contrast, by the early decades of the twentieth century several western European societies had created empires that spanned the globe. The proud assertion that "the sun never sets on the British Empire" was no empty boast: It was a fact. And while the empires created by the French, Germans, Spanish, Portuguese, Dutch, and Belgians were not as large or far flung as the British Empire eventually became, Europeans and their overseas settlements in the New World and Oceania occupied more than three-quarters of the earth's land surface on the eve of World War II. Five centuries earlier, these societies controlled no more than 5 percent.

This phenomenal growth in power, and the corresponding growth in wealth and cultural influence that these societies experienced, poses a striking challenge for sociological theory and theorists: How can these developments be explained? How can one explain the remarkable rise of western European societies from their position of relative disadvantage to their position of unprecedented global power, wealth, and influence? Was this the work of Divine Providence or manifest destiny? Alternatively, was it, perhaps, the result of the Protestant Ethic? Or was it all simply due to chance?

Some Recent Explanations

Over the years sociologists and historians have offered various explanations of this remarkable and seemingly improbable sequence of events; one could write volumes just on the history of such efforts. For present purposes, however, it may suffice to consider just four of the more highly regarded and widely acclaimed efforts of recent years. As will become evident, these explanations, though written by highly knowledgeable authors with widely varying points of view, all ignore, neglect, or minimize one element in the causal process that seems obvious and of extraordinary importance to anyone who approaches the historical record from the perspective of ecological-evolutionary theory.

Few sociologists of the last century enjoyed greater renown in their lifetime than did Talcott Parsons. Late in his career, Parsons decided to join the company of those who have sought to explain western Europe's rise. In a pair of volumes entitled *Societies: Evolutionary and Comparative Perspectives* and *The System of Modern Societies,* Parsons argued that the primary cause of societal development, or lack thereof, lies in the area of religious beliefs and values. Related to this, he attached great importance to legal and moral codes, which he believed were more important than the material interests of people. In his analysis of the process of societal modernization, as in most of his other writings, Parsons drew heavily on ideas developed earlier by Max Weber.

In explaining the evolution of modern western societies, Parsons (1966: ch. 6) argued that the influence of ancient Israel and Greece was critical. Parsons referred to them as "seed-bed societies," saying that while they were not very important in their own day, they have been of "the highest significance" for the subsequent development of modern western societies. Each helped to lay the foundation for a universalistic moral order, which, for Parsons, was the key to the extraordinary success of western societies.

Another notable effort in recent years to explain the rise of the West is found in the work of Immanuel Wallerstein. Building on ideas developed by Lenin and amplified in the 1960s by social scientists in Latin America, Wallerstein explained the rise of the West as a product of the emergence and expansion of a system of international capitalism that has enabled western societies to exploit the peoples and resources, first, of eastern Europe and, then, of more and more of the rest of the world.

In much of Wallerstein's (1974, 1979) writing, descriptive details overwhelm the theoretical analysis. Overall, however, it is clear that Wallerstein's analysis, like Parsons's, is guided by a general theory. But where Parsons's theory all but ignores the role of intersocietal struggles for power and for control of resources, Wallerstein's focuses on them, which is one of its strengths. Unfortunately, however, Wallerstein, like Marx a century earlier, comes close to portraying societal development in the modern world as a zero-sum game, with the gains of western societies being achievable only at the expense of the rest of the world. The role of technological advances in expanding the gross world product, and the implications of this expansion, are largely ignored.

Reacting against Wallerstein's neo-Marxist explanation, one of his former students, Daniel Chirot, developed a neo-Weberian explanation. Chirot (1985: 181) argued that the key to the success of the West lies in its early rationalization of law and religion and in the protection that western European governments provided towns and their fragile early economies. These developments laid a foundation for the emergence of capitalism and for the subsequent emergence of modern industrialism.

Chirot argued that European geography was also a facilitating factor and had, in a variety of ways, enabled Europeans to accumulate a greater degree of wealth than had been possible elsewhere. In part of his analysis, when writing of changes in "the arable land/human ratio," Chirot (1985: 182–183) adopted an ecological-evolutionary perspective, and came closer than either Parsons or Wallerstein to recognizing the influence of a development that may well have been the most important of all in the rise of the West—namely, the discovery and conquest of the New World (see below). Regrettably, however, Chirot's idealistic bias and his eagerness to vindicate Weber diverted him from consideration of the broader ramifications of the geographic and demographic factors.

The most ambitious and widely acclaimed effort to explain the rise of the West has probably been that of William H. McNeill, the noted historian and former president of the American Historical Association. In an 800-page volume entitled *The Rise of the West: A History of the Human Community,* McNeill traced the development of human civilization from its earliest beginnings in the Middle East down to the middle of the twentieth century. In contrast to most earlier efforts by historians and others, McNeill rejected the conventional Eurocentric perspective and adopted a global perspective. McNeill's work challenged the views of earlier writers who had sought to explain the rise and fall of civilizations as the product of internal forces and processes within societies. For McNeill, external forces, especially the processes of intersocietal cultural diffusion, were far more important.

Despite McNeill's impressive achievement, *The Rise of the West* is more a work of description than of explanation. Moreover, where there is explanation, it tends to be particularistic; except for his recurring attention to the role of cultural diffusion, there is no effort to identify underlying general influences (i.e., forces, constraints, etc.) affecting the developmental process.

In this respect, McNeill stands in the classic tradition of historians, the vast majority of whom continue to reject efforts to explain individual events and processes in the light of general theory. This is justified on the grounds that every historical event and every historical process, viewed in its totality, is unique and, therefore, can be explained only in terms of some unique constellation of causes.

While true, this is not the whole truth. Although every historical event and process is necessarily unique, many of the same forces impinge on various sets of them, and it is this fact that makes general theories and the causal explanations based on them not only possible but useful.

"The Greatest Event Since the Creation of the World, Excluding the Incarnation and Death of Him Who Created It"

For those of us who live today, it is all but impossible to view the world through sixteenth-century eyes. Too much has changed, and there are too many things that we either overlook or mistakenly take for granted. We can, however, learn much from accounts written by those who lived at the time, and while we cannot take these accounts at face value, they can enhance our appreciation of certain important aspects of the West's rise to power and affluence that we might otherwise overlook.

Consider, for example, the judgment of the early Spanish historian, or chronicler, Francisco Lopez de Gomara. Writing in the middle of the sixteenth century, he described Columbus's discovery of the New World as "the greatest event since the creation of the world, excluding [only] the incarnation and death of him who created it" (cited in Eliot, 1970: 10).

Even when we make allowance for the hyperbole in this assertion, it is clear that Lopez de Gomara, and those for whom he wrote, regarded the discovery of the New World as an event of extraordinary importance. And this is not surprising. Already by the middle of the sixteenth century, when Lopez de Gomara was writing, the flood of gold and silver pouring in from the Americas had had a profound impact on Spanish society. And it was not Spain alone that was affected: Thanks to trade and commerce, and thanks also to piracy, all of western Europe felt the impact.

To appreciate the impact of this flood of precious metals, one needs to consider a few statistics. For example, between 1500 and 1650, 180 tons of gold and 16,000 tons of silver arrived in Spain according to the records of the Spanish government (Braudel, 1973: 355). In addition, large amounts of gold and silver entered Europe through other channels: English pirates seized substantial quantities and countless tons arrived illegally in Spain. By one account, New World production of precious metals during this period was ten times that of the rest of the world combined (Crow, 1980: 267–273). Small wonder that Lopez de Gomara and his contemporaries were awed by the consequences of the discovery of the New World!

The enormous infusion of gold and silver into the economies of western Europe obviously meant a tremendous increase in the wealth of western European societies. But, important as that was, it was not as important as the huge increase in Europe's money supply that resulted. Between the sixteenth and eighteenth centuries, it is estimated, the stock of precious metals for the world as a whole increased fifteen-fold (Braudel, 1973: 350), indicating that the rate of increase in western Europe was far more spectacular.

This rapid growth in money supply set in motion a process of economic and political change that still continues. As more and more money came into circulation, western Europe began to conduct more and more of its business on a monetary basis. It was no longer forced to rely on the cumbersome older and much less efficient modes of exchange, such as barter and payments in kind. The vast infusion of silver was especially important in this connection, because silver met a vital need, the need for a medium of exchange appropriate to middle-range transactions—namely, coins whose value was considerably less than that of gold coins but substantially greater than that of copper ones.

Not surprisingly, the tremendous expansion of the money supply became a powerful stimulus to trade and commerce throughout much of western Europe. As the wealth and purchasing power of elites increased, so, too, did their demand for goods and services. As a result, wealth spread to other parts of the population, especially merchants, and, in time, its impact rippled through much of society. Even the lower classes benefited as opportunities for employment increased.

Inflation was another important early result of the growth in money supply. This was a natural consequence of the great increase in the money supply and the much more limited increase in the production of goods. Prices doubled, tripled, even quadrupled within a century, and as is always the case when this happens, some prospered while others were hurt. In general, those with fixed incomes, especially the landed aristocracy, were hurt, while merchants and entrepreneurs who could adjust prices in response to the declining value of money tended to benefit. This meant that far more of the economic resources of western European societies wound up in the hands of people who were oriented toward economic innovation and change—a development the importance of which is difficult to exaggerate. As R. H. Tawney (1926: 117) once wrote, the rise in prices in the sixteenth century was simultaneously a stimulant to feverish enterprise and an acid dissolving many traditional relationships.

Finally, with the increasing monetization of economic transactions, merchants found it easier to calculate their costs, revenues, and profits (or losses) in a precise way. Thus, business records became increasingly systematic, techniques of bookkeeping were gradually improved, and a foundation was laid for the development of modern systems of accounting. In short, the monetization of the economies of western Europe and the new economic calculus it made possible provided the critical technical underpinning for a new type of economic system that Weber (1981: 86–91) would later refer to as modern rational capitalism, one of the most powerful instruments of economic growth and expansion ever devised (see also Sombart, 1967: 125–127; Schumpeter, 1950: 123).

Other Treasure

Important as they were, gold and silver were only the first of the treasures of the New World that western Europeans were able to exploit to their advantage. Over the years, the economic value and commercial possibilities of numerous other natural resources were discovered.

Furs were one of the first. Populations of fur-bearing animals had declined greatly in Europe by the time of the discovery and conquest of the Americas. In contrast, large numbers of such animals abounded in parts of the New World, especially in what is now Canada and the United States. At first, the supply of furs was limited and furs were luxury items available only to the wealthy. In time, however, as the supply increased and prices declined, markets expanded. As one historian describes it, what had been a trickle of beaver fur before 1600 became a stream by 1650 and a flood by 1700 (Davis, 1974: 174). By the end of the seventeenth century and the beginning of the eighteenth, the flood of furs had grown so great, and prices were driven so low, that the trade became unprofitable and many furs rotted or were burned to dispose of them.

Tobacco, fish, and sugar also figured prominently in the expansion of European economies from an early date (ibid.: ch. 4). As with furs, the volume of tobacco and sugar shipped to Europe became so great that prices were driven down to the point where profits all but vanished. In response, steps were taken to broaden the economic base and other products became increasingly important. These included rice, coffee, cocoa, cotton, and timber. Timber was especially important since by the seventeenth century Europe's supply was badly depleted. For western Europeans, the massive virgin forests of the New World provided a new and relatively inexpensive source of one of the most useful materials then available.

As forests were cleared, farms took their place and an ever-growing supply of food and fibers became available for export. Still later, western Europeans and North Americans were able to exploit the vast mineral wealth of the New World—coal, iron, petroleum, and natural gas, the critical resources that fueled the Industrial Revolution.

For those who take the time and trouble to review the history of the last five centuries, it is hard to avoid the conclusion that the discovery and conquest of the New World had a *revolutionary impact* on the economies of western European societies and on their place in the global system of societies. Control of the vast resources of the Americas transformed the economies of these societies from ones in which, as in most traditional agrarian societies, scarcity and high prices were the norm to ones in which sufficiency became increasingly common and abundance and even overabundance were not unknown. In addition, this new wealth provided western European societies with the economic and other resources needed to become the dominant players in the international arena.

Equations 3 and 4 Revisited

When we think of the discovery and conquest of the New World in terms of our respecified versions of the equations of Malthus and Sumner (see Equations 3 and 4 in Chapter 4), we see even more clearly how important these events were. Thanks to the discovery and conquest, western European societies experienced a fantastic increase in the resources under their control. The land mass of the New World is *more than thirty times* that of western Europe, and it is safe to say that the value of the natural resources of the Americas exceeded the value of the natural resources then available to western Europeans by at least as much. In fact, with respect to several important resources the ratio was almost certainly much greater than thirty to one. As we have noted, by the end of the fifteenth century western Europe had already consumed many of its own key resources, such as timber, with which it had once been endowed, and it had never been well endowed in terms of others, such as gold and silver. In addition, most of the land that was suitable for cultivation was already under cultivation.

One does not need to be a mathematician to appreciate the enormous importance of a thirty-fold increase in one of the terms on the right-hand side of Equations 3 and 4—or even a ten- or twenty-fold increase. If other things held constant, this would mean a ten-, twenty-, or thirty-fold increase in productivity and in the size of the economic surpluses of western European societies.

Other things, of course, did not remain constant. Populations grew, technologies advanced, and capital, both financial and human, increased. These developments, it should be noted, were themselves largely in response to the acquisition of new resources and the increased productivity of these societies and their overseas extensions. While population growth had a negative impact on the size of surpluses, technological advance and the growth of capital reinforced the impact of the new resources to a degree that more than offset the effect of population growth. Thus, the acquisition of the vast resources of the Americas had a *multiplier effect*, with these derivative effects serving, in balance, to magnify the impact of the resources themselves.

One other point should be noted. As we have seen, the vast resources of the New World did not all become immediately available to western Europeans. On the contrary, the process of discovery and exploitation extended over centuries, and still goes on. Deposits of the most valuable resources by modern standards—coal, iron ore, petroleum, and natural gas, for example—were not even discovered, and technologies for their efficient extraction and utilization were not developed, until the nineteenth and twentieth centuries. This is, of course, what we might expect in view of the fact that the rise of the West itself extended over centuries.

Looking at the history of the last five centuries from the standpoint of our respecified versions of the equations of Malthus and Sumner, we find it hard to avoid the conclusion that *the discovery and conquest of the New World provided a small group of otherwise relatively undistinguished societies in western Europe with a wealth of new resources, without which their rise to power and wealth would have been most improbable.* Thus, ironically, had Christopher Columbus been correct in his belief that Europe was separated from Asia only by open seas, the rise of the West would probably not have occurred.

A Mental Experiment

To appreciate fully the critical importance of the discovery and conquest of the New World for the economic and political development of western Europe, one needs to ask what difference it would have made if the Chinese, rather than western Europeans, had gotten to the New World first and won control of its vast resources. Would scholars today be pondering the rise of the West? Or would they, instead, be debating the causes of the rise of the East?

This question is not as fanciful as it may seem. China was an advanced agrarian society in the fifteenth century. Moreover, Chinese sailors and merchants had traveled as far as the east coast of Africa, and while the Chinese never developed the ships and navigational tools required for trans-Pacific travel, marine technology in China was not far from that level of development. And if the Chinese had reached the New World, they would not have had great difficulty in conquering it.

So what would have happened to western Europe if the Chinese had arrived first and won control of the vast untapped treasure house of resources that was the New World? Without the centuries-long flow of gold, silver, timber, cotton, food-stuffs, and other products, how would Europe have fared? Would the economic surplus have increased nearly as rapidly as it did? And would there have been the expanding wealth of economic opportunities that ensured the survival and spread of the Protestant work ethic once the enthusiasm, dedication, and commitment of the first generations of Protestants were replaced by the more routinized and conventional adherence of later generations? Would the resources have been available to challenge potential inventors and innovators, those whose work became so important later in the early stages of the Industrial Revolution? *Is it not even probable that the relative positions of western Europe and eastern Asia in recent centuries would have been reversed?*

The per capita benefits to China of the discovery and conquest of the New World would, of course, have been considerably less than the per capita benefits to western Europe, since China had a population at least three times larger than that of western Europe at the end of the fifteenth century. One suspects, therefore, that the chief beneficiaries of a Chinese discovery and conquest would have been those Chinese who settled the New World rather than their countrymen who remained behind.

To some extent, a similar pattern developed even in the case of the Europeans. By the late nineteenth or early twentieth century, those who had migrated to North America enjoyed a standard of living surpassing that of their former countrymen who remained behind in Europe—and for the same reason. In other words, the ratio of population to resources was more favorable in North America than in western Europe. This difference in levels of affluence would probably have been even greater had Europe not for so long enjoyed an enormous advantage in terms of political power and capital accumulation (both of which are essential in the development and exploitation of most natural resources). Western Europe's advantage, especially in terms of capital accumulation, enabled its societies to continue to benefit greatly from the exploitation of New World resources long after European political control had ended.

Other Factors in the Rise of the West: The Larger Model

As crucial as the conquest of the New World has been in the West's rise to power and wealth, it was, of course, not the whole story. Numerous other factors were involved, some more important than others. There is good reason to believe, however, that the influence of these other factors has been largely dependent on the discovery and conquest of the New World. In other words, some are important because they contributed to the discovery and conquest of the New World while others are important because they enabled western Europeans to use the new re-sources under their control in ways that enhanced their power and wealth. Thus, had the New World not existed, or had some Asian society discovered and con-quered it, these other factors either would have been irrelevant or, at best, would have contributed only modestly to the benefit of western societies. In short, if western Europeans had not gained control of the New World and its wealth of resources, there would have been no "rise of the West" to explain.

But the New World was there and western Europeans were the ones who discovered and conquered it. Thus, these other factors and their place in the causal process need to be considered if we are to gain an adequate understanding of this enormously important sequence of events. What is needed, then, is a model of relationships among at least the more important elements in the causal chain.

Technology's Role

If the discovery and conquest of the New World was as critical to the rise of the West as I have suggested, one of the questions that ecological-evolutionary theory raises is why this happened *when and where* it did. Why, for example, did the discovery and conquest of the New World elude the Romans, whose vast imperial ambitions carried them well beyond the traditional frontiers of civilization? And why were the merchants of Asia and the Middle East not the ones to discover the New World? In brief, what new developments occurred during the fifteenth cen-tury that allowed western Europeans of this period to achieve what their predeces-sors and their Asian and Middle Eastern rivals were unable to achieve?

Francis Bacon, the late sixteenth- and early seventeenth-century philoso-pher and statesman, provided one of the better answers to this question. He said that three inventions—the mariner's compass, the printing press, and gunpow-der—"had changed the whole face and state of things throughout the world" (cited in Mann, 1986: 445). And he was right: These inventions laid the founda-tion for a vast social and cultural revolution. Already in Bacon's day, the world was a very different place than it had been just a century and a half earlier; the rise of the West was already under way.

Ironically, Bacon had a far better grasp of the causes of this revolutionary process than many scholars today. Writing under the continuing spell of Weber and Marx, the latter all too often focus on developments in ideology and social organization, to the neglect of technological innovation, in their search for expla-nations of the West's extraordinary transformation. Yet, as a number of historians have noted, the advances in technology that Bacon identified were critical, espe-cially in the early stages of the West's rise. Each extended the limits of the possible, and western Europeans were not slow to take advantage of the new opportunities they afforded.

Before the introduction of the compass in Europe late in the twelfth cen-tury, navigation beyond sight of land was so hazardous that it was undertaken only for short distances or over short and familiar routes, as in crossing the English Channel or the Mediterranean Sea. Acquisition of the compass was followed over the next several centuries by a series of important advances in the technology of ship-building. These included the invention of the stern rudder (which replaced steering oars attached to the sides of ships), the construction of larger ships with multiple masts, the substitution of several smaller sails for a single large sail on each mast, and a reduction in the width of ships relative to their length (McNeill, 1963: 570–571). All of these innovations made ships more responsive, more manageable, and, therefore, safer on stormy seas.

With improved ships at their command and with compasses to aid them, western European sailors increasingly ventured out into open seas for longer periods. During the fifteenth century they undertook a series of extended voyages in an effort to find a new trade route to India and China—a route that would enable them to bypass the merchants of the Middle East. Instead, as we know, their efforts led to the startling discovery of a vast new world whose very existence had previously been unknown.

In the conquest of the New World, and in the subsequent exploitation of its resources, the other two inventions noted by Bacon also proved important. While neither was a factor in the voyages of discovery, both were important in other ways. Although it now appears that gunpowder was less important in the conquest than the diseases that Europeans brought with them (McNeill, 1976; Diamond, 1997), it was not unimportant. The early European conquistadors and settlers were far outnumbered by native Americans and would have been hard put to win and maintain control of such vast territories if they had been armed only with traditional weapons. Later, as commercial interests and imperial ambitions brought Europeans to Asia and Africa, areas where European diseases were of little or no importance militarily, gunpowder was extremely important.

The printing press was important in a very different way and has been important at almost every stage of the West's rise to wealth and power. Above all, it has been a powerful agent of change, amplifying and extending in dozens of ways the impact of other forces that were cracking open the tough shell of tradition in the western world (see, e.g., Eisenstein, 1979). In the sixteenth century, the printing press was critical to the success of the Protestant reformers' challenge to established ecclesiastical authority (Dickens, 1966). This, in turn, greatly facilitated the spread of literacy, which the reformers strongly advocated (e.g., Herman, 2001: 22–24). Later, in the eighteenth, nineteenth, and twentieth centuries, the printing press took on greatly added importance by making possible the rapid dissemination of new technologies in agriculture and industry and by creating the necessary foundation for the rise and spread of modern science.

In a preliminary way, one can sum up much of technology's contribution to the rise of the West in two propositions. First, two very specific sets of technological innovations, the invention and subsequent refinements of the compass and the various advances in the technology of ship-building, were essential preconditions to, and catalytic agents for, the discovery and conquest of the New World.

Prior to these advances, sustained and effective interaction between our planet's two hemispheres was impossible. Second, a succession of later technological advances (i.e., the advances that were the basis of the Industrial Revolution) enabled western European societies to increase enormously the magnitude of the benefits they were able to extract from the New World's vast store of untapped resources. Without these later advances, the value of the conquest would have been far, far less than it was. It is no exaggeration to say that the West would not have benefited from the discovery of the New World nearly as greatly as it did were it not for this continuing and expanding stream of technological innovations.

The Protestant Ethic and the Spirit of Capitalism

What, then, are we to say about the role of the much-heralded Protestant Ethic in the rise of the West? What part did it play?

For many sociologists, Max Weber's essay on the Protestant Ethic and the spirit of capitalism provides the definitive explanation not simply of the rise of the West but also of the emergence of modern societies and the modern era. Weber argued that the Protestant Ethic was chiefly responsible for the new spirit of rational capitalism, which he saw as the critical and distinctive feature of western societies and the modern era.

Viewed from the perspective of ecological-evolutionary theory, however, one is inclined to be skeptical that new theological doctrines, by themselves, can have such enormous impact.[1] At a minimum, one would expect other factors to be involved. For example, if our most general model of the determinants of the characteristics of individual societies (see Figure 4.2, p. 76) is correct, one would expect to find prior or concomitant changes of a significant nature in social organization, technology, demography, and/or the biophysical and sociocultural environments. And, if we go on to consider the implications of Equation 3, our attention is focused more narrowly on the possibility of significant changes in the relation of environmental resources and technology to population size.

Viewed from this perspective, the role of the Protestant Ethic appears in a rather different light from that suggested by Weberians and neo-Weberians. Instead of being the effective cause of the modern era, as it has so often been made to appear, it becomes *at best* one among a number of necessary causes—and, perhaps, not even that.

I believe that a very strong case can be made for the thesis that the Protestant Ethic spread as successfully as it did in the western world, and survived as

---

1. It should be noted that I am not arguing here that Weber's essay on the Protestant Ethic and the spirit of capitalism represents the entirety of his contribution to our understanding of the rise of the West. Clearly, it is not. I am arguing, however, that Weber never properly amended his basic thesis in the way that seems to be required, and, as a result, many sociologists today have a mistaken and exaggerated view of the role of the Protestant Ethic in the rise of the West.

long as it has, only because the vast wealth of the Americas enormously strengthened the previously feeble linkage between hard work, frugality, and integrity on the one hand and worldly success on the other. Had sociologists been around to measure these relationships in the sixteenth, seventeenth, and eighteenth centuries, they would have found substantial increases over those obtained in earlier centuries, even if there had been no Protestant Reformation. Moreover, these increases would have been great enough for the masses of ordinary people to become conscious of the change and, therefore, to be influenced in terms of their behavior. Thus, I believe that a good case can be made for the thesis that the discovery and conquest of the New World had the effect of *validating the Protestant Ethic* in a way that would not have been possible in earlier centuries—and in a way that was not possible in China, India, or other traditional agrarian societies of the period. Had Protestantism not supplied a new work ethic,[2] it is likely that one would have emerged in some other guise as people became increasingly aware of the new economic opportunities created by the tremendous flow of wealth from the New World.

Toward an Ecological-Evolutionary Model of the Rise of the West

Creating a model of the West's rise to wealth and power is a daunting task and one that is not likely to be completed any time soon. This does not mean, however, that we should not be working at it. Moreover, if the preceding analysis has any merit, many of the major elements of such a model can already be specified.

As Figure 9.1 indicates, the basic causal sequence appears to have been initiated by (1) advances in the technologies of navigation and water transportation beginning late in the twelfth century, which stimulated the many voyages of exploration in the fifteenth century and made the discovery of the New World possible, and (2) subsequent advances in military technology, in combination with the tremendous impact of diseases brought to the Americas by Europeans, which made the conquest of these two vast continents possible; (3) this, in turn, provided western European societies with a wealth of new resources that (4) vastly increased the money supply, stimulated trade and commerce, led to the rapid expansion of markets, and strengthened the merchant class while weakening the old landed aristocracy, thus (5) laying a foundation for revolutionary advances in agricultural and industrial technology in the eighteenth, nineteenth, and twentieth centuries, which (6), in combination with the wealth of resources controlled by western societies, became the basis of their vastly expanded power, prestige, and wealth in the late nineteenth and twentieth centuries.[3]

---

2. In this connection, one is reminded of R. H. Tawney's thesis that the Protestant Ethic itself was a product of changes that were already under way in western Europe.

3. Obviously, many factors beside those indicated in this paragraph or in Figure 9.1 have contributed to the rise of the West. A comprehensive model of the total process is the last thing that

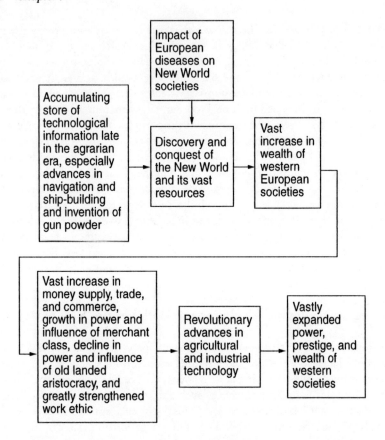

Figure 9.1 Ecological-evolutionary model of the basic determinants of the rise of the West

In this process, *the discovery and conquest of the New World appears to have been the critical development, providing as it did the enormous surge of new resources on which all of the more important later developments depended.* For the first time in the whole of the agrarian era, wealth increased far more rapidly than population over a vast territory and for an extended period, thus leading to extraordinarily

---

should be attempted at this point. My aim here is much more modest, but more appropriate, I believe, under the circumstances. I simply want to draw attention to certain elements in the process that are too often overlooked or underestimated, but appear to have been critical.

rapid growth in the economic surpluses of a small set of societies.[4] Because of this, all kinds of new developments occurred, including the tremendous growth in power and influence of the societies in western Europe.

It should be emphasized, however, that while the discovery and conquest of the New World were critical in the rise of the West, they were not some kind of uncaused source of all that followed. Rather, as Figure 9.1 indicates, the discovery and conquest of the New World would not have happened were it not for the significant advances in the technologies of navigation and ship-building that made trans-Atlantic shipping *on a sustained basis* reasonably safe and profitable, and had not advances in military technology and the scourge of European diseases made the conquest possible.

Figure 9.1 is not meant to be an exhaustive or comprehensive model of the causes of the West's dramatic rise to power and influence, and the countless inter-relations among those causes. We are still far from that point in our understanding of all that was involved.

What can be done, however, and what I have attempted here, is the identification of the most important of the causes and the specification of the more important relations among them. Obviously, the model is incomplete, and it may be flawed in other ways as well. New elements will have to be added and existing ones may have to be respecified. Yet despite its limitations and shortcomings, the model has, I believe, two redeeming features. First, it gives to the discovery and conquest of the New World the importance it deserves. And, second, the model, by virtue of its formal nature (i.e., the unambiguous specification of variables and their interrelations), stands as a challenge to those who can improve upon it. In short, it could provide a foundation for more sustained and cumulative attacks on a problem of enormous interest and importance.

Policy Implications

Before we turn to other matters, it may be well to note the relevance of certain aspects of the preceding analysis for present-day public policy. In recent years, policymakers around the world (except in China) have largely ignored the influence of population growth on standards of living and quality of life. Many, for ideological reasons, fight efforts to limit population growth, arguing—like the late Julian Simon (1981)—that since population growth has been accompanied by rising standards of living in the past we can assume that this will continue to be

---

4. The nearest thing to this that occurred in agrarian societies of the past was the relatively brief period that sometimes followed in the wake of natural disasters such as plagues and famines (as in Europe after the great plagues of the fourteenth century), when societies and their economies were recovering and overpopulation and its attendant evils were temporarily not a problem.

true in the future.[5] Others argue that salvation lies in reliance on market mechanisms and a market economy; and still others (Catholics and Muslims), that population control is contrary to the will of God.

What our policymakers and their supporters fail to recognize is that the experience of the last five centuries cannot be used as a guide to policymaking in today's world or in the years ahead. Certain elements that have been critical to the successes of western nations in recent centuries can never be repeated. No society, or set of societies, is likely ever again to gain control over such vast resources at so little cost. The only unexploited continent remaining is Antarctica, and, while it contains considerable mineral wealth, the costs of extraction will be enormous, and *net* profits of the undertaking will not begin to compare with those derived from the Americas. Underseas mineral deposits are another largely untapped resource, but the technology required to extract them profitably has yet to be developed. Moreover, even when it is developed, the benefits will almost certainly be divided among a much larger number of societies than were the resources of the Americas, thus greatly reducing the impact. Finally, there are the resources of the moon and other planets, but the technology needed for their profitable exploitation lies far in the future. In short, policymakers should not base their plans for the future on mindless extrapolations of economic growth patterns of the past; nor should they assume that correlations that held in the past will necessarily hold in the future. The experience of the last five centuries is not likely soon to be repeated.

Although easy gains now seem a thing of the past, substantial improvements in standards of living will still be possible. To achieve this, however, public policies will have to focus on the four major terms on the right-hand side of Equation 4: resources, technology, capital, and population. In other words, societies will have to develop policies that promote advances in resources and technology, growth of economic and human capital, and restraints on population growth. In poorer countries, the creation of effective programs of contraception and abortion have become imperative if gains in productivity and jobs are not to be more than offset by the increased number of desperate people seeking jobs and the vital necessities of life; in more affluent societies, the primary need today is for effective controls on immigration, if the swelling flood of immigrants from poorer nations is not to wipe out all of the potential benefits of increased productivity and declining birth rates. Those who fail to understand the exceptional and transitory nature of the circumstances responsible for the West's extraordinary rates of economic growth in the past do a profound disservice to society when they focus on the benefits of population growth while ignoring its costs, and mistake a *correlate* of the West's successes with its cause.

Finally, societies and their members must learn to look with greater skepticism at the seductive programs of ideologues, on both the left and the right. Prom-

---

5. Simon, of course, went even further, making the bold claim that population growth has been a (or the) major force responsible for rising standards of living.

ises of salvation through ideology (e.g., by changing the consciousness of the masses, *à la* Mao and others) or through changes in social organization (e.g., by adopting market mechanisms or by expanding state ownership of the means of production) are basically mechanisms for *redistributing* wealth, not for adding to it. This is a distinction we can no longer afford to ignore.

10

TRAJECTORIES OF DEVELOPMENT AMONG SOCIETIES

(coauthored with Patrick D. Nolan)

One of the notable features of the last half-century has been the striking variability in the rates of economic growth of societies.[1] A few have enjoyed extremely rapid growth. Most have experienced more modest gains, and some have had little or no growth, or have even regressed.

This variability has been especially evident among the less developed countries (LDCs) that we once referred to as the "Third World." Both the highest rates of economic growth and most of the sharpest declines are found among these nations.

This invites the question of why some have been so much more successful than others, leading to a second and more general question: What are the basic underlying determinants of societal trajectories of development in the modern world?

Various answers have been given to this question. Theorists such as Parsons and Inkeles, following the lead of Weber, have stressed the importance of belief systems and values. World-system and dependency theorists such as Wallerstein

1. This chapter is a revised and updated version of a paper titled "Trajectories of Development: A Test of Ecological-Evolutionary Theory," published in *Social Forces*, 63 (1984): 1–23.

and Frank, drawing on the ideas of Lenin, have emphasized the workings of the capitalist world economy. Ecological-evolutionary theory, although acknowledging the influence of both of these variables, suggests that another type of variable— differences in the technological and economic heritages of societies—may be even more important.

Industrializing Agrarian and Industrializing Horticultural Societies Compared

The most distinctive feature of evolutionary theories in all of the various sciences, as noted earlier, is their emphasis on the *cumulative* nature of the process of change. Earlier developments greatly influence later ones. Thus, to attempt to understand societal change without taking into account major differences in the social and cultural heritages of the societies in question is to invite trouble, or so ecological-evolutionary theory would lead one to believe.

Applying this principle to the study of the developmental trajectories of societies in the modern era, while also taking account of the critical role of subsistence technology in the developmental process, ecological-evolutionary theory leads one to predict significant differences between those less developed societies that entered the industrial era with an agrarian heritage and those that entered with a horticultural heritage. These now-hybridized societies may be designated respectively as "industrializing agrarian" and "industrializing horticultural" societies (Lenski, 1970: ch. 15). The former are societies in which farming has traditionally involved the practice of plow agriculture; the latter, ones in which plow agriculture was absent and farmers traditionally depended on the hoe and/or digging stick.

For scholars raised in a modern urban environment, this distinction may seem of little importance. Research, however, suggests otherwise. Historically, the invention of the plow had revolutionary consequences: It enabled humans to harness the energy of animals in the task of food production, and it enabled them to control, for the first time, the spread of weeds and restore the fertility of soils by bringing within reach of the root systems of cultivated plants the nutrients that tend to sink beyond their reach, especially in semi-arid regions (Childe, 1936). All this meant larger crops, increased populations, and the possibility of an expanded economic surplus. It also meant more permanent settlements, since fields could be kept permanently under cultivation. No longer was cultivation dependent on impermanent gardens, as in the practice of horticulture (from the Latin *horti cultura*, "the cultivation of a garden").

Looking to the preindustrial past, we find that the great majority of agrarian societies became substantially larger and more complex than most horticultural societies. The Incan Empire and the West African state of Songhay were probably the largest horticultural societies ever and they had populations of no more than several million. In contrast, the Roman Empire, with its agrarian technology, appears to have had a population of 70 million at one time, and China achieved a population of several hundred million before industrialization began to make its impact felt.

These differences in size are linked to sociologically more important differences between horticultural and agrarian societies of the preindustrial past, and *many of these differences have been highly relevant to the process of societal development in the modern world.* For example, urban communities (i.e., communities in which the majority of the inhabitants are freed from the necessity of producing their own foods and fibers) were widespread in agrarian societies but rare in horticultural societies. Linked with this, occupational specialization was far more complex and other forms of specialization (e.g., organizational, communal, regional) much more highly developed in agrarian societies. In addition, most agrarian societies had a literate minority from an early date, whereas this was rare in horticultural societies. Agrarian societies usually had standardized currencies; most horticultural societies did not. Many agrarian societies had highly developed administrative bureaucracies with complex systems of record-keeping; horticultural societies generally did not.

One could easily extend this list, but it should already be clear that agrarian societies brought to the modern era many of the social and cultural resources that are essential if a society is to be competitive in the global system and able to enjoy significant economic growth and development. By comparison, horticultural societies have been badly handicapped in this regard. Because of this, and because change is a cumulative process, ecological-evolutionary theory leads one to expect *important, systematic, and predictable differences among industrializing societies.*

Thus, if ecological-evolutionary theory is correct, there should be substantial differences between industrializing agrarian and industrializing horticultural societies, with respect to both their current characteristics and their trajectories of development. As Figure 10.1 illustrates, industrializing agrarian societies were already much more developed by modern standards than were industrializing horticultural societies long before the onset of industrialization, and this difference should persist well beyond the onset of sustained contact with industrial societies despite capital transfers from industrial societies. Ecological-evolutionary theory does not, however, allow us to predict whether the gap between the trajectories of the two sets of societies will ultimately increase, decrease, or simply persist (again, see Figure 10.1), though there are reasons for expecting that *in the long run* (i.e., a century or more) the gap will decrease.

Translated into testable propositions, ecological-evolutionary theory leads one to expect significant differences between industrializing agrarian and industrializing horticultural societies with respect to (1) current levels of economic development and rates of economic growth, (2) informational resources and levels of human capital, and (3) basic demographic patterns. Each of these hypotheses can and will be tested with multiple indicators (see below).

After testing these hypotheses, we will observe the efficacy of the traditional subsistence technology variable relative to that of a measure of the same societies'

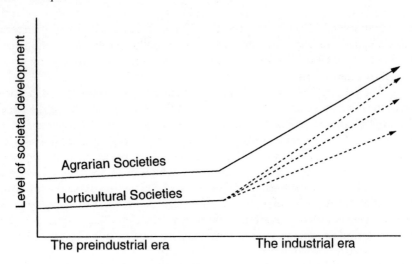

Figure 10.1 Levels and trajectories of development of industrializing agrarian and industrializing horticultural societies in the preindustrial and industrial eras

status in the global economy. In other words, we will compare the predictive power of the distinction between industrializing agrarian and industrializing horticultural societies with that of a distinction between semiperipheral and peripheral societies, as defined by proponents of world-system theory. This should *not* be considered a direct comparison of ecological-evolutionary with world-system theory, since ecological-evolutionary theory acknowledges that the developmental trajectory of societies is influenced by external forces (i.e., the sociocultural environment) as well as by internal forces. Rather, the comparison is designed to provide some idea of the *relative* strength and importance of these two sets of forces, and to indicate how much more of the variation among less developed societies can be accounted for by the inclusion of this almost universally neglected variable. Obviously, the thesis that technoeconomic heritage is important in shaping current rates and directions of development in less developed nations is strengthened if one can show that it has significant effects *independent* of those societies' status in the capitalist world system (currently a widely accepted explanation of differences among poorer nations). Finally, in the last stage of the analysis, one other possible explanation of the findings will be discussed and another tested.

Data and Methods

Fortunately, for purposes of statistical analysis, there are substantial numbers of both industrializing agrarian and industrializing horticultural societies in the world today. A few of these will be excluded from the analysis because of their very small size (e.g., Maldive Islands), their lack of real political autonomy (e.g., Lesotho), or their marginal status with respect to the independent variable (e.g., Ethiopia, Jordan, North Yemen). Taiwan was omitted because the World Bank fails to include it in its reports, and a handful of major oil-exporting nations (e.g., Venezuela, Nigeria, Indonesia) were excluded to remove the potentially biasing effect of this extraordinarily powerful "wild card" variable.[2] The classification of the societies used in the analysis is shown in the Appendix at the end of this chapter.[3]

The data used were drawn from the World Bank, as indicated in the various tables below. The classification of societies in world-system theory is derived from Snyder and Kick (1979).

Analysis of variance and dummy variable regression were used to test the strength and statistical significance of relationships. Category means, the number of cases, the strength of relationships, and the significance of differences are indicated in the tables.[4] In later stages of the analysis, zero-order and partial standardized regression coefficients were compared to determine the relative magnitudes and independence of the effects of status and heritage on the dependent variables. To make this possible, periphery and industrializing horticultural nations were coded *0* and semiperiphery and industrializing agrarian nations were coded *1*.[5] The magnitudes of the standardized regression coefficients indicate the strength of the relationships, and the signs indicate the way in which semiperiphery and industrializing agrarian nations differ from periphery and industrializing horticultural nations on the various dimensions. The partial standardized regression coefficients are indications of how much *independent* impact world-system status and technoeconomic heritage each have on the dependent variables. In a final

---

2. The presence or absence of oil within the territorial boundaries of a nation is irrelevant to our basic hypothesis concerning the importance of technoeconomic heritage, yet it obviously has a substantial effect on many of the dependent variables with which we are concerned. Moreover, since more of the oil-exporting nations fall into the category we expect to be more successful and more highly developed (i.e., industrializing agrarian societies), it is important to remove this potential source of bias that would lend support to our hypotheses.

3. Readers should note that the classification of societies into the two categories of "industrializing agrarian" and "industrializing horticultural" used in this chapter differs slightly from that used in the earlier 1984 paper and in Nolan's paper, "World-System Status, Techno-Economic Heritage, and Fertility" (1988: 9–33). Haiti was moved from the industrializing agrarian category to the industrializing horticultural category for reasons explained in Lenski and Nolan (1986), and several other societies were excluded because of either the importance of petroleum production in those societies or the absence of relevant data.

4. Significance levels in this analysis should not be interpreted as indicative of the probability that findings can be generalized to some larger universe of societies, since the data are derived from the specified universe. As Blalock (1979: 241–243) has noted, in analyses of this type, significance values indicate the probability that observed category differences could be the result of random assignment of cases to categories and, therefore, the likelihood that the observed relationships are due to chance.

5. Industrial societies (the "core nations" in world-system theory) were excluded from the analysis, and *semiperiphery* and *periphery* were defined in the manner indicated by Snyder and Kick (1979: 1110–1116).

step, this analysis is applied to the subset of nations in the sample that achieved independence after 1940.

Before turning to our findings, we should note that our selection of societies for analysis stacks the cards against our hypothesis in one very important respect. By excluding industrial societies, we are excluding a set of societies *all* of which have an agrarian heritage and all of which differ dramatically from industrializing horticultural societies with respect to all of the dependent variables we will be examining. Thus, the tests we make are extremely rigorous and the results *substantially understate* the actual strength of the relationships involved.

Initial Findings

According to our first subhypothesis, industrializing agrarian societies should differ significantly from industrializing horticultural societies in their level of economic development. As Table 10.1 shows, this is, in fact, the case: Average per capita GNP in industrializing agrarian societies is currently nearly seven times that in industrializing horticultural societies, and when the effect of outliers (i.e., atypical cases) is minimized by logging the data, more than 50 percent of the variance in per capita GNP (see R^2) among less developed societies viewed as a whole is accounted for by technoeconomic heritage alone.

In addition, it appears that in recent decades (1965–2002) per capita incomes in industrializing agrarian societies have been rising more than ten times as fast as in industrializing horticultural societies (2.3 percent/year vs. 0.2 percent). This is not something that ecological-evolutionary theory can claim to have predicted. On the contrary, one might have expected by now some erosion of the developmental advantage enjoyed by societies with an agrarian heritage.[6]

---

6. The magnitude of the advantage enjoyed by industrializing agrarian societies has varied from decade to decade, with no consistent trend, but there has been no decade for which data are available in which industrializing horticultural societies as a group have enjoyed a higher rate of economic growth than industrializing agrarian societies.

Table 10.1. Economic Development in Industrializing Agrarian and Industrializing Horticultural Societies Compared

Indicator	Technoeconomic Heritage: Agrarian (N)	Horticultural (N)	Summary Statistics
GDP/capita 2002 (in 1995 US$)	2453.9 (36)	355.9 (25)	R^2=.219 P<.001
Log GDP/capita 2002	3.2 (36)	2.5 (25)	R^2=.524 P<.001
GDP/capita growth rate 1965–2002	2.3 (36)	0.2 (28)	R^2=.317 P<.001

Data Sources: World Development Indicators 2001, and World Development Indicators Online (http://www.worldbank.org/data/).

Table 10.2. Informational Resources in Industrializing Agrarian and Industrializing Horticultural Societies Compared

Indicator	Technoeconomic Heritage: Agrarian (N)	Horticultural (N)	Summary Statistics
Adult Literacy 2002[a]	82.2 (31)	55.1 (20)	R^2=.401 P<.001
Adult Literacy 1975[b]	64.3 (34)	28.3 (22)	R^2=.467 P<.001
Enrollment Sec. Schs. 2001[c]	65.5 (37)	19.9 (13)	R^2=.516 P<.001
Enrollment Sec. Schs. 1975	35.1 (37)	9.4 (28)	R^2=.478 P<.001
Newspapers/1,000 pop. 1995	68.1 (35)	5.4 (27)	R^2=.203 P<.001
Log Newspapers/1,000 pop. 1995[d]	1.6 (36)	0.6 (27)	R^2=.517 P<.001
Computers/1,000 pop. 2002	56.2 (34)	10.6 (22)	R^2=.080 P<.035
Log Computers/1,000 pop. 2002[d]	1.5 (34)	0.8 (22)	R^2=.339 P<.001
Sci.Arts/1,000,000 pop. 1999	15.4 (39)	2.4 (27)	R^2=.090 P<.014
Log Sci.Arts/1,000,000 pop. 1999[d]	0.8 (39)	0.4 (27)	R^2=.143 P<.002

Data Source: World Development Indicators 2001, and World Development Indicators Online (http://www.worldbank.org/data).
[a]Average for years 2000–2002.
[b]Average for years 1974–1976.
[c]Average for years 2000–2001.
[d]A constant of 1 was added before logging to avoid zero values.

One of the major reasons for these differences emerges when the informational and human capital resources of the two sets of societies are compared. Measures of these resources make it clear that, as ecological-evolutionary theory leads one to expect, industrializing horticultural societies lag well behind their agrarian counterparts (see Table 10.2). Literacy rates, percentage of the school-age population enrolled in secondary schools, newspaper circulation rates, frequency of computers, and rates of publication of scientific articles all show substantial differences.[7] Collectively, these constitute a major handicap. Given the enormous importance that ecological-evolutionary theory attaches to informational resources, we should not be surprised to find substantial differences in both the levels of economic development and in economic growth rates. In fact, were the economic development of these societies dependent solely on their own locally developed human capital and informational resources (i.e., as differentiated from those supplied by multinational corporations, the United Nations, and other foreign agencies), they would lag even more.

A second factor that has contributed enormously to the difficulties encountered by industrializing horticultural societies has been their run-away rates of population growth (themselves at least partly a function of limited informational resources). As Table 10.3 indicates, these societies have been far slower than in-

7. The amount of the variance explained by the difference in technoeconomic heritage is least where the publication of scientific articles is involved. This is because the value for this variable for many less developed societies is zero, thus leaving little variance to be explained.

194   Chapter 10

Table 10.3. Demographic Rates in Industrializing Agrarian and Industrializing
Horticultural Societies Compared

Indicator	Technoeconomic Heritage: Agrarian (N)	Horticultural (N)	Summary Statistics
Crude Birth Rate 2002	23.5 (39)	39.4 (28)	R^2=.603 P<.001
Crude Birth Rate 1965	41.8 (39)	48.3 (28)	R^2=.272 P<.001
Total Fertility Rate 2002	2.9 (39)	5.3 (28)	R^2=.599 P<.001
Total Fertility Rate 1965	6.2 (39)	6.8 (28)	R^2=.113 P<.005
Crude Death Rate 2002	7.4 (39)	17.8 (28)	R^2=.693 P<.001
Crude Death Rate 1965	14.7 (39)	23.3 (30)	R^2=.492 P<.001
% Annual Pop. Growth 2002	1.6 (39)	2.3 (28)	R^2=.259 P<.001
% Annual Pop. Growth 1965	2.6 (39)	2.6 (28)	R^2=.001 P<.794
Infant Mortality Rate 2002	37.8 (39)	107.8 (28)	R^2=.595 P<.001
Infant Mortality Rate 1965	109.1 (39)	157.2 (28)	R^2=.304 P<.001
Life Expectancy 2002	67.9 (39)	45.8 (28)	R^2=.745 P<.001
Life Expectancy 1965	54.0 (39)	41.5 (28)	R^2=.481 P<.001

Data Source: World Development Indicators 2001, and World Development Indicators Online (http://www.worldbank.org/data/).

dustrializing agrarian societies in curbing their birth rates (an 18.4 percent reduction between 1965 and 2002 vs. 43.8 percent). As a result, their rates of population growth remain far higher. What is striking in Table 10.3 is the magnitude of most of the R^2 values, especially those for the more recent period.

The implications of this for economic development and for standards of living are difficult to exaggerate. Vast resources are consumed in supporting large numbers of children, many of whom are unlikely ever to be employed productively. Moreover, as these children mature, many come to recognize this fact and the boys, especially, become prime candidates for militias, criminal gangs, and other politically destabilizing organizations. Haiti, Liberia, and Rwanda are classic examples of this, but not the only ones by any means.

As ecological-evolutionary theory would lead one to expect, industrializing agrarian societies have long had much larger urban populations than industrializing horticultural societies (see Table 10.4). As recently as 1980, they appear still to have had more than twice the proportion of their people living in cities of 1 million or more. Industrializing horticultural societies are closing the gap, however. Already in 1965, the rate of growth of their urban populations was nearly half again as great as that of industrializing agrarian societies, and although the rate of urban growth is slowing somewhat in both sets of societies, those with a horticultural heritage are still growing more than half again as fast. In fact, today more of the population in industrializing horticultural societies live in their society's largest city than is the case in industrializing agrarian societies (42.2 vs. 34.6 percent).[8]

8. On first consideration, it may seem puzzling that 42.2 percent of the population of industrializing horticultural societies live in the largest city, but only 15.6 percent live in cities of a million or more. The reason for this is, of course, that in many societies the largest city has a population of less than 1 million.

Table 10.4. Urban Growth Patterns in Industrializing Agrarian and Industrializing Horticultural Societies Compared

Indicator	Technoeconomic Heritage: Agrarian (N)	Horticultural (N)	Summary Statistics
% in cities 1M+ 2000	25.6 (28)	15.6 (12)	R^2=.146 P<.015
% in cities 1M+ 1980	21.5 (28)	9.5 (12)	R^2=.254 P<.001
Log % in cities of 1M+ 2000	1.3 (28)	1.2 (12)	R^2=.137 P<.019
Log % in cities of 1M+ 1980	1.3 (28)	0.9 (12)	R^2=.324 P<.001
% Annual Urban Growth 2002	2.7 (39)	4.2 (27)	R^2=.358 P<.001
% Annual Urban Growth 1965	4.2 (39)	6.0 (32)	R^2=.254 P<.001
% in largest city 2000	34.6 (33)	42.2 (16)	R^2=.046 P<.141
Log % in largest city 2000	1.5 (33)	1.6 (16)	R^2=.060 P<.089

Data Sources: World Development Indicators 2001, General Series and Table 3.10, and World Development Indicators Online (http://www.worldbank.org/data/).

In the long run, this trend could work to the advantage of industrializing horticultural societies, since urbanization historically has created conditions favorable to economic development (e.g., greater access to information of many kinds and the growth of human capital). In the short run, however, overly rapid growth of urban populations tends to be a source of all kinds of social problems, especially political instability.

Possible Alternative Explanations of Findings

Although data such as those just summarized strongly suggest that ecological-evolutionary theory provides important and distinctive insights concerning developmental problems encountered by many less developed societies, we need to consider the possibility of alternative explanations. For example, one might argue that while the differences we have identified are real, they reflect the operation of processes other than those suggested by ecological-evolutionary theory. Thus, the differences may be due to the influence of environmental or genetic factors or to variations in the political histories of the societies involved.

With respect to the first of these alternative explanations, we would note that far from contradicting ecological-evolutionary theory, it is entirely compatible with it. As the label *ecological* indicates, this theory treats relations between societies and their environments as of the utmost importance, and there is ample evidence that the historic "failure" of sub-Saharan societies to adopt plow agriculture was an unavoidable response to constraints imposed by the biophysical environment under preindustrial conditions (Farmer, 1968; Meggers, 1954; Watters, 1960). As one writer (Farmer, 1968: 203) has observed, horticulture constitutes "an adaptation to tropical soil conditions under which continuous cultivation may be highly dangerous in the absence of advanced techniques for conserving soil and maintaining soil fertility [and] . . . it is significant in this connection that

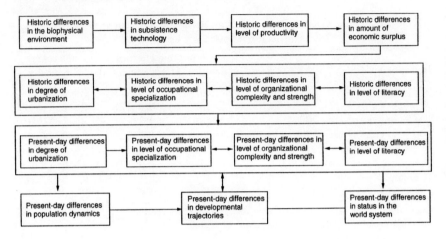

Figure 10.2 An ecological-evolutionary model to explain the differences between industrializing horticultural and industrializing agrarian societies in the contemporary world

European settlers in Brazil have, in some areas, taken to [horticulture]." It might
be added that even in the twentieth century, European colonists and colonial
administrators, armed with modern industrial technology, found it difficult or
impossible in much of sub-Saharan Africa to introduce agriculture, and what
was difficult with the aid of modern technology would obviously have been impossible without it. Furthermore, as William McNeill (1976) has shown, over the
centuries diseases transmitted by micropredators have been far more of a hin-
drance to societal development in Africa than elsewhere.

Hence, far from contradicting ecological-evolutionary theory or providing
a basis for an alternative explanation of our findings, the close association of horticultural societies with sub-Saharan Africa supports it. In short, differences in the
biophysical environment appear to be the explanation of why horticultural societies in Europe and most of Asia successfully made the transition to plow agriculture in the premodern era while those in sub-Saharan Africa did not. Figure 10.2
specifies in somewhat greater detail the links between the environmental variable,
the horticultural vs. agrarian distinction, and the divergent developmental trajectories of modern societies as hypothesized by ecological-evolutionary theory.

Before leaving this subject, we should also note that the practice of horticulture has survived into the modern era in a number of areas far removed from sub-
Saharan Africa—in Papua New Guinea, in Haiti, in parts of southeast Asia, and
in parts of Latin America. In southeast Asia and in Latin America, however, horticulture is no longer the dominant mode of farming, having been displaced by
plow agriculture, except in remote and hilly areas.

Papua New Guinea, however, provides us with an opportunity to test the
thesis that something uniquely African, cultural or genetic, rather than some-

Table 10.5. Characteristics of Papua New Guinea Compared to Average Values for Industrializing Agrarian and Industrializing Horticultural Societies

Indicator	Papua New Guinea More Closely Resembles Average Values of
GDP/capita 2002 (in 1995 US$)	Horticultural Societies
GDP/capita growth rate 1965–2002	Horticultural Societies
Enrollment Secondary Schools 2001	Horticultural Societies
Newspapers/1,000 population 1995	Horticultural Societies
Computers/1,000 population 2002	Agrarian Societies
Crude Birth Rate 2002	Horticultural Societies
Total Fertility Rate 2002	Horticultural Societies
Crude Death Rate 2002	Agrarian Societies
% Annual Urban Growth 1999	Horticultural Societies

Sources: See Tables 10.1 to 10.4.

thing associated with horticulture, is the cause of the patterns described above. If the characteristics of this non-African society resemble those of industrializing agrarian societies, it would suggest that the patterns we have explained in terms of technoeconomic heritage are due to something else more uniquely African. On the other hand, if the characteristics of Papua New Guinea more nearly resemble the characteristics of the largely sub-Saharan set of industrializing horticultural societies, this would support the thesis that horticulture is the critical determinant.

In Table 10.5, we compare the developmental profile of Papua New Guinea with that of industrializing horticultural and agrarian societies presented earlier in Tables 10.1 to 10.4. Our comparison is based on nine nonredundant measures for which data on Papua New Guinea are available. As Table 10.5 indicates, on seven of these variables, the values for Papua New Guinea more nearly resemble the average values for industrializing horticultural societies as a whole than they do the values for industrializing agrarian societies. This is what one would expect if, indeed, technoeconomic heritage is responsible for the differences we have found.

In the case of Haiti, the one other geographically non-African society in which horticulture remains the dominant mode of subsistence, all eight of the variables in Table 10.5 for which data are available resemble the horticultural norm more closely than the agrarian (no data were available for Haiti's Secondary School enrollment). Thus, Haiti, too, lends support to ecological-evolutionary theory, though, unlike the Papuan case, one cannot rule out the possibility of genetics as a causal factor since the population is overwhelmingly of recent sub-Saharan African descent.

Another possible alternative explanation of our findings is that the differences we have identified between industrializing horticultural and industrializing agrarian societies are simply a reflection of forces identified by world-system theory.

Table 10.6. Zero-Order and Partial Regression Coefficients of Dependent Variables Regressed on Ecological-Evolutionary and World-System Dummy Variables

Indicator	Zero-Order		Partial		N
	EET	WST	EET	WST	
GDP/capita 2002 US1995$	.450***	.428***	.350**	.318*	56
Log GDP/capita 2002 US1995$	.715***	.385**	.659***	.178ns	56
GDP/capita growth 1965–2002	.583***	.258*	.558***	.076ns	59
Adult Literacy 1995	.704***	.377**	.650***	.212ns	46
Enrollment Sec. Schools 2001	.680***	.342*	.640***	.233*	43
Newspapers/1,000 pop. 1995	.431**	.435**	.326**	.332**	56
Log newspapers/1,000 pop. 1995	.733***	.349**	.692***	.131ns	56
Computers/1,000 pop. 2002	.283*	.330*	.209ns	.274ns	49
Log Computers/1,000 pop. 2002	.628***	.322*	.584***	.164ns	49
Sci. Articles/1,000 pop. 1999	.294*	.413**	.183ns	.356**	59
Log Sci. Arts./1,000 pop. 1999	.407**	.424***	.305*	.330**	59
Crude birth rate 2002	−.775***	−.374**	−.729***	−.144ns	60
Total fertility rate 2002	−.778***	−.371**	−.734***	−.139ns	60
Crude death rate 2002	−.833***	−.280*	−.827***	−.019ns	60
Population growth 2002	−.547***	−.331**	−.491***	−.176ns	60
Infant mortality rate 2002	−.769***	−.316*	−.744***	−.048ns	60
Life expectancy 2002	−.855***	−.326*	−.836***	−.062ns	60
Urban growth 2002	−.598***	−.340**	−.545***	−.171ns	59

Sources: See Tables 10.1–10.4.
ns = Not statistically significant
* P<.05
** P<.01
*** P<.001

This brings us to our next question: To what extent are the effects of technoeconomic heritage and status in the world-economy independent of one another?

To answer this question, we compared the individual and joint effects of these variables on the various dependent variables examined in Tables 10.1–10.4. As noted earlier, both ecological-evolutionary theory and world-system theory expect societies to be greatly influenced by their social environments. Ecological-evolutionary theory, however, leads one to expect that the technoeconomic heritages of societies have an even more powerful influence on societal development.

As the partial regression coefficients in Table 10.6 indicate, this expectation was confirmed, with the dummy variables derived from ecological-evolutionary theory proving to be better predictors than the dummy variables derived from world-system theory for 14 out of 18 dependent variables. Overall, 16 of the 18 partial regression coefficients based on the dummy variables derived from eco-logical-evolutionary theory were statistically significant, but only 5 of those de-

Table 10.7. Zero-Order and Partial Standardized Regression Coefficients of Dependent Variables Regressed on Ecological-Evolutionary and World-System Dummy Variables for Nations Under Colonial Control Until 1940 or Later

Indicator	Zero-Order		Partial		
	EET	WST	EET	WST	N
GDP/capita 2002 US1995$	.394*	.441*	.228ns	.325ns	32
Log GDP/capita 2002 US1995$	.663***	.504**	.548**	.225ns	32
GDP/capita growth rate 1965–2002	.751***	.458**	.701***	.097ns	33
Adult Literacy 1995	.646**	.545**	.505*	.326ns	22
Enrollment Sec. Schools 2001	.785***	.482*	.703***	.239ns	21
Newspapers/1,000 pop. 1995	.464**	.547**	.249ns	.419*	30
Log newspapers/1,000 pop. 1995	.755***	.669**	.559***	.381**	30
Computers/1,000 pop. 2002	.323ns	.452*	.149ns	.384ns	28
Log computers/1,000 pop. 2002	.570**	.543**	.407*	.358*	28
Sci. articles/1,000 pop. 1999	.341ns	.389*	.193ns	.290ns	32
Log sci. arts./1,000 pop. 1999	.523**	.517**	.351ns	.339ns	32
Crude birth rate 2002	−.818***	−.527**	−.744***	−.143ns	33
Total fertility rate 2002	−.811***	−.520**	−.739***	−.138ns	33
Crude death rate 2002	−.721***	−.520***	−.626***	−.171ns	33
Population growth 2002	−.592***	−.362*	−.552***	−.077ns	33
Infant mortality rate 2002	−.791***	−.513**	−.717***	−.143ns	33
Life expectancy 2002	−.881***	−.514**	−.839***	−.081ns	33
Urban growth 2002	−.613***	−.384*	−.562**	−.099ns	32

Sources: See Tables 10.1–10.4.
ns = Statistically not significant
* P<.05
** P<.01
*** P<.0001

rived from world-system theory. Moreover, none of the latter were significant at the .001 level while 13 of the former reached that level of significance.

Clearly, then, the distinction between semiperipheral and peripheral societies, as established by world-system theory, does not explain the differences we have found between industrializing agrarian and industrializing horticultural societies. On the contrary, a comparison of the zero-order and partial coefficients in Table 10.6 indicates that many of the differences among developing societies that proponents of world-system theory have attributed to the operation of the capitalist world economy have, in reality, been due to differences in the technoeconomic heritages of these societies. This is especially important in the case of the measure of per capita economic growth in the years between 1965 and 2002. The slow rate of economic growth in peripheral societies appears to have been due far more to their lack of the advantages of an agrarian heritage than to their status in the capitalist world system. Overall, only 5 of the 18 statistically significant zero-order relationships based on world-system theory in Table 10.6 remain significant when the influence of technoeconomic heritage is taken into account.

Finally, a third alternative that has been suggested is that our findings reflect differences in the *political* heritages of our two sets of societies, with industrializing horticultural societies having been under European colonial control more often than industrializing agrarian societies. Once again, it should be noted that such differences are not inconsistent with ecological-evolutionary theory, since the theory leads one to expect stronger and more powerful governments in agrarian societies and, therefore, greater ability to resist foreign colonialism. Thus, it would not be surprising if the effects of colonial control were also implicated in the problems of industrializing horticultural societies.

To test this possibility, we repeated the analysis in Table 10.6 with a more limited sample of societies, all of which were under colonial control until at least 1940. This procedure eliminated only one industrializing horticultural society, but it eliminated more than half of the industrializing agrarian societies.

The results of this analysis are summarized in Table 10.7, which parallels Table 10.6. The first column in the table indicates the effects of technoeconomic heritage with political heritage controlled (because of the nature of the sample of societies involved), and the third column indicates the effects of technoeconomic heritage with both political heritage and status in the world-system of societies controlled.

The picture that emerges in this table is much the same as that in Table 10.6. Although all 18 of the zero-order coefficients based on world-system theory are statistically significant, only 3 of them remain significant after controls are introduced for the influence of technoeconomic heritage. In contrast, 13 of the 18 coefficients based on ecological-evolutionary theory remain significant after controlling for the influence of status in the capitalist world system. Thus, it appears that the differences between industrializing agrarian and industrializing horticultural societies found in Tables 10.1–10.4 reflect only minimally either the influence of differences in their political (i.e., colonial) heritages or differences in their statuses in the capitalist world-system.

Conclusions

In this chapter we have tested a set of interrelated hypotheses derived from ecological-evolutionary theory. These hypotheses were based on the premise that the past is not dead history and that differences in the technoeconomic heritages that societies bring to the modern era from the preindustrial past exercise a powerful influence on them still today, especially on their patterns and trajectories of development. Specifically, industrializing horticultural societies were predicted to have (1) lower levels of technological and economic development, (2) lower rates of economic growth, (3) more limited informational resources, and (4) less favorable demographic patterns than their industrializing agrarian counterparts.

Each of these hypotheses was confirmed with multiple indicators. In addition, it was shown that the effects attributed to technoeconomic heritage are largely independent of the kinds of influences identified by world-system theory and also of the influence of earlier colonial control. Contrary to the expectations of those who emphasize these external forces, our findings point to the greater importance of *internal* forces and the cultural heritage of each society.

Our findings also contradict the widespread view (implicit in the use, *without qualification,* of terms such as "the Third World," "the LDCs," and "the periphery") that today's less developed societies are a homogeneous group except for secondary characteristics and developmentally unimportant idiosyncratic differences. This view ignores an important, though largely overlooked, fault line within the world of less developed societies that profoundly affects both their current levels of development and other characteristics as well as their prospects for the future.

In summary, the data support a three-stage model in which (1) historic differences in the biophysical environment gave rise to historic differences in subsistence technology, which (2) caused differences in the social and economic development of societies in the premodern era, and these, in turn, (3) are responsible for similar or derivative social and economic differences today (see Figure 10.2).[9] Additional research is obviously needed to explore and test all of the implications of this model, but clear and compelling evidence indicates its importance and utility in explaining significant differences in current levels and rates of development among less developed societies. Moreover, to our surprise, several lines of evidence suggest that the importance of the variables in our model may still be *increasing* rather than declining, as one would expect in the case of variables that reflect conditions in the past. Thus, Dubos's assertion about the importance of the past finds striking confirmation in the developmental trajectories of societies today.

Appendix: Cases in the Analysis

Industrializing Agrarian

Dominican Republic, Jamaica, Guatemala, Honduras, El Salvador, Nicaragua, Costa Rica, Panama, Colombia, Guyana, Ecuador, Peru, Brazil, Bolivia, Paraguay, Chile, Argentina, Uruguay, Morocco, Tunisia, Turkey, Egypt, Syria, Lebanon, Afghanistan, China, North Korea, South Korea, India, Pakistan, Burma, Sri Lanka, Nepal, Thailand, Cambodia, Laos, Vietnam, Malaysia, Philippines.

Industrializing Horticultural

Haiti, Mali, Senegal, Benin, Burkina Faso, Mauritania, Niger, Ivory Coast, Guinea, Upper Volta, Liberia, Sierra Leone, Ghana, Togo, Central African Republic, Chad, Congo, Uganda, Kenya, Tanzania, Burundi, Rwanda, Somalia, Mozambique, Zambia, Zimbabwe, Malawi, Malagasy Republic, Papua New Guinea.

---

9. For a very similar analysis, arriving at very similar conclusions, see Jared Diamond's important recent volume, *Guns, Germs, and Steel: The Fate of Human Societies.*

11

AN EXPERIMENT THAT FAILED

Not long ago, roughly a third of the world's population lived in societies controlled by followers of Karl Marx. Guided by his ideas, the leaders of these societies sought to establish a radically new kind of social order, one in which all of the more serious evils of existing societies would be eliminated and societal resources redeployed so that freedom, equality, justice, and affluence would be the birthright of every human being.

Because of their virtual monopoly of power, these leaders were able to convert Marx's ideas into institutional realities in their societies, and thus put to the test important, but previously untested, ideas about human nature and human societies. In effect, they were able to carry out a series of radical social experiments on a scale, and of a scope, never before attempted.

From the standpoint of social theory, it is difficult to exaggerate the importance of these experiments and the ideas that guided them. Above all, they put to the test the important assumption that selfishness and self-assertive behavior, in all their manifestations, are products of social experience rather than an expression of genetically programmed elements of human nature.

Following Marx, the leaders of Marxist societies assumed that selfishness and greed are merely responses that people have been forced to adopt because of the conditions of life in societies in which the means of production are privately owned. By abolishing the institution of private property, they believed they would not only eliminate such behaviors, they would also rid society of the many evils that flow from them: exploitation, oppression, inequality, poverty, crime, alcoholism, alienation. In socialist societies, work would become a joy, people would live and work together in harmony, and they would soon come to enjoy unprecedented levels of affluence and freedom. In short, by abolishing the pernicious institution of private property, and by reeducating the masses through control of schools, the mass media, and the arts, they would usher in a golden age. Although others have shared these goals, only the leaders of Marxist societies have had the power and resources at their command that were needed to implement them and, thus, to put these ideas to a meaningful test.[1]

They also put to the test one other proposition of great importance for social theory, and of special relevance to ecological-evolutionary theory—namely, that ideologies have greater influence on societal development than do material forces. This may seem ironic, since Marxist theory is commonly regarded as a materialist theory. Even in its earliest formulations, however, Marx attached great importance to ideology, as in his discussions of "false consciousness." Twentieth-century Marxist leaders, such as Lenin, Mao, and Castro, placed even greater emphasis on ideology, as have most academic Marxists who commonly refer to materialist interpretations as "vulgar Marxism."

Unfortunately, sociologists have been slow to appreciate the relevance of Marxist societies for social theory. For many years, one could justify this inattention to "really existing socialist societies" because of the difficulties of obtaining reliable data about them.[2] The leaders of these societies showed little interest in making accurate information available to outsiders. Social and economic data were treated either as state secrets or as material to be manipulated for propaganda purposes. Even such things as telephone directories, maps, and censuses were often treated in this way.

Following Stalin's death in 1953, however, conditions began to improve. During the period known as "the thaw," novelists and journalists began to find it possible to write a bit more honestly about daily life in the Soviet Union, and sociological research was legalized in Poland and Yugoslavia. By the late 1950s, it even became possible for sociologists in Poland to begin exploring certain aspects of the highly sensitive subject of social inequality. Nevertheless, a decade later one could still plausibly argue that it was impossible to draw conclusions about Marxist societies, since the evidence was frequently contradictory and the conclusions of experts in the West were often distorted by their own ideological biases (i.e., sympathetic scholars found the rosy reports issued by the authorities generally credible, while critics dismissed them as propaganda).

---

1. To be sure, Marxist elites never had total control, nor have their experiments been conducted under totally ideal conditions. But significant social experiments have rarely been conducted under ideal conditions. Were one to ignore or reject conclusions other than those based on perfectly executed experiments, one would be obliged to ignore or reject virtually the whole of modern social science.

2. The terms "really existing socialism" and "really existing socialist societies" were coined by eastern Europeans. Although the Marxist-Leninist societies to which they applied the terms have represented but one version of socialism, they cannot be ignored since they incorporated the critical socialist principle of public ownership of the means of production far more thoroughly than other societies that have been labeled socialist (e.g., Sweden, which for decades has been governed by a social democratic, or socialist, party).

Ecological-Evolutionary Theory and the Marxist Experiments

During the 1950s and early 1960s, at a time when I was regularly teaching a graduate seminar on social inequality, I was confronted anew each year with the question of how to deal with the Soviet Union and the other Marxist societies of eastern Europe. Should they be treated as a totally new type of society, products of a new stage in societal development, as Marxists insisted, or should they be treated as simply a variant form of modern industrial society?

Obviously, there was something to be said for both points of view; in some respects these societies were unique, but in others they resembled western industrial societies. Viewed from a journalistic perspective (which is often hard to escape when dealing with contemporary societies), the differences seemed far greater and far more important than the similarities. In a period when the cold war often threatened to become a shooting war, one was bombarded by daily reminders of the differences.

On the other hand, if one stepped back and viewed these two sets of societies in broader historical and comparative context, the differences between them seemed less striking and the similarities more impressive. If one compared Soviet and American societies with hunting and gathering or horticultural societies, for example, the differences between Soviet and American societies seemed almost trivial. Even when compared with agrarian societies of the not-so-distant past, the similarities seemed much greater than the differences. Both had far higher levels of urbanization than any agrarian society ever had, vastly larger and better educational systems, much higher levels of literacy, smaller families, much larger numbers of women employed outside the home, much higher standards of living for the masses of ordinary people, longer life spans, and lower levels of economic inequality. In addition, work activities in Soviet and American societies were organized around factories and offices, not family groups, as in traditional agrarian societies; giant bureaucracies were commonplace; and both had republican governments. In short, in the modern world, as in the past, a society's basic mode of subsistence seemed to be a more powerful determinant of more of its basic attributes than either ideology or politics.

During the early 1960s, at a time when my primary interest was in theories of social inequality and its causes, I gradually came to believe that it was a mistake to attempt to build theories largely on the experience of modern western societies, as was then customary in sociology. Increasingly it seemed to me that the power and value of theories are a function of the range and breadth of the sources that have been taken into account in their formulation. In other words, much could be learned by comparing modern western societies with nonmodern and nonwestern societies. But I also came to believe that unsystematic, apples-and-oranges comparisons of the kind popularized by Margaret Mead among others (i.e., simplistic comparisons of the practices of a highly complex western industrial society with those of some tiny, largely undifferentiated, preliterate society, without taking account of the larger social matrices in which these practices were embedded) usually did more harm than good.

For the comparative method to be effective, I felt that the social sciences needed a comprehensive map of the universe of human societies, both past and present. Such a map would enable one to recognize which relevant variables were controlled, and which were not, in a given comparison—thus minimizing, or at least reducing, the frequency of inappropriate comparisons and flawed interpretations. The creation of such a map, however, presupposes an ability to specify its basic parameters.

Based on all I had been able to learn by the time that I wrote *Power and Privilege,* it seemed clear that the most basic differences in power and privilege among societies were linked to differences in societal modes of subsistence: The most egalitarian societies were those with the least advanced technologies, while those with the greatest inequalities in power and privilege were ones with much more advanced technologies (Lenski, 1966: 46ff.). As one of the corollaries of this, it seemed that Soviet-type societies and the western democracies were best understood if viewed as two subsets of societies within the more basic set defined by its members' utilization of, and dependence on, modern industrial technology.[3]

Despite numerous clear and unequivocal statements to the contrary throughout the volume (see especially the summary discussion of the basic theoretical model in the final chapter), some critics professed to find in *Power and Privilege* another regrettable expression of "technological determinism" or, worse yet, "vulgar Marxism." In an effort to set the record straight, I confronted this issue directly in the first edition of *Human Societies* (Lenski, 1970: 139–142). In a discussion titled "Technological Determinism?" I stated that ecological-evolutionary theory takes a probabilistic, *not* a deterministic, approach to the role of technology in social change. I said that it views a society's basic subsistence technology as but one force in a field of forces that collectively determine the totality of the society's various characteristics. More precisely, "it [ecological-evolutionary theory] regards basic subsistence technology as *the most powerful single force in the field, not with respect to the determination of every single characteristic, but rather with respect to the total constellation of characteristics*" (emphasis in original).

In keeping with this principle, subsistence technology was again used to establish the first-order division of societies (i.e., hunting and gathering societies,

---

3. In the original design of *Power and Privilege,* I planned to include several additional chapters on individual societies. In this way, I hoped to draw attention even more clearly to the multilevel nature of the theory I was proposing. In other words, the theory was grounded in a small number of propositions believed to be applicable to human societies as a whole (Lenski, 1966: chs. 1–4 and 13). This general theory established the necessary covering principle (i.e., the critical importance of subsistence technology) that laid a foundation for a series of more powerful special theories (ibid.: chs. 5–12). These, in turn, identified the covering principles needed to guide the analysis of individual societies (e.g., the importance of ideological differences among technologically similar societies). This section of the book was to have included separate chapters on the Soviet and American systems of stratification. Unfortunately, because of time constraints, these chapters were never written. I still believe, however, that this is the kind of conceptual framework that is required if the study of human societies is ever to become an enterprise in which knowledge cumulates.

horticultural, industrial, etc.), and ideology was again treated as the basis for a second-order division in more advanced societies (i.e., agrarian and industrial: see Figure 6.5 in Chapter 6 of the present volume). In other words, it was again assumed that the industrial technology that the Soviet Union, Poland, Hungary, and Czechoslovakia shared to such a great degree with the western democracies was having, and would continue to have, an even greater impact on their development overall than would their distinctive Marxist ideology.

Thus, in discussing the polities of industrial societies, I began by asserting that "[o]ne of the most striking changes associated with the emergence of industrial societies has been the rise of democratic government" (1970: 354). I went on to say that while not all industrial societies have had democratic polities,

> some of [these nondemocratic polities] have been eliminated (e.g., [Nazi] Germany and [Fascist] Italy), while others have been liberalized, so that a larger proportion of the population has some influence in the political process (e.g., Yugoslavia, Hungary, and even, to some degree, the Soviet Union). Though the level of democratic participation achieved in these nations falls far short of what exists elsewhere, the *trend* is important. (1970; emphasis in original)

In discussing the causes of this trend, I argued that

> it is doubtful that the democratic movement would have succeeded without the technological contribution of the Industrial Revolution. To begin with, industrialization eliminated the traditional need for large numbers of unskilled and uneducated workers living at or near the subsistence level. As new sources of energy were tapped and machines were built to perform the more routine tasks, societies had to start producing more skilled and educated workers. People like these, however, are much less likely to be politically apathetic and servile. On the contrary, they tend to be self-assertive, jealous of their rights, and politically demanding. Such characteristics are essential in a democracy for they counterbalance and hold in check the powerful oligarchical tendencies present in any large and complex organization.

Industrialization also made possible the remarkable development of the mass media. To a great extent, this has been a response to the spread of literacy and to the increased demand for information generated by the rising level of education. Through newspapers, magazines, radio, and television, the average citizen of a modern industrial society stays in far closer touch with political events than his counterpart in agrarian societies could possibly be. While much of the information he receives is extremely superficial and distorted, nevertheless it generates interest and concern. Thus the media not only satisfy a need, they also stimulate it.

Finally, industrialization stimulated the growth of urban communities and this, too, strengthened democratic tendencies. Isolated rural communities have long been noted for their lack of political sophistication and for their patriarchal and paternalistic political patterns. Urban populations, by contrast, have always been better informed and more willing to challenge established authority. Thus, merely by increasing the size of urban populations, industrialization contributed to the democratic trend (1970: 357–358).

Convergence in a variety of other aspects of life in industrial societies was also discussed, but with the proviso that this did not always mean movement toward historic western norms. By way of summarizing and explaining economic trends, I wrote,

> [I]n the future there will probably be less variation in this important aspect of industrial societies than in the past. Both Communist and non-Communist societies are moving toward a more balanced type of economy in which both market and command will play important roles. Market forces will be used to achieve greater efficiency, while command will be used to protect the corporate interests of society and to limit the growth of inequality. This is not to say, of course, that differences between economic systems will be eliminated . . . but they will probably be reduced. (1970: 376)

Tendencies toward convergence and parallel trends in development resulting from industrialization were noted in a number of other areas, ranging from the increasing participation of women and the growing importance of educational credentials in the labor force to the weakening of family ties and the emergence of generational cleavages. Summing up, I wrote,

> Industrial societies are not, of course, moving toward a single uniform pattern. Differences will certainly remain; but they will probably be less marked than those that separated Hitler's Germany or Stalin's Russia from the western democracies. (1970: 427)

Events of the past twenty years surely seem to support not only this very general prediction but also most of the more specific predictions on which the general prediction was based. Although I cannot claim that ecological-evolutionary theory anticipated the astonishing events of 1989, 1990, and 1991, it did provide the basis for accurate forecasts of the *direction of change* in the economies, polities, and other areas of life in eastern Europe and China. The same cannot be said of some of the other theories of societal development to which sociologists have been much attached in recent years.

Fatal Flaws in the Marxist Program

Since the 1980s, our knowledge of Marxist societies has grown enormously. Thanks to Gorbachev's policy of *glasnost,* and even more to the revelations that have followed in the wake of the dramatic political changes in 1989, 1990, and 1991, we know far more about the inner dynamics of these societies than was known previously.

Today, for example, we have a greatly expanded body of information about the wealth and lifestyles of the ruling elites in Marxist societies of the past. Thus, following the overthrow of Bulgarian Communist Party leader Todor Zhikov, we learned that during his years in power he acquired no less than thirty homes as well as a yacht that was later sold for $1.85 million, and that he and other top Party leaders had accumulated millions of dollars in secret foreign bank accounts (Laber, 1990). We also learned that the long-time leader of the Romanian Communist Party, Nicolae Ceausescu, did even better for himself and his family, amassing forty villas and twenty palaces, all at a time when most Romanians were living without heat or light. Ceausescu was also reported to have deposited $40 million in Swiss bank accounts (*Washington Post*, May 6, 1990). From East Germany, we learned further that Erich Honecker accumulated millions in Swiss bank accounts by skimming profits from arms sales to Third World nations, while at the same time using $42 million of public funds to create for himself and a handful of other top East German Party leaders a fine private estate outside Berlin that was carefully hidden from the rest of the population (*Bild am Sonntag*, August 25, 1990). Even a lesser Party official, Harry Tisch, appears to have misappropriated more than a million dollars of public funds to create for himself his own personal hunting lodge and vacation home.

While it had long been known that Communist Party elites reserved for themselves a variety of privileges that were denied to others (Matthews, 1978; Voslensky, 1984), the extent of these privileges proved far greater than most western experts had imagined. That these were not merely aberrations of *eastern European* Marxism is indicated by the fact that in Nicaragua, the Sandinistas converted the villas and other property previously owned by Somoza and his associates into their own personal property, while in Vietnam a high-ranking Party official was sentenced for his involvement in an $8 million bank fraud, and in China and Vietnam Communist Party elites continue to live in closely guarded compounds, similar to those that long hid the private lives of Marxist leaders in eastern Europe from public view (Salisbury, 1992). Recently, China's National Audit Office estimated that $15 billion a year, or more than 1 percent of the nation's annual economic output, is embezzled, and the evidence points to high Party officials as the principal culprits (*Washington Post*, January 10, 2002).

At the other extreme, poverty was much more widespread in Marxist societies than western observers were generally aware. Reports released by Soviet authorities during the Gorbachev era indicated that, for years, at least 20 percent of the population had been living at or below the official poverty level (Fein, 1989). Homelessness was also reported to have been a problem in Moscow and other Soviet cities long before the collapse of the Communist regime, while studies in Hungary toward the end of the Communist era found that a quarter of the population was living in poverty (Kamm, 1989).

Despite all this, it still appears that the level of economic inequality in Marxist societies never was as great as that in most non-Marxist societies. Wealthy and privileged though the Zhikovs, Ceausescus, and Honeckers were by comparison with their fellow countrymen, the magnitude of their wealth never matched that amassed by leading western and Japanese businessmen and by oil-rich Middle Eastern elites. Moreover, passing accumulated wealth on to succeeding generations was more difficult in Marxist societies than elsewhere, as the experience of the Brezhnev family and others reminds us.[4]

Looking back, it is clear that the internal, systemic problems of the command economies and one-party polities of Marxist societies have been far more serious than western observers suspected. In fact, it now appears that the greatest success of these societies was their ability to *dissimulate*—a success that was too often achieved because of the readiness of many western journalists, scholars, and others to accept the glowing reports of socialist successes uncritically (Hollander, 1981).[5] The Czech philosopher Erazim Kohak summarized the situation best when he wrote that "[t]he entire world of 'real socialism' was one vast Potemkin village."

Now, however, thanks to all that has been learned in recent years, we know that the economies of these societies had been stagnating for a long time and that much of the population had grown disaffected and hostile. Worse yet, Marxism and Marxist regimes had lost whatever legitimacy they once enjoyed in the minds of many, and even Party members had often become disillusioned (Andorka, 1992).[6] In short, a moral, economic, and political crisis was developing that some leader would have to confront. If not Andropov, then Gorbachev, and if not Gorbachev, then someone else. The crisis was so pervasive that even in Hungary, long an island of relative prosperity and less repressive Marxism, the Marxist regime was unable to survive.

Everything that we have learned over the years about the inner workings of the Marxist regimes of eastern Europe has reinforced ecological-evolutionary theory's assumption concerning the importance of our species' genetic heritage as a factor influencing societal life and development. With the wisdom of hindsight, it is now easier to see how fundamental miscalculations concerning human nature led to insoluble operational problems that eventually undermined these regimes. These problems were of two basic types: (1) undermotivation of ordinary workers, and (2) misdirected motivation of managers, bureaucrats, and other decisionmakers.

---

4. Shortly after Brezhnev's death, his son-in-law was arrested and sentenced to prison for illegal financial activities.

5. When Jonathan Mirsky, a British reporter, returned to China in the less repressive period following Chairman Mao's death, he met one of his former guides, who was also a translator, and asked him why he had deceived him so badly about the true nature of conditions during the Mao era. The man replied that he had done so because Mirsky himself wanted to be deceived. To Mirsky's credit, he told this story on himself and frankly acknowledged the validity of the charge (*New York Review of Books*).

6. Ironically, this was at a time when Marxist ideology was becoming fashionable among western scholars and intellectuals.

The first of these problems was identified long ago by eastern European workers themselves when they began to say, "They pretend to pay us, and we pretend to work" (Dobbs, 1981). Workers had concluded that the rewards for most kinds of work simply did not justify more than minimal, perfunctory effort (Shlapentokh, 1989: ch. 2). Shoddy workmanship, sullen workers, absenteeism, corruption, and bureaucratic pathologies of various kinds came to typify worker performance in Marxist societies (*The Economist,* 1988). While these problems are present in every society to some degree, they became far more prevalent and far more serious in the economies of Marxist societies than in most. They became so serious, in fact, that they had demoralizing consequences for the vast majority of citizens: endless hours spent in lines queuing for merchandise that was usually of poor quality, frequent confrontations with surly state employees, unsatisfactory housing, an inadequate health care system, and more. Adding insult to injury, most citizens became aware that the ruling elite and its allies in the *nomenklatura* were exempted from most of these problems: For them, there were well-stocked stores with better-quality merchandise in ample supply and more responsive employees, better housing, better health care facilities, better schools for their children, second homes, travel opportunities, household servants, and countless other "perks" (Voslensky, 1984). Rubbing salt in the wound, this elite preached socialism and the need for sacrifice while enjoying all of these special privileges.

For many years, Marxist elites in eastern Europe and their sympathizers in the west explained away the failures and shortcomings of these societies on the grounds of *external factors:* the historic backwardness of eastern Europe, the damage to the Soviet economy caused by the civil war that followed the revolution, the devastation caused by World War II, and the pressures of the cold war. Although there was some truth to these claims, it became increasingly clear that *internal, systemic factors* had become a more serious source of problems. By the late 1980s, this was obvious even to leaders of these societies, and many of them became advocates of major changes, and some abandoned Marxist principles altogether (Hollander, 1999).[7]

Over the years, Marxist societies experimented with a variety of incentive systems. Sometimes, guided by socialist ideals, Party leaders reduced wage differentials among workers and sought to rely more heavily on moral incentives; at other times, in an effort to improve economic performance, they turned to material incentives and increased wage differentials. The egalitarian nature of Marxist ideology, however, severely limited the possibilities for reform of the incentive system.[8]

---

7. This loss of faith in Marxist principles by large numbers of the ruling elite, and their resulting loss of self-confidence, may well have been the primary factor responsible for their weak and ineffective resistance as opposition began to mount in the 1980s.

8. The official salaries of Party leaders were also kept quite low, in seeming conformity with Marxist ideology, but these leaders were always compensated generously in a variety of other ways. Stalin's daughter, Svetlana Alliluyeva, for example, reported that her father, like monarchs in agrarian societies, simply treated the public treasury as his own private resource. One suspects that the same has been true of most other top Party leaders, and is still true of Fidel Castro and Kim Jong-Il.

Several times, in an excess of ideological zeal, wage differentials for the masses were virtually eliminated: In Czechoslovakia in the early 1960s, for example, wage differences were reduced to the point where engineers and highly skilled workers were being paid only 5 percent more than the least skilled (Machonin, 1968). Because of this, large numbers of talented young people dropped out of school, feeling that it was not worth the effort required, and the income that would be sacrificed, to continue their studies. Severe morale problems also developed among skilled workers, engineers, and other professionals (Machonin, 1997). Within several years, problems had grown so acute that authorities were forced to reverse themselves and increase rewards for better-educated and more highly skilled individuals. A similar crisis developed in the Soviet Union in the early 1930s in response to a wage-leveling program initiated by Stalin, and he, too, was forced to reverse course and increase material incentives and wage differentials substantially (Inkeles, 1950). More recently, the political and economic crisis that led to the collapse of the Soviet Union appears to have had its origins in a process of wage leveling initiated by Brezhnev.

The ultimate source of each of these crises as well as the chronic economic problems of Marxist societies appears to have been the much-too-optimistic Marxian view of human nature. Marx, who adopted the eighteenth-century view of Enlightenment thinkers in this regard, saw the unattractive aspects of human nature as merely products of corrupting social institutions that could all be eradicated by the elimination of those institutions. But where the French *philosophes* blamed the defects in human nature on the influences of church and state, Marx saw private property as the ultimate source of societies' ills: If it were abolished, he argued, human nature would soon be transformed. Once socialism was established, and the means of production owned by all, greed and selfishness would disappear. Moral incentives could replace material incentives, and workers would find work intrinsically rewarding: They would work for the sheer joy of working and for the satisfaction of knowing that they were contributing to society's needs, not simply to acquire the necessities of life for themselves and their families.[9]

Unfortunately, the abolition of private property failed to produce this happy transformation of human nature. Instead, freed from the fear of unemployment and lacking adequate material incentives, worker performance deteriorated and production stagnated or declined in Marxist societies everywhere (*The Economist*, 1988; Greenhouse, 1989; Huberman and Sweezy, 1967; Kamm, 1989; Jones, 1981; Machonin, 1997; Scammel, 1990; Shlapentokh, 1989; Silk, 1990; Zeitlin, 1970). The most compelling evidence of this came from the two Germanys, which, because they initially shared a common heritage of pride in work, provided an unusual experimental test case. During and following the collapse of the German Democratic Republic, evidence of the deterioration of work standards under the Marxist regime became all too evident. For example, a western reporter who vis-

---

9. Marx's idealized view of work is reminiscent of Luther's view, and seems to have been a reflection of his Germanic heritage.

ited a large construction site in East Berlin shortly before the collapse found only a single worker present early in the afternoon. When he inquired where everyone was, the man shrugged and replied, "Quitting time." Prior to reunification, East German workers were often quoted as saying how fearful they were that they would not be able to adapt to the demanding standards in West German industry.

Equally telling, President Gorbachev's close associate Aleksandr Yakovlev asserted at the last Communist Party Congress in the Soviet Union that labor productivity in capitalist South Korea was ten times higher than in socialist North Korea (New York Times News Service, 1990).

Already in the early 1980s, Tatiana Zaslavskaia, a leading Soviet sociologist, discovered that as many as a third of Soviet workers hated their work and were unresponsive to incentives of any kind (Shlapentokh, 1987). Others have come to similar conclusions regarding both the Soviet Union and other socialist societies (e.g., Kennan, 1988; Pravda, 1988).

Related to this, graft and corruption became widespread. As one observer commented, "Money passes under the table everywhere [in socialist societies]—from the surgical office to the housing authority's office. Inventory shrinkage is a preoccupation for accountants at enterprises from agricultural collectives to construction materials producers" (Keresztes, 1987). While one might expect this in capitalist societies, it is hardly what Marx leads one to expect under socialism.

But the motivational problems of workers in Marxist societies were due not only to faulty assumptions about human nature. They also developed in response to defective organizational arrangements spawned by the command economies of those societies. Lacking the automatic checks and balances on production and consumption that operate in a market economy under truly competitive conditions, planners were forced to assign arbitrary prices and production quotas for goods and services of every kind. To ensure fulfillment of the quotas, managers were awarded substantial bonuses for meeting or exceeding them and were penalized severely for any shortfall.

Unfortunately, this seemingly rational procedure had an important, but unanticipated, consequence: Managers found that they could maximize their rewards, and minimize their risks, by stockpiling essential resources of every kind—*including labor* (Greenhouse, 1989; Kostakov, 1989; H. Smith, 1976). Since there was no penalty attached to the employment of excess numbers of workers, labor resources were used very inefficiently, adding to worker cynicism.

Managers also developed a variety of other unfortunate adaptations to the system of central planning. They learned, for example, that quantity, not quality, was what their bosses, the central planners, cared about (Parkhomovsky, 1982).[10]

---

10. Quality controls are most likely to develop when producers are obliged to compete for the support of consumers, and when consumers can penalize the producers of inferior products by turning to competitors. The massive loss of market share by American automobile manufacturers during the 1970s and 1980s is an example of this. When people are using their own money to purchase goods and services, they are not nearly so willing to accept inferior products as when they are using other people's money (i.e., as when politicians and governmental bureaucrats use public funds).

They learned, too, that production figures could be inflated without much risk since those above them in the hierarchy were also rewarded for good statistics and no one had any vested interest in seeing if actual performance matched the claims being made (G. Medvedev, 1989; Z. Medvedev, 1990).

Managers also learned that the risks of exercising initiative far exceeded any likely rewards. As one Czech scholar (Kohak, 1992: 200) described conditions,

> the adaptive strategy [in Marxist societies] is necessarily one of low profile, avoiding initiative, avoiding responsibility, avoiding standing out in any way. Even picking up windblown trash before the house is unwise: it makes one stand out. So is refusing to sign a petition—or volunteering to sign it. The wise strategy is to sign it when instructed to do so. Holding an opinion is equally unwise. The adaptive strategy is to think nothing until told, then agreeing, though not too vehemently.

Finally, they learned that there were only minimal rewards for reinvestment in plant and for technological innovation. Lacking pressures from direct economic competition, Party leaders and planners failed to appreciate the importance of continuous modernization of their society's industrial plant. According to one account, Soviet managers received bonuses of 33 percent for fulfilling production quotas, but only 8 percent for fulfilling the plan for new technology (*The Economist*, 1988: 11). Thus, capital investment and technological advance were badly neglected, with the result that the command economies of Marxist societies became less and less competitive in world markets.

Several striking examples illustrate the kinds of problems that developed. For example, one of the most important technological advances in the steel industry in the twentieth century, continuous casting, was the work of Soviet engineers. But twenty-seven years after this new technology was first introduced at the Novolipetsk metallurgical factory, it had been adopted by only 12 percent of the Soviet steel industry. In contrast, by then the new technology was in use in 62 percent of the West German steel industry and 79 percent of the Japanese.

That this was not some isolated case is indicated by the fact that only 23 percent of patented Soviet inventions were put to use within a two-year period, compared to 66 percent of American inventions and 64 percent of West German (ibid.). As one Czech economist observed recently, his country's industrial plant was technologically only about three years behind that of western Europe when the Communists seized power in the late 1940s, but by the time the Communists relinquished power less than half a century later, it was twenty-five years behind.

Another of the gross malfunctions of Marxist economies stemmed from the overconcern of politicians and planners with production statistics and their lack of concern with distribution and delivery to consumers. Thus, following a wonderfully bountiful grain harvest in the Soviet Union in 1990, as much as 2 million tons per day rotted away on farms and at collection points around the nation because of inadequate storage and transportation facilities, and the nation was forced to import grain from abroad (Remnick, 1990). In the case of potatoes, only 24 million tons out of a harvest of 90 million tons actually reached consumers (Pear, 1990). Similar problems have plagued most other Marxist societies. In Cuba, for example, "diplomats estimate that almost a third of fresh produce bound for city markets spoils because of inefficient management and lack of refrigeration" (Schauche, 1990).

Although it is not possible to explore this matter in depth here, several observations are in order. First, a substantial majority of the citizens in most of the once-socialist societies of eastern Europe rejected the system when given the chance. Even one-time Party leaders often lost faith in central planning and the command economy. As one member of the Soviet Congress of People's Deputies said on the floor of that body, his nation had taught the world a valuable lesson by testing, at great cost to itself, what proved to be "an impossible system of economic development" (Zakharov, 1990).

Second, there have been remarkable similarities in the performance of command economies in otherwise widely diverse Marxist societies. Most of the pathologies found in eastern Europe—absenteeism, poor work discipline, low levels of productivity, inattention to quality, failure to reinvest in plants and to encourage innovation, indifference to the needs and interests of consumers—have also been reported in China, North Korea, Cuba, and elsewhere.

Finally, and perhaps most telling of all, many of these same problems are evident in the public sector of non-Marxist societies. Government workers and workers in state-owned western enterprises are widely perceived as less diligent, innovative, enterprising, responsive, and responsible than workers in private industry: Negative associations with the term "bureaucrat" are almost as strong in non-Marxist societies as in Marxist. In addition, government agencies in these societies are noted for their inefficient use of human and other resources. Managers in these bureaucracies quickly learn that they are much more likely to maximize their own rewards by enlarging the size of the work force and other resources under their supervision (*regardless of need*) than by using these resources efficiently.[11]

Many have argued that the massive failures of the socialist economies of eastern Europe and elsewhere demonstrate the superiority of capitalism and indicate that the future lies with it. That conclusion, however, seems unwarranted. Those societies that are commonly referred to as "capitalist," have, in reality, very *mixed economies*.[12] To paraphrase Marx, they are societies in which rewards are

---

11. This is a lesson that most who work for government agencies learn quickly. My early mentors were officers under whom I served during World War II and supervisors in the Veterans Bureau and the Customs Service shortly thereafter. The lesson was reinforced by subsequent experience over forty years at two state universities. It should be noted, however, that bureaucratic pathologies are not limited to governmental agencies; they also flourish in many large corporations in the private sector.

12. Unfortunately, many successful politicians and many economists in the United States in recent years have failed to recognize this. In fact, many today seem to be nearly as blinded by ideology as Marxists of the recent past.

allocated partly on the basis of *need,* partly on the basis of *work,* and partly on the basis of *property* (Lenski, 1984: 199ff.). In short, they are societies that combine elements of communism, socialism, and capitalism, a combination resulting from an extended process of trial-and-error experimentation guided by a spirit of pragmatism. It is a system that recognizes the need for material incentives and acknowledges the benefits of at least a certain degree of economic inequality. But it is also a system that recognizes the necessity of allocating a part of the economic product on the basis of need, and much on the basis of work.[13] In short, the conventional view of societies as being either capitalist or socialist has become increasingly inappropriate.

If the assumptions concerning human nature that undergird ecological-evolutionary theory are correct, debates over the proper allocation of the economic product will almost certainly continue indefinitely in democratic societies, since what appears equitable from the perspective of one person or group commonly appears less than equitable from the perspective of others. Moreover, societies will surely find it necessary to make changes in the light of future experience (i.e., in response to the impact of new technologies, changing demographics, changing levels of affluence, changes in international relations, etc.). In the near future, however, such changes are likely to be more in the nature of "fine-tuning" than the radical reordering of economic systems envisioned by Marx and his followers.

What Have We Learned from Marxist Experiments? What Might We Learn?

What have we, as western sociologists, learned from the enormously costly (in terms of human suffering) efforts of Marxists in eastern Europe and elsewhere to create a new social order and to remake human nature?

Not nearly as much as we should have, I am afraid. Focused as we have been on our own societies and their problems, we have largely ignored the important experiments in "really existing socialist societies."

What might we learn?

Much, I believe, that could be of enormous value to sociology and, more important, to society. For example, the experience of Marxist societies everywhere provides a powerful demonstration of the fact that it is far easier to conceive of utopia than to create it. In fact, this experience demonstrates that efforts to create such societies can easily have disastrous consequences. Noble ends all too often become a justification for ignoble means, and noble goals, such as justice and freedom, all too easily become a justification for tyranny. If nothing else, the expe-

---

13. Data collected by the Internal Revenue Service of the United States indicate that in recent years approximately 10 percent of GDP has been allocated on the basis of need (public health and education expenditures, public welfare), 70 percent on the basis of work (wages and salaries), and 20 percent on the basis of property rights (interest, rents, dividends, capital gains) (Lenski 1984: 202).

rience of Marxist societies in the twentieth century should remind us of the wisdom of Lord Acton's assertion that "power tends to corrupt and absolute power corrupts absolutely."

The experience of Marxist societies also demonstrates that the abolition of private ownership is not the panacea many have imagined it to be. It does not bring most of the benefits that its proponents have promised; it does not mean an end to inequalities in power and control within societies; and it does not even ensure an equitable distribution of material rewards among their members. On the contrary, public ownership of the means of production (i.e., state control[14]) in Marxist societies has given rise to a system of political stratification in which a tiny, unified elite comes to exercise all of the many powers previously divided among a diversity of elites, economic, political, religious, and intellectual—and other members of society find their rewards dependent largely on the value placed on their service to this elite rather than on the value of their service to society at large or their contributions to its welfare (Andorka, 1992: 12; Kennedy and Bialecki, 1989: 316–318).[15]

Finally, *and most important of all,* the experience of Marxist societies warns of the dangers of underestimating the refractory elements in human nature. Marx, who lived in the nineteenth century, knew nothing of the new science of genetics. Thus, like other progressive thinkers of the eighteenth and nineteenth centuries he believed that all of the unattractive features of human life were due to the influence of corrupt and corrupting social institutions. Change the social environment, and you would change human nature; abolish private property, and you would remove the basic source of greed and selfishness and pave the way for the emergence of the "new socialist man."

Unfortunately, this did not happen. Greed and selfishness survived and even flourished in Marxist societies, though often they were expressed in new and innovative ways.[16] But what has been most depressing about these societies has been

---

14. Some would still like to believe that public ownership of the means of production does not have to become, in reality, state ownership. To date, however, no one has found a way in which huge populations of the size found in modern societies can effectively exercise control over property held in their name. The real issue involved is not who "owns" a given property (i.e., who holds legal title) but who "controls" it. Even in societies that are far more democratic than any Marxist society has ever been, the public has rarely achieved effective control over the operation of public properties.

15. More than a century ago, and more than twenty years before the first Marxist society was established, Gaetano Mosca (1930: 284ff.) predicted that if private property were ever abolished, the chief effect would be to concentrate all of the powers previously divided among the owners of various enterprises in the hands of a tiny governing elite, making them vastly more powerful than their capitalist predecessors. In many respects, this is one of the most successful predictions ever made by a social scientist. What makes this prediction so impressive is the fact that it was thoroughly grounded in a theory, and, in addition, it dealt with a set of conditions that had never yet been observed. Most social science predictions, in contrast, anticipate the recurrence of some previously existing sequence of events—often, in fact, a well-established sequence.

16. The most creative of these innovations was the establishment of a dual system of currency, with one special form of the currency (e.g., the so-called golden rubles in the old Soviet Union) providing Marxist elites with access to more varied, and better-quality, goods in special stores that

the conduct and character of those most involved in, and most exposed to, the system, those most honored by it, the Brezhnevs, the Honeckers, the Zhikovs, the Ceausescus, and the thousands of others elevated within the Party to positions of responsibility. These men (there were few women) were products of the Marxist system, people who had been immersed in the Communist Party from early in life, and they were the ones who were selected by the Party itself to be its leaders.

Thus, although many of Marx's ideas continue to have a following in the social sciences, the judgment of history on the societies created by his followers will almost certainly be harsh. Tragically, the leaders of these societies, like most social scientists still today, grossly underestimated the constraints imposed on human societies and their development by our species' genetic heritage.[17]

These constraints also help us to understand one other important feature of Marxist societies. Marx promised that after the revolution the state would wither away. Instead, wherever his followers came to power, the state expanded enormously, concentrating power in the top leader or leaders, and thus became even more repressive than it had been before. Viewed from the perspective of ecological-evolutionary theory, this is not surprising. When a society's leaders expect people to act in ways that are contrary to their basic nature, they soon discover that there is no alternative to the use of force and coercion. Thus, instead of an increase in freedom, Marxist experiments have resulted in its curtailment.

This is not to suggest that human societies cannot be improved or that we must accept the world as we find it. The experience of western industrial societies makes it clear that this is not the case: Real and substantial improvements are possible. But the massive social experiments conducted by Marxists in eastern Europe and elsewhere demonstrate that we are still a very long way from being able to create the ideal society of which we so easily dream. More important still, those experiments should teach us that premature efforts to create such a society, especially when based on overly optimistic assumptions about human nature, can cause incalculable harm. One hopes that in the years ahead, sociologists and others who share a concern with human welfare will come to appreciate the immense importance of the experiments undertaken by Marx's followers and will begin to use the evidence produced by those experiments to test their assumptions about human societies and the forces shaping them. This should enable us to provide far better guidance to social engineers and policymakers than we have been able to provide thus far.

---

were closed to nonelites. Thus, while government data showed only minimal inequality in incomes measured in number of rubles received by elites and rank-and-file workers, gross inequalities actually flourished. For decades, most western observers were fooled by this arrangement and were greatly impressed by Communist "successes" in reducing economic inequality.

17. The importance of these constraints is also demonstrated by the growing body of evidence concerning the influence of genetics on behavior. See, for example, Matt Ridley's *Genome: The Autobiography of a Species in 23 Chapters* (1999).

PART III

Epilogue

12

RETROSPECT AND PROSPECT

It is no secret that many sociologists are unhappy with the public image of their discipline and the low esteem in which it is commonly held. Too often academic colleagues and others whose good opinion we value have either unflattering or confused ideas about the field. Some of us are also troubled by the fact that the field fails to attract its fair share of the best undergraduates, many of whom see sociology as little more than common sense dressed up in arcane jargon or, alternatively, as slightly disguised ideology.

For a long time, many of us excused the inadequacies of our discipline on the grounds that sociology was still a new science and had not yet had sufficient time to demonstrate what it could do. Although comforting, this has been a dubious claim. It is now more than 200 years since Turgot, Millar, Ferguson, and others laid the foundations of a science of human societies and nearly as long since Comte gave it a name. Thus, sociology is at least as old as chemistry and biology.

What we ignore or overlook when we attempt to explain away the shortcomings of our discipline are the problems that we have created for ourselves. Above all, we have failed to recognize the need for a theory that is both comprehensive (i.e., addresses the full range of phenomena within the discipline) and testable.

Most sociological theories in recent decades meet only one of these criteria. A few, like Parsons's theory, are comprehensive, but shot through with ambiguities that make meaningful testing all but impossible (Black, 1961). Most, while testable, are extremely limited in scope (i.e., they apply only to some narrow range of phenomena). Such theories, while having a useful and legitimate place in science, are no substitute for the kind of comprehensive theory that *Webster's Third New International Dictionary* has in mind in its definition of "theory" as "the coherent set of hypothetical, conceptual, and pragmatic principles *forming the general frame of reference for a field of inquiry*"[1] (emphasis added).

Lacking such a frame of reference, sociology has tended to become what Gilbert and Sullivan might have called "a thing of shreds and patches," hardly more than the sum of its many diverse and fragmented parts. Unless and until sociologists recognize the importance of a unifying "general frame of reference" comparable to the neo-Darwinian framework in biology, our discipline is not likely to realize its full potential.[2]

Retrospect

My primary aim in this volume (and in other things I have written in recent decades) has been to revive and stimulate interest in the kind of comprehensive theory of human societies and their development that was the hallmark of sociology in an earlier era. Years ago, I came to the conclusion that sociology had lost its way.[3] After sociologists ceased to concern themselves with the larger social universe and its long-term history, teaching and research came to be focused primarily on various aspects of the current life of their own society,[4] and the discipline became hardly more than a patchwork of concepts, data, disjointed middle range theories, conventional wisdom, and thinly veiled (or not so thinly veiled) ideology.

Can a macro-organizational, macro-chronological, ecological-evolutionary theory provide a way out of these difficulties? As should be clear by now, I believe it can, but I readily admit that I am not an unbiased observer. There are, however, certain objective criteria that can be used to judge a theory's promise in this regard, and these can be framed as a series of questions.

First, does the theory offer a set of principles capable of providing a coherent frame of reference for the analysis of human societies and their development, both individually and collectively, over the long span of human history? Second, is the theory testable? Third, is it amenable to refinement and modification? And,

---

1. I believe that this definition might be improved a bit if it read "a coherent set of concepts and principles that form the general frame of reference for a field of inquiry."

2. This is not (repeat *not*) a call for sociologists to adopt the methods of the physical sciences as a whole. But it is a call for sociologists to recognize our discipline's desperate need for a comprehensive theory of human societies that is sufficiently unambiguous that its various principles are operationalizable and testable.

3. I came to this conclusion largely as a result of teaching the introductory course year after year and finding it impossible to provide students with a coherent view of the social world and of the discipline of sociology. My frustration with the introductory course was reinforced by experience with a graduate seminar in social stratification, during which all of the problems of the larger discipline were repeated (see the preface to this volume).

4. This pattern developed first in American sociology under the influence of the Chicago school in the period around World War I. Since World War II, it has become equally characteristic of sociology in most other countries.

finally, is it capable of generating research that yields insights into social phenomena that go beyond common sense and the conventional wisdom?

In my opinion, in the case of ecological-evolutionary theory each of these questions can be answered in the affirmative. First, the theory contains a set of logically coherent principles that enable one to map the universe of human societies from prehistoric times to the present. This map may be flawed in some respects, and it is certainly still incomplete (i.e., many important details are missing), but it is no more flawed and no more incomplete than the maps of geographers in the eighteenth century, or the Linnaean map of the biological universe in the nineteenth century—maps that provided those disciplines with the foundations required for subsequent advances in theory and research.

Second, is the theory testable? Again, an affirmative answer seems warranted, though an important qualification has to be added. The theory cannot easily be falsified by a single critical test, as is possible with certain deterministic theories in the physical sciences. Ecological-evolutionary theory is couched in probabilistic terms, and therefore, like evolutionary theory in biology, cannot be falsified merely by evidence from a single exceptional case (J. M. Smith, 1992: 35). Judgments concerning the validity of probabilistic theories usually require evidence from multiple tests employing diverse data sets.

Third, ecological-evolutionary theory is clearly subject to refinement and modification. Many of its propositions are underspecified, and all of them are subject to challenge and refutation; there are no articles of faith to which "true believers" must unreservedly subscribe, as is true of certain ideologically based theories.

Finally, I hope that the analyses in Part II of this volume provide at least some indication of the theory's potential for shedding new light on old issues. Each of the problems dealt with in those chapters has been studied and debated intensively by a variety of knowledgeable specialists over many years. In the process, much has been learned, but what has been learned has been limited by the kinds of questions asked and by the kinds of assumptions made. For a variety of reasons, these have resulted in the neglect of certain types of variables and constants, which, with hindsight, appear to have been extremely important. Thus, *the greatest strength of ecological-evolutionary theory may well be that it compels us to take seriously certain important aspects of the human condition that other theories allow one to neglect or even ignore.*

Before turning to problems for future research, it may be well to draw attention to one important area where ecological-evolutionary theory has already provided fruitful new insights, namely, the origins and causes of *gender inequality.* The work in this area has by now become so extensive that I cannot hope to do justice to all of it, nor can I even claim to be familiar with all of it. All I can do here is to draw attention to some of the work with which I am familiar and to encourage readers to follow up for themselves by consulting current work in the field.

To my knowledge, the first to see the relevance of ecological-evolutionary theory for the understanding of gender inequality were Robert Winch and Rae

Lesser Blumberg. In a volume titled, *Familial Organization: A Quest for Determinants,* published in 1977, Winch and Blumberg developed and tested, with good results, a model of familial organization that drew heavily on ecological-evolutionary theory. The following year, Blumberg published another volume, *Stratification: Socioeconomic and Sexual Inequality,* in which she dealt in greater depth with the issue of sexual inequality viewed from the perspective of ecological-evolutionary theory.

Blumberg's work proved to be only the beginning. In the years that followed, she and others drew on ecological-evolutionary theory in varying degrees to explain the origins and sources of gender inequality (Blumberg, 1984, 1989, 2004; Chafetz, 1980, 1984, 1988, 1989, 1990, 2004; Collins et al., 1993; Huber, 1976, 1988, 1991, 1999, 2004). In summarizing this work, Janet Saltzman Chafetz (2004: 16) recently argued that by adding a number of important new elements to the more general theory "we now have a much more robust understanding of how systems of [gender inequality] arise and vary over time and space." If true, this bodes well for the future of ecological-evolutionary theory—or, perhaps more accurately, this family of theories.

An Agenda for Future Research

If the promise of ecological-evolutionary theory is to be realized fully, however, a more active program of research will have to be undertaken than is currently under way. For various reasons, sociologists have been slow to explore the implications of the theory in research.

This is not because the theory has been tested and found wanting; on the contrary, it has generally been ignored, misrepresented,[5] or simply dismissed out of hand on the grounds that it embraces "obviously" erroneous—even dangerous (from a disciplinary standpoint)—assumptions about the importance and relevance of "nonsociological" factors, such as human nature, technology, and the biophysical environment. In addition, for the more ambitious advocates of social engineering, it draws attention to powerful constraints on human action that are not easily overcome by political manipulation. In short, ecological-evolutionary theory tends to draw attention to things that are inconvenient, or even embarrassing.

While these are surely fatal flaws for many, others may find in ecological-evolutionary theory a potentially fruitful new perspective and paradigm. However, as I noted in the introduction to Part II of this volume, sociologists who have been trained in recent decades primarily to conduct sophisticated quantitative analyses of data from a single contemporary society may find it difficult to see the many varied kinds of research possibilities and data suggested by ecological-evo-

5. See, for example, Sanderson (1990: 145–153).

lutionary theory. For this reason, it may be helpful to conclude with brief sketches of several lines of research that seem promising or important.

The Arts and Technological Innovation

Art is an aspect of life that many think of as a world apart from technology. Great works of art are products of the human spirit, not something to be explained away by a reductionist materialist theory. As E. T. A. Hoffman, the nineteenth-century composer and poet once wrote, "effective composition is *nothing but* [emphasis added] the art of capturing with a higher strength, and fixing in the hieroglyphs of tones, what was received in the mind's unconscious *ecstasis.*"

There is, of course, an element of truth in this widely held point of view. But like all half-truths, it neglects much that is critical to an understanding of the matter in question.

My own interest in the importance of technology in the world of art was stimulated initially many years ago by an article by the noted organist and student of the organ, E. Power Biggs (1968). In it, he argued that music written for the organ reflected the technology of the instruments available to individual composers to a far greater degree than critics recognized. Thus, Handel's compositions, for example, were written for eighteenth-century English organs, noted for their bright and gay tones. In contrast, Bach's famed Toccata and Fugue in D Minor was written to display and employ the massive power and range of the organ at the Johanniskirche in Lueneberg, where he was a student in his early years. The most telling feature of Biggs's article, however, was the account of his own discovery that Spanish organ music, long judged inferior to its German counterpart, revealed unexpected zest and color when played on the Spanish instruments for which it had been written. In short, Biggs concluded, composers were profoundly influenced by the characteristics of the instruments available to them.

The impact of technology on musical composition is more evident to most of us in the contrast between the classic symphonies of the seventeenth and eighteenth centuries and the romantic symphonies of the nineteenth—differences that reflect the many advances made in the design and construction of musical instruments. These newer instruments opened up a vast new world of possibilities for composers—possibilities denied to even the most talented of their predecessors. The impact of these advances can also be seen in compositions for keyboard stringed instruments, as the clavichord was displaced by the harpsichord and the harpsichord by the pianoforte. Each new technological advance opened up challenging and exciting new possibilities for composers.

In the case of painting, many of the most important developments have reflected advances in the technology of optics. Research on the role of the camera obscura strongly suggests (though not all experts agree) that this device was largely responsible for the emergence of visual realism and accuracy in perspective in the work of artists such as da Vinci, Caravaggio, Velazquez, Van Eyck, and Vermeer

(Hockney, 2001; Steadman, 2001). There is evidence, too, that major artists such as Ingres employed the camera lucida, which was invented in 1807 specifically for the purpose of facilitating more accurate sketching of objects (Hockney, 2001).

It is also no coincidence that the first truly modern camera was the product of work by Nicephore Niepce, who was trying to devise an alternative method of producing lithographs, and by a painter, L.-J.-M. Daguerre. From the standpoint of art history, however, the real importance of the modern camera seems to have been the dramatic shift from realism to impressionism and then on to expressionism and other increasingly abstract styles of painting. Photography, in effect, became the new mode of visual artistic realism, largely displacing painting. In short, it would appear that two of the most important developments in the history of painting have been responses to technological innovations that created, first, dramatic new possibilities, and then, later, a disturbing new challenge for artists.

There is today a vast amount of scattered material available that illustrates the impact of technology on all of the creative arts. As one art historian has observed, "To varying degrees, the arts depend on technological evolution for the very techniques used to create works of art—literature the least, music considerably, and architecture most of all" (Kavolis, 1987). However, the definitive analysis of the complex interplay between technological innovation and artistic creation remains to be written.

Science and Technological Innovation

In a speech in New Delhi in 1944, Winston Churchill asserted that "[s]cience has given to this generation the means of unlimited disaster or of unlimited progress" (*New York Times,* January 3). In putting the matter this way, Churchill gave expression to the popular view that science is the great engine of change that has shaped the modern world.

Without denying or minimizing the importance of scientific advance in the process of change in the modern era, the popular view reflects a failure to appreciate the degree to which scientific advances themselves have been dependent on prior technological innovation. Modern medical science and the germ theory of disease, for example, would not exist were it not for the invention of the microscope and a host of subsequent instruments employed in medical research. Similarly, the science of astronomy rests on a foundation of discoveries that only became possible with the invention of the telescope, the radio telescope, and other technological innovations.

In science, as in the arts, and in the whole of human life, technological innovations expand the limits of what is possible—both for good and for ill. Applied science puts these tools to use in experimental tests of abstract general theories derived from pure science (see, for example, Galison [1997]). Even the most important of these theories, from the general theory of relativity to theories of biological evolution and plate techtonics, would almost certainly never have been formulated had it not been for prior technological innovations.[6] Einstein, for example, is reported to have said late in life that his work with applications for technological patents when he was a young man employed by the Swiss patent office had been an important stimulus to his thinking about physics (Dyson, 2003: 43).[7]

To the best of my knowledge, the story of this important relationship in all its ramifications has yet to be written, but when it is, I suspect it will support ecological-evolutionary theory. To say this is not to deny that feedback occurs, or that this feedback is important in the total process of change; scientific advances raise questions as well as answer them, and the new questions frequently create the need and demand for new technologies. Thus, the emergence of modern science has been an important stimulus to technological innovation, but major advances in scientific knowledge appear to have been dependent in nearly every instance on prior advances in technology.

Religion and Technological Innovation

During the nineteenth century, sociologists and anthropologists wrote extensively about the evolution of religion from the animistic faiths of hunters and gatherers to the polytheistic and monotheistic faiths of agrarian peoples (e.g., Spencer, 1896; Tylor, 1958) and about the linkages between social experience and religious beliefs and practices (e.g., Weber, 1963). One could well argue, therefore, that there is little new that can be said on the subject.

I believe, however, that we badly need an updated treatment of the subject, one that takes account of certain significant developments in the recent past and is based on a reconceptualization of religion itself. With respect to the latter, I have in mind the more encompassing view of religion proposed by Talcott Parsons (1968, vol. II: 566–567, 667–668, 717). According to Parsons, the essence of religion is the effort of people to make sense of the totality of their experience.

Defining religion in this way helps one to see the interconnections between traditional religions on the one hand and certain secular modern ideologies and certain aspects of modern science on the other. Traditional religions, all in their

---

6. The modern theory of biological evolution provides a less obvious instance of scientific theory's dependence on prior technological advance, but I believe that even here the dependence exists. For example, the technologies that made the discovery of DNA possible were critical to the demonstration of the interconnectedness of life forms as diverse as humans and worms or bacteria. Moreover, it is probably no coincidence that both Darwin and Wallace developed their original insights as a result of travels to distant places, taking advantage of relatively recent advances in maritime technology. It would be no easy task to identify all of the technologies that have been required to produce the highly sophisticated theory of biological evolution that exists today.

7. As a young man, Einstein worked in the Swiss patent office in Bern and his earliest work involved applications for patents concerned with electric clocks and their coordination by the distribution of electric time signals (Dyson, 2003).

own ways, have obviously sought to make sense of the totality of human experience. But so, too, have certain modern secular ideologies such as Communism and Nazism. As the French political scientist Maurice Duverger once observed,

> Marxism is not only a political doctrine, but a complete philosophy, a way of thinking, a spiritual cosmogony. All isolated facts in all spheres find their place in it and the reason for their existence. It explains equally well the structure and evolution of the state, the changes in living creatures, the appearance of man on earth, religious feelings, sexual behavior, and the development of the arts and sciences. And the explanation can be brought within the reach of the masses as well as being understood by the learned and by educated people. [It] can easily be made into a catechism without too serious a deformation. In this way the human spirit's need for fundamental unity can be satisfied. (1959: 118–119)

Much the same could be said of Nazism, though its substantive content was radically different. To put the matter another way, these ideologies were, for the faithful, the functional equivalent of traditional religion (which is, I believe, why they were so intolerant of the older faiths).

Modern secular religions clearly reflect the influence of modern science, which has gradually undermined key elements of traditional theistic faiths and motivated many to seek alternative explanations of human experience.[8] In fact, science itself provides the basic intellectual underpinning for the beliefs of most contemporary agnostics and atheists.[9] Thus, to the degree that modern science itself has been dependent on technological innovation, these newer efforts to make sense of the totality of human experience are dependent on the advances in technology and would not have occurred to the degree and on the scale that they have without these advances.[10]

War and Human Nature

War and its causes are subjects that mainstream sociologists have largely ignored or avoided (Garnett, 1988, 1996; Nolan, 2003). For more than half a century, from 1950 to 2000, less than 1 percent of the more than 2,000 articles published in the three leading journals of the discipline dealt with the subject. Sociologists are not alone in this respect. Archaeologists apparently share this tendency (LeBlanc,

---

8. Even Nazism reflected the influence of modern science in its utilization of late nineteenth- and early twentieth-century racialist theory, which was in its day the prevailing scientific view.

9. Atheism, of course, has origins that predate the modern scientific movement, but in the prescientific past it appears to have been confined to a minuscule number of philosophers, and even among philosophers and intellectuals it was the belief of only a small minority.

10. It is noteworthy that the concept "agnostic" was the invention of T. H. Huxley, Darwin's famous advocate and popularizer, and was his way of responding to the new elements of human experience that resulted from the Darwinian revolution (Desmond and Moore, 1991: 568).

2003a, 2003b), and there is evidence suggesting that anthropologists and primatologists are not too different.[11]

In view of the importance of warfare throughout history and in the modern world, this neglect is shocking. One would suppose that something as consequential as war would be the object of intense concern.

One reason for this neglect in sociology has almost certainly been the abandonment of the broadly inclusive, comparative perspective that was the hallmark of the older evolutionism. By focusing on the internal processes of a single society, as is now common practice, it becomes impossible to say to what extent the various features of that society's way of life are due to its own unique characteristics and to what extent they are products of more universal human tendencies, or human nature itself.

This latter possibility, it must be noted, is one that *most* social scientists do not like to contemplate. Having fought and won the battle against a reductionist biological determinism nearly a century ago, most social scientists are loathe to concede more than the barest minimum to biological factors. In fact, many have adopted the view that reality is entirely a social construction.

Unfortunately, this flies in the face of a growing body of evidence that all aspects of human life are ultimately products of the interaction of environment and genetics, and that the influence of genetics on human action is far greater than most social scientists have wanted to believe (e.g., Ridley, 1999). While there is almost certainly no gene for making war, self-serving behavior (both individual and collective) is so widespread among humans that it would be surprising if deadly conflicts between societies did not emerge when their interests came into conflict or when war promised to serve the interests and ambitions of their leaders.

The relevant materials on this subject are widely scattered in fields that range from history and archaeology to primatology and ethology, so it will be no small matter to pull them all together. But it will be worth the effort, and ecological-evolutionary theory may prove useful in that endeavor.

Population Growth and Quality of Life

During the 1980s, the late Julian Simon (1981) popularized the view that population growth stimulates economic growth and thus improves the quality of life for people. To support his view, Simon focused heavily on the experience of the United States and western Europe, where rapid population growth was linked with rapid economic growth and rapidly rising standards of living. From this, Simon concluded that the former had made the latter possible.

Earlier, in Chapter 9, I proposed a different explanation of the American–western European experience, based on ecological-evolutionary theory. I argued

---

11. Among anthropologists, the hostile reaction of other anthropologists to the work of Napoleon Chagnon points in this direction. In the case of primatologists, Jane van Lawick-Goodall had to discover for herself that contrary to well-established opinion in the discipline, our chimpanzee cousins did, in fact, engage in warfare and even practiced the chimpanzee equivalent of genocide.

that population growth, economic growth, and the rising standard of living in this country were all ultimately dependent on the European conquest of the New World and the acquisition of the vast material resources it contained.

Skeptics and critics may, of course, legitimately argue that my explanation, while plausible, remains unproven, and I have to agree. I believe, however, that the case can be substantially strengthened by further research, especially by studies that examine other instances of the relationship between population growth, economic growth, and quality of life, thereby testing the validity of Hypothesis 4 (see Chapter 4), which was the basis of my ecological-evolutionary explanation of the rise of the West.

It is common knowledge today that those nations that are having the greatest economic difficulties are generally also those that are experiencing the most rapid population growth. This should give pause to advocates of Simon's view as well as to Catholic and Muslim religious leaders who denounce the use of modern technologies for controlling reproduction.

To move closer to a resolution of the issue, we need to look much more closely at the relationship between various measures of quality of life on the one hand and population growth and economic growth on the other. This needs to be done, moreover, while controlling for the level of societal development. In other words, we should compare Third World societies with other Third World societies, or, better yet, industrializing horticultural societies with other industrializing horticultural societies and industrializing agrarian societies with other industrializing agrarian societies. In this way, we could determine if, indeed, curbs on the growth of population (as in China) facilitate improvements in quality of life, as ecological-evolutionary theory leads one to expect.

The Social Impact of Advances in the Technologies of Health and Sanitation

The immediate effects of the revolutionary advances in the technologies of health and sanitation are well known today and well documented: massive declines in deaths from infectious diseases in advanced industrial societies and most industrializing agrarian societies, as well as greatly reduced infant and maternal mortality, and substantially increased life expectancy. In addition, there are the secondary and tertiary effects of these advances in medicine and sanitation, such as the extraordinary growth in numbers of elderly persons. This, in turn, has spawned an array of increasingly urgent social problems ranging from the economic issue of financing the costly needs of the elderly, especially with respect to health care, to the moral issues of deciding under what circumstances, and on whose say-so, life-support systems are to be denied or withdrawn in the case of the terminally ill.

Ethics, like art, often seems far removed from the mundane world of technology, and governed by different forces. Yet hardly a month goes by that we are not reminded of the illusory nature of such a view: With ever-increasing frequency, the media report new controversies generated by the application of new medical technologies. By creating new possibilities for human action, these new technologies often challenge and subvert existing codes of morality.

New life-support systems, for example, have provided a dramatic challenge to the traditional interpretation of the ancient Hippocratic oath of physicians. Should these new systems be used to sustain the lives of individuals who are brain-dead? Should they be used to keep alive grossly malformed infants who have no possibility of ever leading anything remotely resembling a pain-free life? Where should the line be drawn in such cases, and who should make decisions about such matters? Questions like these are forcing physicians, both individually and collectively, to rethink and, in many cases, revise their ethical code.

Traditional religious principles have also been challenged by the changes brought about by the new technologies of health care and sanitation. Thanks to the decline in child and infant mortality, the ancient biblical injunction to be fruitful and multiply can no longer be understood as it traditionally was. Similarly, the invention of the pill and other contraceptive devices, and advances in the technology of abortion, have dramatically altered sexual practices and even to some considerable degree normative standards. Most of the major Protestant denominations have by now revised their teachings in these areas to accommodate the new realities, and while the leadership of the Roman Catholic Church continues to fight to preserve its traditional moral code, it has paid a heavy price in loss of credibility and respect within its own constituency. For many years now, surveys have indicated that the actions of rank-and-file Catholics with respect to contraception and abortion are indistinguishable from those of non-Catholics. Even in that most Catholic of countries, Ireland, ethical standards in matters of sexual morality appear to be changing in response to the impact of the new technologies.

In Third World societies, the new technologies of health and sanitation have generated a very different set of problems. Thanks to these new technologies and the failure to adopt the new technologies for controlling reproduction, most of these societies now have very youthful populations. This creates enormous strains on their educational systems and their economies as they struggle to educate the rapidly growing numbers of young people. Rapid population growth has also led to serious problems of unemployment and underemployment, and these, in turn, commonly lead to political unrest and authoritarian governance. This relationship between rates of population growth and average age of populations on the one hand and political instability and authoritarian government on the other merits far greater attention than it is currently receiving either by social scientists or by policymakers.

Concluding Remarks

One could easily extend this list of topics that invite study from an evolutionary perspective. The impact of innovations in the technologies of transportation and communication is an obvious example. Less obvious, but equally promising, would be a study of the historic impact of maritime societies on the evolution of the global system during the agrarian era. Mention should also be made of the potential of studies of other uncommon types of societies, such as fishing societies, herding societies, horticultural societies embedded in agrarian societies (such as the hill country peoples of Vietnam and Myanmar), and unusual hybrid societies, such as the Plains Indians of nineteenth-century America, hunters and gatherers or horticulturalists who suddenly acquired horses and guns from much more advanced European societies with striking results (Lenski, 1966: 93, 95). The unique features of each of these types of societies are likely to provide unique insights into basic processes of societal development.

In short, the possibilities for advancing our understanding of human societies seem endless. What is required is simply curiosity, imagination, and a willingness to look beyond the here-and-now and beyond the narrow self-imposed limits of contemporary sociology as evolutionary theory invites us to do. In so doing, we will come to appreciate anew the profound wisdom of the assertion of the distinguished biologist Rene Dubos (1968: 270) when he wrote, "The past is not dead history; it is the living material out of which man makes himself and builds the future."

REFERENCES

Aitchison, Leslie. 1960. *A History of Metals.* London: MacDonald and Evans.

Albright, William F. 1956. *The Archaeology of Palestine.* London: Penguin.

Alliluyeva, Svetlana. 1967. *Twenty Letters to a Friend.* New York: Harper.

Alt, Albrecht. 1966. *Essays on Old Testament History and Religion.* Translated by R. A. Wilson. Oxford: Blackwell.

Anderson, Gary A. 1987. *Sacrifices and Offerings in Ancient Israel,* Harvard Semitic Monographs, vol. 41. Atlanta: Scholars Press.

Andorka, Rudolf. 1992. "Economic, Social and Political Causes of the Collapse of the Socialist System." Unpublished manuscript, Budapest.

Baldus, Bernd. 1990. "Positivism's Twilight," *Canadian Journal of Sociologyy,* 15: 149–163.

Bell, Daniel. 1973. *The Coming of Post-Industrial Society: A Venture in Social Forecasting.* New York: Basic Books.

Bellah, Robert. 1957. *Tokugawa Religion: The Values of Pre-Industrial Japan.* New York: Free Press.

Biggs, E. Power. 1968. "Dr. Schweitzer's Intuition Confirmed," *Saturday Review,* August 31, 41–43.

Billington, Ray Allen. 1973. *Frederick Jackson Turner: Historian, Scholar, Teacher.* New York: Oxford University Press.

Black, Max. 1961. *"Some Questions About Parsons' Theory."* In Max Black (ed.), *The Social Theories of Talcott Parsons: A Critical Examination.* Englewood Cliffs, NJ: Prentice-Hall.

Blalock, Hubert M. 1979. *Social Statistics,* 3d ed. New York: McGraw-Hill.

Blau, Peter. 1977. *Inequality and Heterogeneity: A Primitive Theory of Social Structure.* New York: Free Press.

Blum, Jerome. 1961. *Lord and Peasant in Russia from the Ninth to the Nineteenth Century.* Princeton: Princeton University Press.

Blumberg, Rae Lesser. 1978. *Stratification: Socioeconomic and Sexual Inequality.* Dubuque, IA: William Brown.

————. 1984. "A General Theory of Gender Stratification," *Sociological Theory,* 2: 23–101.

————. 1989. "Toward a Feminist Theory of Development." In Ruth Wallace (ed.), *Feminism and Sociological Theory.* Newbury Park, CA: Sage.

————. "Extending Lenski's Schema . . . ," *Sociological Theory* 22: 278–291.

Bock, Kenneth. 1978. "Theories of Progress, Development, Evolution." In Tom Bottomore and Robert Nisbet (eds.), *A History of Sociological Analysis.* New York: Basic Books.

Bollen, Kenneth. 1983. "World System Position, Dependency, and Democracy: The Cross-National Evidence," *American Sociological Review,* 48: 468–479.

Boserup, Ester. 1970. *Women's Role in Economic Development.* New York: St. Martin's Press.

Boulding, Kenneth. 1970. *A Primer on Social Dynamics: History as Dialectics and Development.* New York: Free Press.

————. 1978. *Ecodynamics: A New Theory of Societal Evolution.* Beverly Hills, CA: Sage.

Braidwood, Robert J. 1960. "Levels in Prehistory: A Model for the Consideration of the Evidence." In Sol Tax (ed.), *Evolution After Darwin,* vol. 2, pp. 143–152. Chicago: University of Chicago Press.

Braudel, Fernand. 1973. *Capitalism and Material Life, 1400–1800.* Translated by Miriam Kochan. New York: Harper & Row.

Bright, John. 1972. *A History of Israel,* 2d ed. Philadelphia: Westminster.

Brinton, C. Crane. 1933. *English Political Thought in the Nineteenth Century.* London: Benn.

Brown, Harrison. 1954. *The Challenge of Man's Future.* New York: Viking Compass.

Buss, Martin J. 1980. Essay Review of Norman Gottwald, *The Tribes of Yahweh, Religious Studies Review,* 6: 271–274.

Calvin, M. 1969. *Chemical Evolution: Molecular Evolution Towards the Origins of Living Systems on the Earth.* New York: Oxford University Press.

Carter, Charles. n.d. "The Emerging Frontier in the Highlands of Canaan: New Models for An Old Problem." Unpublished paper.

Catton, William R., Jr. 1966. *From Animistic to Naturalistic Sociology.* New York: McGraw-Hill.

Chafetz, Janet Saltzman. 1980. "Toward a Macro-Level Theory of Sexual Stratification and Gender Differentiation." In Scott McNall and G. Howe (eds.), *Current Perspectives in Social Theory,* vol. 1. Greenwich, CT: JAI Publications.

————. 1984. *Sex and Advantage: A Comparative Macro-Structural Theory of Sex Stratification.* Totowa, NJ: Rowman & Allenheld.

————. 1988. "The Gender Division of Labor and the Reproduction of Female Disadvantage," *Journal of Family Issues,* 9: 108–131.

————. 1989. "Gender Equity: Toward a Theory of Change." In Ruth Wallace (ed.), *Feminism and Sociological Theory.* Newbury Park, CA: Sage.

————. 1990. *Gender Equity: A Theory of Stability and Change.* Newbury Park, CA: Sage.

————. 2004. "Gendered Power and Privilege: Taking Lenski One Step Further," *Sociological Theory* 22: 269–277.

Chaney, Marvin. 1983. "Ancient Palestinean Peasant Movements and the Formation of Premonarchic Israel." In David Freedman and David Graf (eds.), *Palestine in Transition: The Emergence of Ancient Israel.* Sheffield: Almond.

————. 1986. "Systematic Study of the Israelite Monarchy." In Norman Gottwald (ed.), *Social Scientific Criticism of the Hebrew Bible and Its World, Semeia,* 37: 53–76.

Chang, Chung-li. 1955. *The Chinese Gentry: Studies in Their Role in Nineteenth Century Chinese Society.* Seattle: University of Washington Press.

Charlesworth, B., and D. Charlesworth. 2002. "Hitchhiking." In M. Pagel (ed.), *Encyclopedia of Evolution*, pp. 471–473. New York: Oxford University Press.

Childe, V. Gordon. 1936. *Man Makes Himself.* New York: Mentor Books. Reprinted in 1951.

Chirot, Daniel. 1985. "The Rise of the West," *American Sociological Review*, 50: 181–195.

Chomsky, Noam. 1957. *Syntactic Structures.* The Hague: Mouton.

Cohen, Mark Nathan. 1977. *The Food Crisis in Prehistory.* New Haven: Yale University Press.

Collins, Randall, J. S. Chafetz, R. L. Blumberg, S. Coltrane, and J. Turner. 1993. "Toward an Integrated Theory of Gender Stratification," *Sociological Perspectives*, 36: 185–216.

Connor, Walter. 1972. *Deviance in Soviet Society: Crime, Delinquency, and Alcoholism.* New York: Columbia University Press.

Cooper, Vaughan S., and Richard E. Lenski. 2000. "The Population Genetics of Ecological Specialization in Evolving E. Coli Populations," *Nature*, 407: 736–739.

Crossan, John Dominic. 1991. *The Historical Jesus: The Life of a Mediterranean Jewish Peasant.* San Francisco: Harper.

———. 1994. *Jesus: A Revolutionary Biography.* San Francisco: Harper.

———. 1998. *The Birth of Christianity.* San Francisco: Harper.

Crow, John. 1980. *The Epic of Latin America*, 3d ed. Berkeley: University of California Press.

Curtis, Helena. 1975. *Biology*, 2d ed. New York: Worth.

Davidson, Basil, and F. K. Buah. 1966. *A History of West Africa: To the Nineteenth Century.* Garden City, NJ: Doubleday Anchor.

Davis, K. G. 1974. *The North Atlantic World in the Seventeenth Century.* Minneapolis: University of Minnesota Press.

Davis, Kingsley. 1953. "Reply [to Tumin]," *American Sociological Review*, 18: 394–397.

Davis, Kingsley, and Wilbert Moore. 1945. "Some Principles of Stratification," *American Sociological Review*, 10: 242–249.

de Graaf, Nan Dirk. 1988. *Post-Materialism and the Stratification Process: An International Comparison.* Dissertation submitted at the University of Utrecht.

Desmond, Adrian, and James Moore. 1991. *Darwin.* New York: Norton.

Diamond, Jared. 1997. *Guns, Germs, and Steel: The Fate of Human Societies.* New York: Norton.

Dickens, Arthur G. 1966. *Reformation and Society in 16th Century Europe.* New York: Harcourt, Brace.

Dickerson, Richard E. 1978. "Chemical Evolution and the Origin of Life," *Scientific American*, 239: 70–86.

Divale, William. 1972. "Systematic Population Control in the Middle and Upper Paleolithic: Inferences Based on Contemporary Hunter-Gatherers," *World Anthropology*, 4: 222–243.

Dobbs, Michael. 1981. "They Pretend to Pay Us, We Pretend to Work, East Europeans Say," *Washington Post*, April 22.

Dobzhansky, Theodosius, Francisco Ayala, G. Ledyard Stebbins, and James W. Valentine. 1977. *Evolution.* San Francisco: Freeman.

Dubos, René. 1968. *So Human an Animal.* New York: Scribners.

Dumond, Don. 1975. "The Limitations of Human Population: A Natural History," *Science*, 187: 713–721.

Duncan, Otis Dudley. 1964. "Social Organization and the Ecosystem." In R. E. L. Faris (ed.), *Handbook of Modern Sociology.* Chicago: Rand McNally.

Durkheim, Emile. 1893. *The Division of Labor in Society.* Translated by G. Simpson. New York: Macmillan. Reprinted in 1933.

———. 1897. *Suicide.* Translated by J. Spaulding and G. Simpson. New York: Free Press. Reprinted in 1951.

———. 1912. *The Elementary Forms of the Religious Life.* Translated by J. W. Swain. London: Allen & Unwin. Reprinted in 1915.

Duverger, Maurice. 1959. *Political Parties: Their Organization and Activity in the Modern State.* Translated by Barbara and Robert North. London: Methuen.

Dyson, Freeman. 2003. "Clockwork Science," *New York Review of Books,* November 6, 2003: 42–44.

Eberhard, Wolfram. 1952. *Conquerors and Rulers: Social Forces in Medieval China.* Leiden: Brill.

———. 1960. *A History of China,* 2d ed. Berkeley: University of California Press.

The Economist. 1988. "The Soviet Economy," April 9, pp. 3–18.

Eisenstein, Elizabeth. 1979. *The Printing Press as an Agent of Change,* 2 vols. Cambridge: Cambridge University Press.

Eliot, J. H. 1970. *The Old World and the New, 1492–1650.* Cambridge: Cambridge University Press.

Ember, Carol, and Melvin Ember. 1981. *Anthropology.* 3rd ed. Englewood Cliffs, NJ: Prentice-Hall.

Emerson, Alfred E. 1959. "Social Insects," *Encyclopedia Britannica.*

Evans, A. B. 1977. "Developed Socialism in Soviet Ideology," *Soviet Studies,* 29: 409–428.

Ewers, John C. 1955. "The Horse in Blackfoot Indian Culture, With Comparative Material from Other Western Tribes," Smithsonian Institution Bureau of American Ethnology, *Bulletin,* 159.

Farmer, B. H. 1968. "Agriculture: Comparative Technology," in *International Encyclopedia of the Social Sciences,* 1: 202–208.

Fein, Esther. 1989. "Glasnost Is Opening Door on Poverty," *New York Times,* January 29.

Forbes, R. J. 1964. *Studies in Ancient Technology.* 9 vols. Leiden: Brill.

Frank, Andre Gunder. 1966. "The Development of Underdevelopment," in R. I. Rhodes (ed.), *Imperialism and Underdevelopment.* New York: Monthly Review Press.

Fried, Morton. 1967. *The Evolution of Political Society.* New York: Random House.

Frisbee, W. Parker, and Clifford Clarke. 1979. "Technology in Evolutionary Perspective," *Social Forces,* 58: 591–613.

Fritz, Volkmar. 1987. "Conquest or Settlement? The Early Iron Age in Palestine," *The Biblical Archaeologist,* 50: 84–100.

Galbraith, Kenneth. 1958. *The Affluent Society.* Boston: Houghton Mifflin.

Galison, Peter. 1997. *Image and Logic: A Material Culture of Microphysics.* Chicago: University of Chicago Press.

Garnett, Richard. 1988. "The Study of War in American Sociology: An Analysis of Selected Journals," *American Sociologist,* 19: 270–282.

———. 1996. "The Neglect of War in American Sociology: Findings from Leading Journals." Unpublished paper presented at the annual meeting of the Southern Sociological Society.

Goldschmidt, Walter. 1959. *Man's Way: A Preface to the Understanding of Human Society.* New York: Holt.

Gottwald, Norman. 1979. *The Tribes of Yahweh: A Sociology of the Religion of Liberated Israel 1250–1050 B.C.* Maryknoll, NY: Orbis.

———. 1983. *"Two Models for the Origins of Ancient Israel: Social Revolution or Frontier*

Development." In H. B. Huffmon, F. A. Spina, and A. R. W. Green (eds.), *The Quest for the Kingdom of God: Studies in Honor of George E. Mendenhall.* Winona Lake, IN: Isenbrauns.

Gould, Stephen Jay. 1976. "Human Babies Are Embryos," *Natural History,* 85 (February).

Granovetter, Mark. 1979. "Advancement in Theories of Social Evolution and Development," *American Journal of Sociology,* 85: 489–515.

Grauman, John. 1968. "Population Growth," *International Encyclopedia of the Social Sciences,* 12: 376–381.

Greenhouse, Steven. 1989. "Can Poland's Dinosaur Evolve?" *New York Times,* November 27.

Harris, Marvin. 1968. *The Rise of Anthropological Theory.* New York: Crowell.

———. 1974. *Cows, Pigs, Wars and Witches: the Riddles of Culture.* New York: Random House.

———. 1977. *Cannibals and Kings.* New York: Vintage Books.

———. 1979. *Cultural Materialism.* New York: Random House.

Hassan, Fekri. 1981. *Demographic Archaeology.* New York: Academic Press.

Hawkes, Jacquetta. 1963. *Prehistory.* New York: Mentor.

Hawley, Amos. 1950. *Human Ecology.* New York: Ronald.

Heise, David, Gerhard Lenski, and John Wardwell. 1976. "Further Notes on Technology and the Moral Order," *Social Forces,* 55: 316–337.

Herman, Arthur. 2001. *How the Scots Invented the Modern World.* New York: Three Rivers.

Hockney, David. 2001. *Secret Knowledge: Rediscovering the Lost Techniques of the Old Masters.* New York: Viking.

Holland, H. 1984. *The Chemical Evolution of the Atmosphere and the Oceans.* Princeton: Princeton University Press.

Hollander, Paul. 1981. *Political Pilgrims: Travels of Western Intellectuals to the Soviet Union, China, and Cuba, 1928–1978.* New York: Oxford University Press.

———. 1999. *Political Will and Personal Belief: The Decline and Fall of Soviet Communism.* New Haven: Yale University Press.

Hopkins, David. 1987. "Subsistence Struggles in Early Israel," *The Biblical Archaeologist,* 50: 178–191.

Huber, Joan. 1976. "Toward a Sociotechnological Theory of the Women's Movement," *Social Forces,* 23: 371–388.

———. 1988. "A Theory of Family, Economy, and Gender," *Journal of Family Issues,* 9: 9–26.

———. 1991. "Macro-Micro Linkages in Gender Stratification." In Joan Huber (ed.), *Macro-Micro Linkages in Sociology.* Newbury Park, CA: Sage.

———. 1999. "Comparative Gender Stratification." In Janet S. Chafetz (ed.), *Handbook of the Sociology of Gender.* New York: Plenum.

———. 2004. "Lenski Effects on Sex Stratification Theory," *Sociological Theory* 22: 258–268.

Huberman, Leo, and Paul Sweezy. 1967. *Socialism in Cuba.* New York: Modern Reader Paperbacks.

Hughes, Everett C. 1961. "Ethnocentric Sociology," *Social Forces,* 40: 1–4.

Hymes, Dell. 1968. "Linguistics: The Field," *International Encyclopedia of the Social Sciences,* 9: 351-71.

Inglehart, Ronald. 1971. "The Silent Revolution in Europe: Intergenerational Change in Post-Industrial Societies," *American Political Science Review,* 65: 990–1017.

———. 1977. *The Silent Revolution.* Princeton: Princeton University Press.

Inkeles, Alex. 1950. "Social Stratification and Mobility in the Soviet Union," *American Sociological Review,* 15: 465–479.

———. 1966. "Making Men Modern: On the Causes and Consequences of Individual Change in Six Developing Countries," *American Journal of Sociology,* 75: 208–225.

———. 1974. *Becoming Modern: Individual Change in Six Developing Countries.* Cambridge, MA: Harvard University Press.

Inkeles, Alex, and Larry Sirowy. 1983. "Convergent and Divergent Trends in National Educational Systems," *Social Forces,* 62: 303–333.

Inkeles, Alex, and David Smith. 1974. *Becoming Modern: Change in Six Developing Countries.* Cambridge, MA: Harvard University Press.

Jones, T. Anthony. 1981. "Work, Workers, and Modernization in the USSR," *Sociology of Work,* 1: 249–283.

———. 1983. "Models of Socialist Development," *International Journal of Comparative Sociology,* 24: 86–99.

Kamm, Henry. 1989. "Hungarians Shocked by News of Vast Poverty in Their Midst," *New York Times,* February 6.

Kautsky, John. 1982. *The Politics of Aristocratic Empires.* Chapel Hill: University of North Carolina Press.

Kavolis, Vytautus. 1987. "Social and Economic Aspects of the Arts," *Encyclopaedia Britannica,* 15th ed., vol. 14, p. 131.

Keller, Albert G. 1920. *Societal Evolution.* New York: Macmillan.

Kennan, George. 1988. "The Gorbachev Prospect," *New York Review of Books,* January 21, pp. 3–7.

Kennedy, Michael, and Ireneusz Bialecki. 1989. "Power and the Logic of Distribution in Poland," *East European Politics and Societies,* 3: 300–328.

Keresztes, Peter. 1987. "In Hungary, Taxes and Tears," *Wall Street Journal,* December 16.

Kerr, Clark, and John Dunlop, Frederick Harbison, and Charles Myers. 1960. *Industrialism and Industrial Man.* Cambridge, MA: Harvard University Press.

Kohak, Erazim. 1992. *The Embers and the Stars: A Philosophical Inquiry Into the Moral Sense of Nature.* Chicago: University of Chicago Press.

Kostakov, Vladimir. 1989. "Employment: Scarcity or Surplus?" In Anthony Jones and William Moskoff (eds.), *Perestroika and the Economy,* pp. 159–175. Armonk, NY: Sharpe.

Krader, Lawrence. 1968. "Pastoralism," *International Encyclopedia of the Social Sciences,* vol. ll: 453–460.

Krakauer, D. C. 2002. "Genetic Redundancy." In M. Pagel (ed.), *Encyclopedia of Evolution,* pp. 413–415. New York: Oxford University Press.

Kummer, Hans. 1971. *Primate Societies.* Chicago: Aldine-Atherton.

Laber, Jeri. 1990. "The Bulgarian Difference," *New York Review of Books,* May 17, pp. 34–36.

Lapidus, Gail. 1987. "Gorbachev and the Reform of the Soviet System," *Daedalus,* vol. 116.

Lapp, P. W. 1969. *Biblical Archaeology and History.* New York: World.

Laszlo, E. 1987. *Evolution: The Grand Synthesis.* Boston/London: New Science Library.

Leavitt, Gregory. 1977. "The Frequency of Warfare: An Evolutionary Perspective," *Sociological Inquiry,* 14 (January): Appendix B.

LeBlanc, Steven A. 2003a. *Constant Battles.* New York: St. Martin's Press.

———. 2003b. "Prehistory of Warfare," *Archaeology,* 56(3): 18–25.

Lee, Richard, and Irven DeVore (eds.). 1969. *Man The Hunter.* Chicago: Aldine.

Lenski, Gerhard. 1966. *Power and Privilege.* New York: McGraw-Hill.

———. 1970. *Human Societies.* New York: McGraw-Hill.

———. 1976. "History and Social Change," *American Journal of Sociology,* 82: 548–564.

———. 1980. Essay Review of Norman Gottwald, *The Tribes of Yahweh, Religious Studies Review,* 6: 275–278.

———. 1984. "Income Stratification in the United States: Toward a Revised Model of the System," *Annual Review of Research in Social Stratification and Mobility,* 3: 173–205.

———. 1988. "Rethinking Macrosociological Theory," *American Sociological Review,* 53: 163–171.

Lenski, Gerhard, and Jean Lenski. 1974–1987. *Human Societies,* 2d to 5th eds. New York: McGraw-Hill.

Lenski, Gerhard, Jean Lenski, and Patrick Nolan. 1991–1995. *Human Societies,* 6th and 7th eds. New York: McGraw-Hill.

Lenski, Gerhard, and Patrick Nolan. 1984. "Trajectories of Development: A Test of Ecological-Evolutionary Theory," *Social Forces,* 63: 1–23.

Lerner, Daniel. 1958. *The Passing of Traditional Society.* Glencoe, IL: Free Press.

Levine, Donald. 1982. "On the Heritage of Sociology." Unpublished paper presented at a conference honoring Morris Janowitz, University of Chicago, May 14–15.

Lewis, John C. 1942. "The Effects of White Contact Upon Blackfoot Cullture," *Monographs of the American Ethnological Society,* vol. 6.

Lewontin, R. C. 1983. "Darwin's Revolution," *New York Review of Books,* June 16, 21–27.

Leyburn, James G. 1936. *Frontier Folkways.* New Haven: Yale University Press.

Linton, Ralph. 1936. *The Study of Man.* New York: Appleton-Century.

———. 1952. "Universal Ethical Principles." In Ruth Anshen (ed.), *Moral Principles of Action.* New York: Harper & Row.

Lynd, Robert, and Helen Lynd. 1937. *Middletown in Transition.* New York: Harcourt, Brace.

Lyttle, T. W. 2002. "Meiotic Distortion." In M. Pagel (ed.), *Encyclopedia of Evolution,* pp. 708–713. New York: Oxford University Press.

Machonin, Pavel. 1968. Personal communication.

———. 1997. "Social Structures of Communist Societies 'Apres la Lutte,'" *Sisyphus: Social Studies,* 10: 17–39.

Mann, Michael. 1986. *The Sources of Social Power,* vol. 1. Cambridge: Cambridge University Press.

Marx, Karl. 1964. *Pre-Capitalist Economic Formations.* Translated by J. Cohen and edited by E. Hobsbawm. London: Laurence and Wishart. Originally published in 1857–1858.

———. 1970. *A Contribution to the Critique of Political Economy.* New York: International Publishers. Originally published in 1859.

Maryanski, Alexandra, and Jonathan H. Turner. 1992. *The Social Cage: Human Nature and the Evolution of Society.* Stanford: Stanford University Press.

Maslow, A. H. 1954. *Motivation and Personality.* New York: Harper & Row.

Matthews, Mervyn. 1978. *Privilege in the Soviet Union.* London: George Allen & Unwin.

Mayr, Ernest. 1978. "Evolution," *Scientific American,* 239: 46–55.

———. 1982. *The Growth of Biological Thought: Diversity, Evolution, and Inheritance.* Cambridge, MA: Belknap.

McNeill, William H. 1963. *The Rise of the West: A History of the Human Community.* Chicago: University of Chicago Press.

————. 1976. *Plagues and Peoples.* New York: Doubleday Anchor.

Mead, Margaret. 1928. *Coming of Age in Samoa.* New York: Morrow.

————. 1930. *Growing Up in New Guinea.* New York: Blue Ribbon.

————. 1935. *Sex and Temperment in Three Primitive Societies.* New York: Morrow.

Medvedev, Grigorii. 1989. *Chernobyl'skaia Kronika.* Moscow: Sovremennik. Cited by David Holloway, "The Catastrophe and After," *New York Review of Books,* July 19, p. 5.

Medvedev, Zhores. 1990. *The Legacy of Chernobyl.* New York: Norton.

Meggers, Betty. 1954. "Environmental Limitation of the Development of Culture," *American Anthropologist,* 56: 801–824.

Mendenhall, George E. 1962. "The Hebrew Conquest of Palestine," *Biblical Archaeologist,* 25: 66–87. Reprinted in *The Biblical Archaeologist Reader,* 3 (1970), pp. 100–120.

————. 1973. *The Tenth Generation: The Origins of the Biblical Tradition.* Baltimore: Johns Hopkins University Press.

Merrill, Robert S. 1968. "Technology: The Study of Technology," *International Encyclopedia of the Social Sciences,* vol. 15, pp. 576–589.

Merton, Robert. 1949. *Social Theory and Social Structure.* Glencoe, IL: Free Press.

Michels, Robert. 1915. *Political Parties.* New York: Dover. Reprinted in 1959.

Mishkin, Bernard. 1940. *Rank and Warfare Among the Plains Indians.* Monographs of the American Ethnological Society, vol. 3.

Montesquieu. 1748. *The Spirit of Laws.* Translated by T. Nugent. New York: Hafner. Reprinted in 1949.

Moore, Barrington, Jr. 1966. *Social Origins of Dictatorship and Democracy.* Boston: Beacon Press.

Moore, Wilbert. 1963. *Social Change.* Englewood Cliffs, NJ: Prentice-Hall.

Mosca, Gaetano. 1896. *The Ruling Class.* Translated by Hannah Kahn. New York: McGraw-Hill. Reprinted in 1930.

Murdock, George Peter. 1967. "Ethnographic Atlas: A Summary," *Ethnology,* 6: 154–233.

Nemeth, Roger S., and David A. Smith. 1985. "International Trade and World System Structure: A Multiple Network Analysis," *Review,* 8: 517–560.

New York Times News Service. 1990. "Gorbachev Checks Headstrong Congress," July 8.

Neyrey, Jerome H. 1996. "Luke's Social Location of Paul." In B. Witherington (ed.), *History, Literature, and Society in the Book of Acts.* Cambridge: Cambridge University Press.

Nisbet, Robert. 1969. *Social Change and History.* New York: Oxford.

Nolan, Patrick D. 1983a. "Status in the World System, Income Inequality, and Economic Growth," *American Journal of Sociology,* 89: 410–419.

————. 1983b. "Status in the World Economy and National Structure and Development: An Examination of Developmentalist and Dependency Theories," *International Journal of Comparative Sociology,* 24: 109–120.

————. 1988. "World-System Status, Techno-Economic Heritage, and Fertility," *Sociological Focus,* 21: 9–33.

————. 2003. "Toward an Ecological-Evolutionary Theory of the Incidence of Warfare in Preindustrial Societies," *Sociological Theory,* 21: 18–30.

————. n.d. "Complexity, Structural Resistance to Change and Sociocultural Evolution." Unpublished paper.

Nolan, Patrick, and Gerhard Lenski. 1985. "Techno-Economic Heritage, Patterns of Development, and the Advantage of Backwardness," *Social Forces* 64: 341–358.

————. 1999. *Human Societies.* 8th ed. New York: McGraw-Hill.

————. 2004. *Human Societies,* 9th ed. Boulder, CO: Paradigm Publishers.

Noth, Martin. 1960. *The History of Israel.* Translated by P. R. Ackroyd. New York: Harper & Row.

Novikov, I. D. 1983. *Evolution of the Universe.* Translated by M. M. Basko. Cambridge: Cambridge University Press.

Ogburn, William F. 1922. *Social Change.* New York: Viking.

Parkhomovsky, Elrad. 1982. "Can't Anybody Here Make Shoes?" *Izvestia,* reprinted in *World Press Review,* July.

Parsons, Talcott. 1951. *The Social System.* Glencoe, IL: The Free Press.

———. 1966. *Societies: Evolutionary and Comparative Perspectives.* Englewood Cliffs, N.J.: Prentice-Hall.

———. 1968. *The Structure of Social Action.* New York: Free Press. Originally published in 1937.

———. 1971. *The System of Modern Societies.* Englewood Cliffs, NJ: Prentice-Hall.

Pear, Robert. 1990. "Soviet Experts Say Their Economy Is Worse Than U.S. Has Estimated," *New York Times,* April 24.

Peel, J. D. Y. 1971. *Herbert Spencer: The Evolution of a Sociologist.* New York: Basic Books.

Pfeiffer, John E. 1972–1978. *The Emergence of Man.* 2d and 3d eds. New York: Harper & Row.

Phillips, Claude S. 1971. "The Revival of Cultural Evolution in Social Science Theory," *Journal of Developing Areas,* 5: 337–369.

Plato. n.d. *The Republic.* Translated by Benjamin Jowett. New York: Modern Library.

Pravda, Alex. 1988. "Still Under Ice After Two Decades," *Wall Street Street Journal,* August 22.

Remnick, David. 1990. "Soviet Grain Rots as Food Shelves Stay Bare," *Washington Post,* August 6.

Ridley, Matt. 1999. *Genome: The Autobiography of a Species in 23 Chapters.* New York: Harper Collins.

Sagan, Carl. 1977. *The Dragons of Eden.* New York: Ballentine Books.

Sahlins, Marshall, and Elman Service. 1960. *Evolution and Culture.* Ann Arbor, Michigan: University of Michigan Press.

Salisbury, Harrison. 1992. *The New Emperors: China in the Era of Mao and Deng.* Boston: Little, Brown.

Sanderson, Stephen K. 1990. *Social Evolutionism.* Cambridge, MA: Blackwell.

Sawyer, Jack. 1967. "Dimensions of Nations," *American Journal of Sociology,* 73: 145–172.

Scammel, Michael. 1990. "Yugoslavia: The Awakening," *New York Review of Books,* June 28, pp. 42–47.

Schauche, Don. 1990. "Cuban Leadership Scrambles to Revamp Slumping Economy," *Los Angeles Times,* August 4.

Schmandt-Bessert, Denise. 1978. "The Earliest Precursor of Writing," *Scientific American,* 238 (January): 50–59.

Schumpeter, Joseph. 1950. *Capitalism, Socialism, Democracy.* New York: Harper Torchbooks.

Service, Elman. 1962. *Primitive Social Organization.* New York: Random House.

———. 1971. *Cultural Evolutionism: Theory in Practice.* New York: Holt, Rinehart and Winston.

———. 1975. *Origins of the State and Civilization: The Process of Cultural Evolution.* New York: Norton.

Shlapentokh, Vladimir. 1987. "Soviet People: Too Rich for Reform," *New York Times,* November 23.

―――. 1989. *Public and Private Life of the Soviet People.* New York: Oxford University Press.

Silk, Leonard. 1990. "Soviet Crisis Worse, Economists Declare," *New York Times,* March 15.

Simon, Julian L. 1981. *The Ultimate Resource.* Princeton: Princeton University Press.

Simpson, George Gaylord. 1951. *The Meaning of Evolution.* New Haven: Yale University Press.

Skocpol, Theda. l979. *States and Social Revolutions: A Comparative Analysis of France, Russia and China.* New York: Cambridge University Press.

Smith, Hedrick. 1976. *The Russians.* New York: Quadrangle.

Smith, John Maynard. 1992. "Taking a Chance on Evolution," *New York Review of Books,* May 14.

Snow, C. P. 1961. *The Two Cultures and the Scientific Method.* Cambridge: Cambridge University Press.

Snyder, D., and E. Kick. 1979. "Structural Position in the World System and Economic Growth 1955–1970: A Multiple Network Analysis of Transnational Interactions," *American Journal of Sociology,* 84: 1096–1126.

Sombart, Werner. 1967. *The Quintessence of Capitalism.* New York: Fertig.

Spencer, Herbert. 1896. *Principles of Sociology.* New York: Appleton. Originally published in 1876.

Spitz, Rene. 1945. "Hospitalism," *The Psychoanalytic Study of the Child,* 1: 53–72. New York: International Universities.

―――. 1946. "Hospitalism: A Follow-Up Report," *The Psychoanalytic Study of the Child,* 2: 113–117. New York: International Universities.

Stager, L. E. 1985. "The Archaeology of the Family in Ancient Israel," *Bulletin of the American Schools of Oriental Research,* 260: 1–35.

Statistical Abstract of the United States, 2002.

Steadman, Philip. 2001. *Vermeer's Camera: Uncovering the Truth Behind the Masterpieces.* New York: Oxford University Press.

Strom, Stephen, and Karen Strom. 1979. "The Evolution of Disk Galaxies," *Scientific American,* 248: 72–82.

Sumner, William Graham. 1906. *Folkways.* New York: Mentor. Reprinted in 1960.

Sumner, William Graham, and Albert G. Keller. 1927. *The Science of Society,* 4 vols. New Haven: Yale University Press.

Tawney, R. H. 1926. *Religion and the Rise of Capitalism.* New York: Mentor Books. Reprinted in 1947.

Taylor, Charles, and David Jodice. 1983. *World Handbook of Political and Social Indicators,* 3d ed. New Haven: Yale University Press.

Tilly, Charles. 1964. *The Vendee.* Cambridge, MA: Harvard University Press.

Tomasson, Richard F. 1980. *Iceland: The First New Society.* Minneapolis: University of Minnesota Press.

Tumin, Melvin. 1953. "Some Principles of Stratification: A Critical Analysis," *American Sociological Review,* 18: 387–394.

Turgot, A. R. J. 1973. "On Universal History." In Ronald L. Meel (ed.), *Turgot on Progress, Sociology and Economics.* Cambridge: Cambridge University Press. Originally written in 1750.

Turner, Frederick Jackson. 1894. "The Significance of the Frontier in American History," *Report of the American Historical Association for 1893*: 199–227. Reprinted in F. J. Turner, *The Frontier in American History*, pp. 1–38. New York: Holt, 1920.

———. 1920. *The Frontier in American History*. New York: Holt.

Turner, Jonathan H. 2000. *On the Origins of Human Emotions: A Sociological Inquiry into the Evolution of Human Affect*. Stanford: Stanford University Press.

Tylor, E. B. 1958. *Primitive Culture*. New York: Harper Torchbooks. Originally published in 1871.

Utz, Pamela. 1973. "Evolutionism Revisited," *Comparative Studies in Society and History*, 15: 227–240.

Vaidyanathan. 1982. "Bovine Sex and Species Ratios in India," *Current Anthropology*, 23: 365–384.

von Hagen, Victor. 1961. *The Ancient Sun Kingdoms of the Americas*. Cleveland: World.

Voslensky, Michael. 1984. *Nomenklatura: The Soviet Ruling Class*. Garden City, NY: Doubleday.

Wallerstein, Immanuel. 1974. *The Modern World System: I.* New York: Academic Press.

———. 1979. *The Modern World System: II.* New York: Academic Press.

Washburn, Sherwood. 1978. "The Evolution of Man," *Scientific American*, 239: 194–208.

Watson, William. 1961. *China Before the Han Dynasty*. New York: Praeger.

Watters, R. F. 1960. "The Nature of Shifting Cultivation: A Review of Recent Research," *Pacific Viewpoints*, 1: 59–99.

Weatherford, Jack. 1988. *Indian Givers: How the Indians of the Americas Transformed the World*. New York: Crown.

Webb, Walter Prescott. 1949. "The Frontier and the 400–Year Boom." In Walter P. Prescott, *The Turner Thesis*. Boston: Heath, pp. 131–143.

Weber, Max. 1958. *The Protestant Ethic and the Spirit of Capitalism*. Translated by Talcott Parsons. New York: Scribners. Originally published in 1904.

———. 1963. *The Sociology of Religion*. Translated by Ephraim Fischoff. Boston: Beacon Press. Originally published in 1922.

———. 1981. *General Economic History*. New Brunswick, NJ: Transaction Books, 1981. Originally published in 1927.

Weippert, M. 1971. *The Settlement of Israelite Tribes in Palestine*. Translated by J. D. Martin. In *Studies in Biblical Theology*, 2d ser., 21, pp. 1–146. London: SCM.

Weisz, Paul B. 1967. *The Science of Biology*. 3d ed. New York: McGraw-Hill.

Wesolowski, Wlodzimierz. 1966. *Classes, Strata and Power*. London: Routledge & Kegan Paul.

Whiting, John. 1964. "Effects of Climate on Certain Cultural Practices." In Ward Goodenough (ed.), *Explorations in Cultural Anthropology: Essays in Honor of George Peter Murdock*. New York: McGraw-Hill.

Williams, Robin. 1951. *American Society*. New York: Knopf.

Wilson, Edward O. 1971. *The Insect Societies*. Cambridge, MA: Harvard University Press.

———. 1975. *Sociobiology: The New Synthesis*. Cambridge, MA: Harvard University Press.

Wright, G. Ernest. 1957. *Biblical Archaeology*. Philadelphia: Westminster.

Zakharov, Mark. 1990. "A Glimpse into 1990: Politics and Democracy," *Literaturnaya Gazetta* (international edition), March, p. 5.

Zeitlin, Maurice. 1970. *Revolutionary Politics and the Cuban Working Class*. New York: Harper & Row.

INDEX

ABOUT THE AUTHOR

Gerhard Lenski, Professor Emeritus of Sociology at the University of North Carolina, Chapel Hill, is the author of *Power and Privilege* and *The Religious Factor* and coauthor with Patrick Nolan of *Human Societies* 9th ed. (Paradigm 2004). He is a recent recipient of the ASA Distinguished Career Award.